How to Sound Cultured

MASTER THE 250 NAMES
THAT INTELLECTUALS
LOVE TO DROP INTO
CONVERSATION

**Thomas W. Hodgkinson
and Hubert van den Bergh**

ICON

Published in the UK in 2015 by Icon Books Ltd,
Omnibus Business Centre,
39–41 North Road, London N7 9DP
email: info@iconbooks.com
www.iconbooks.com

Sold in the UK, Europe and Asia
by Faber & Faber Ltd, Bloomsbury House,
74–77 Great Russell Street,
London WC1B 3DA or their agents

Distributed in the UK, Europe and Asia
by TBS Ltd, TBS Distribution Centre, Colchester Road,
Frating Green, Colchester CO7 7DW

Distributed in Australia and New Zealand
by Allen & Unwin Pty Ltd,
PO Box 8500, 83 Alexander Street,
Crows Nest, NSW 2065

Distributed in South Africa by
Jonathan Ball, Office B4, The District,
41 Sir Lowry Road, Woodstock 7925

Distributed in India by Penguin Books India,
7th Floor, Infinity Tower – C, DLF Cyber City,
Gurgaon 122002, Haryana

Distributed to the trade in the USA
by Publishers Group West,
1700 Fourth Street, Berkeley, CA 94710

Distributed in Canada
by Publishers Group Canada,
76 Stafford Street, Unit 300, Toronto, Ontario M6J 2S1

ISBN: 978-184831-930-1

Typeset in Minion by Marie Doherty

Printed and bound in the UK by

Contents

CONTENTS

About the authors

Thomas W. Hodgkinson is the author of the novel *Memoirs of a Stalker* (Silvertail Books, 2016). He writes regularly for *The Spectator* and the *Daily Mail*, and is a contributing editor at *The Week*.

Hubert van den Bergh is the author of *How to Sound Clever* (Bloomsbury, 2010). He has written for the *Daily Telegraph* and *The Guardian* and appeared on Vanessa Feltz's BBC Radio 2 show.

Acknowledgements

Joint acknowledgements: Sheila Ableman; Duncan Heath; Leena Normington; Andrew Furlow; Steve White.

Thomas's acknowledgements: Anna Yermakova; Thomas Fink; Alastair Hall; Charles Campbell; Peter Philipp Földeáky; Tom Stevens; Mia More; Ray Monk; Stephen Fry; Nick Thompson; Theo Tait; Martina Caruso; Emma Castagno; Jeremy O'Grady; Thomas Leveritt; Alexander Fiske-Harrison; Alex Preston; Russell Brand; Jocelyn Baines; Julia Hodgkinson; Dominic Hodgkinson; Nicholas Allen; Virginia Price; Philip O'Mahony; Woody Allen; James Price; Richard Curtis.

Hubert's acknowledgements: My wife Louisa; my parents and my ten wonderful siblings and their spouses: John and Marion van den Bergh; Antonia and Olivier Hopkes; James and Louisa van den Bergh; Mary and Guy van der Westhuizen; John, George, Billy, Benedict, Caroline, Sarah Jane, and Lucy van den Bergh; James and Viviane Mayor; Claude Reed; Sue Ginsberg; Timothy Baum; Crispin Odey; Alex Buchanan; Feras Al-Chalabi; Piers Ouvaroff; Patrick Long; Dom Waugh; Louisa Elder; Michael Davies; Jasper Thornton; John Bentley; Lady Murton.

Please contact the authors with views, criticisms and
all else at:

thomaswhodgkinson@gmail.com
hubert_vandenbergh@yahoo.co.uk

Introduction

A friend of ours was recently at a dinner party. It was given by an artist and there were intellectual types dotted around the table. After what seemed like hours of the other guests discussing intimidating figures such as Chomsky and Wittgenstein, she was relieved when the conversation turned to Rambo. Finally: a chance for her to join in. She started to talk about the gun-toting muscleman as played by Sylvester Stallone in the 1980s action movies, mentioning (a point she was particularly pleased with) that the US government at the time had taken the films seriously, viewing their popularity as an implied critique by the public of the administration's foreign policy.

Everyone stared at her.

'Actually,' one messy-haired academic eventually drawled, 'we were discussing Rimbaud, the 19th-century decadent poet.'

Yet when she told us this story, it got us thinking. Rimbaud isn't the only one, not by a long shot. There are, for most of us, literally hundreds of cultural names we are expected to know something about, but about whom we actually don't have much of a clue – apart from possibly recognising the name. Stefan Zweig. Bertrand Russell, Friedrich Engels. (Could you hold forth for a minute about any of these?) Then there's Bertolt Brecht, Denis Diderot and Michel Foucault. All slippery customers. Journalists constantly cite names such as these, as proof of their cultural credentials. Intellectuals just love to drop them into conversation, like a badge of membership to some elite club, tossed onto the tabletop. We decided to listen out for these names; round them up; and then pluck out the heart of their mysteries.

We learnt a few surprising things along the way. When you look into it, it turns out these formidable individuals are usually known mainly for just one thing. For example, all you really need to know about Virginia Woolf's achievement as an author is that she employed a stream-of-consciousness technique. (This basically involves recording what you think, unedited. Oversharing can be the result.) That he started the anti-consumerism movement – by going and living in a forest by himself – is what Henry David Thoreau was about. And Ayn Rand devoted her life to arguing that governments had no business interfering in the lives of their citizens; they shouldn't even ask for taxes. All intriguing concepts. And a lot less intimidating than many intellectuals would have you believe.

Another thing we learnt is that a lot of these characters knew each other, or at least crossed paths at some point. Some of them even went to bed together. Others contented themselves with a swift punch-up.

And we stumbled on a lot of surreal or surprising connections, which we've used to divide up our book into short chapters. Take, for example, the chapter entitled 'Gruesome Deaths' (page 234). This comprises three of our 250-odd cultural names, all of whom met a particularly unpleasant end:

Isadora Duncan, Fedérico García Lorca, and Che Guevara. Apart from dying horribly, Che, when alive, smelt terrible. In fact, his hygiene was so careless his friends nicknamed him 'The Pig' – which is why he connects to the following chapter: 'Stinkers'. The other 'Stinkers' are Mao, who died without ever having brushed his teeth, and the sweaty novelist Ernest Hemingway – who connects to the next chapter, 'Plane Crashes'. (In fact, Ernest was unlucky enough to have experienced two such accidents, the pain of which drove him to suicide.) And so it goes on …

That's one way of approaching *How To Sound Cultured*: to keep turning the pages, letting these chapter groupings and their links propel you forward. Or else you could just turn to the index, pick out a few names that have always troubled you, and take it from there. Either way, if we've done our job properly, you should find that this book is a quick and easy read – and that it slays a whole host of intellectual dragons, who by the time you've finished reading, will lie in a heap, underneath a cloud of cultural smoke.

Party Throwers

There's a talent in recognising talent in others – and it may be that it's for this, above all else, that the following characters will be remembered by posterity. They all threw fantastic parties, to which they invited the most gifted artists and writers of their time.

Peggy Guggenheim, art collector (1898–1979)

USAGE: In reference to any struggling artist, you might observe, 'What he needs is a Peggy Guggenheim figure to come along.'

Peggy Guggenheim was once asked how many husbands she had had. 'My own, or other people's?' she replied. Sex seems to have been a major preoccupation of the American heiress's life, with art running it a close second. Sometimes the two coincided. She slept with the Surrealist painter Max Ernst* (who didn't?) and even went so far as to marry him, although the union didn't last long.

Generally, however, men didn't treat Peggy well. Her first husband beat her and the Expressionist painter Jackson Pollock* once observed that she was so ugly, you'd first have to put a towel over her head if you wanted to make love

---

* If a name has an asterisk next to it, this means it has its own entry in the book and is therefore in the index.

to her. (Alas, Peggy had a bulbous nose, which she tried unsuccessfully to improve by plastic surgery.) You'd think that Pollock, who never put his theory to the test, would have been more grateful, since Guggenheim persistently invited him to the famous parties she threw, where he got to meet the great and the good of his day. Despite her huge wealth, her tightfistedness meant she famously served only dreadful scotch and ready-salted potato chips at these soirées. She did, though, became one of Pollock's most generous patrons.

The original poor little rich girl, Guggenheim found a purpose in life when she travelled around Europe spending her dough on magnificent works of art by the geniuses of her day, including Picasso*, Kandinsky*, Klee*, Dalí, Magritte and Mondrian, to name a few. These eventually found a permanent home in a palazzo in Venice, which was renamed the Guggenheim Museum (not to be confused with the Guggenheim Museum in New York, which was created by her uncle, Solomon R. Guggenheim). There's some debate over whether Peggy had a real eye for artistic excellence herself, or if the quality of her collection can largely be attributed to her experienced advisors.

Gertrude Stein, writer (1874–1946)

USAGE: If you're unimpressed by someone's garden, but don't wish to be rude, you could quote Stein's most famous line: 'A rose is a rose is a rose is a rose.'

Woody Allen's film *Midnight in Paris* seems to have been inspired by the thought: wouldn't it be great to go to one of Gertrude Stein's parties! Stein, a wealthy gay Jewish author, moved to Paris when she was 29 with her brother Leo. They soon put together such an amazing art collection, people started dropping by at all hours, just to see the pictures (and also, if they were artists, to try to sell their works). Finally the Steins decreed that they would welcome visitors only on Saturday evenings – and thus began their famous 'salons', which became an institution in Paris.

After falling out with her brother, Gertrude carried on the tradition with her lover, Alice B. Toklas. When guests turned up – Picasso*, Matisse, Hemingway*, Fitzgerald, and the rest – they would talk shop with Stein, while Alice entertained their wives and girlfriends in another room. For Stein was a serious author in her own right, even if her writing was almost incomprehensible. She took the idea of stream-of-consciousness to an extreme, apparently believing that, if something occurred to her, she should jot it down. She also favoured repetitions to ensure she got her message across. Her best-known line of verse was 'A rose is a rose is a rose is a rose.' ('In that line,' she later congratulated herself, 'the rose is red for the first time in English poetry for a hundred years.') Or here's another sample: 'Out of kindness comes redness and out of rudeness comes rapid same question.' Crazy, right? But Stein failed to see that if something made no sense, it couldn't be interesting for long.

Her biggest commercial success was the more straightforward prose work *The Autobiography of Alice B. Toklas*. With typical modernist tricksiness, it told not Alice's life story but Gertrude's. Stein's legacy has been tarnished by claims she kowtowed to the Nazis during the Second World War. Even her gifts as an art collector have been called into question. One critic claimed she had a knack for 'collecting geniuses'. But some have argued it was actually Leo who had the eye for truly talented artists, and that after the siblings parted, Gertrude's art collection went downhill.

Stéphane Mallarmé, poet (1842–98)

USAGE: On seeing a film that's rich in stirring imagery but isn't quite logically coherent, you could say that it takes its place in a fine tradition that goes back to Stéphane Mallarmé.

The French *littérateur* Stéphane Mallarmé spent most of his life struggling to make ends meet. Yet he still managed to cobble together a few *sous* so he could throw a drinks party once a week at his home in the rue de Rome in Paris. The regular guests at these salons became known as the Mardistes – after the French word for Tuesday, which was when they met – and they included many of the most gifted authors of the time. W.B. Yeats, André Gide* and Paul Valéry*, to name but a few. Edgar Degas and Auguste Rodin used to shamble along too.

If you're a poet, a good way of ensuring your legacy is to persuade a great composer to put your words to music. And that was what Mallarmé, staggeringly well connected as he was, managed to do. His poem 'L'Après-midi d'un faune' was set to music by Claude Debussy, and later choreographed for a notorious ballet by Vaslav Nijinsky*. Ravel and Boulez also wrote scores for poems by Mallarmé. Musicality was something he aimed for in his work. He was less interested in what words meant than in how they sounded. Indeed, he liked to introduce homophones (words that sounded exactly like other words) into his verse, so that, if it was read aloud, the listener wouldn't be sure what was actually being said. He or she could only listen to, and enjoy, the music of the words.

Mallarmé's emphasis on style over substance was one of his qualifications for membership of the literary movement known as Symbolism in late 19th-century France. This basically meant having interests that ran counter to those of the Realists, who wanted to depict life as accurately as possible. Mallarmé's influence, by all accounts, was vast, and not only in literature. He inspired the Cubist and Futurist artists, and the Dadaists, and the Surrealists. More dubiously, perhaps, the British rock group Coldplay claimed to have had Mallarmé in mind when they wrote their song 'Viva la Vida', thereby establishing their high cultural credentials. They didn't, however, go as far as the pop singer Lady Gaga, who for the sleeve design of one of her albums recruited the services of one of America's best-known contemporary artists …

Album Artists

The contemporary art scene can seem a bit recherché, with few artists having much of an impact on the younger generation (or anyone else for that matter). One way to avoid this trap is to have one of your artworks used as the cover for an album by a trendy singer or rock band.

Jeff Koons, artist (b. 1955)

USAGE: A divisive figure, Koons is usually referred to in tones of contempt or adoration. Be controversial: say you think he's 'fine'.

In 2013, Jeff Koons designed the artwork for the album *ArtPop* by the pop star Lady Gaga. Some might say that 'Gaga' is the appropriate word here. For Koons' artworks incorporate elements that seem designed to appeal to the pre-speech toddler: the shiny, squeaky, kitsch and cartoon. A huge balloon dog made out of chrome metal. A basketball suspended in a fish-tank of water. Sculptures of Michael Jackson and the Incredible Hulk.

A former broker, Koons has brought a Wall Street savvy to his work, turning his creative output into an industry. Some 100 assistants are employed at his factory-like studio in New York. His masterstroke has been to combine his infantile attributes with references to art's grand tradition. As a result, serious art museums can display his works, knowing they'll have as wide an appeal as an exhibition of erotica – which they can resemble in other respects too. His *Made in Heaven* series (1991) consisted of explicit photos of Koons having sex with his wife, the Hungarian porn star La Cicciolina (the word means 'woman who appeals to fat little boys'). Obviously titillating, the arrangements were deliberately similar to those found in paintings by the 18th-century French artists Boucher and Fragonard.

The decision to feature himself in his works points to another key Koonsian feature. He is not only interested in celebrity, he's a celebrity himself. If it's all a confidence trick, it has been highly successful. In 2013, his *Balloon Dog (Orange)* became the most expensive work by a living artist ever sold at auction, after it fetched $58.4m. Whatever else one might want to say about Koons, his brazen commercialism can seem rather fun.

Gerhard Richter, artist (b. 1932)

USAGE: If someone asks you your favourite artist, you might respond, 'I'm tempted to say Richter. But he's worked in such a variety of styles ...'

Since the death of Lucian Freud, the German artist Gerhard Richter is often said to be the world's greatest living painter. What has he done to deserve this accolade? Crucially, he has stayed interested in using paint at a time when many regard the medium as a bit old-fashioned. An obvious example would be his *Abstrakte Bilder* series of the 1980s and 90s (the term just means 'abstract pictures'). Typical examples involve a photograph printed on a large canvas, with paint thickly applied on top and then smeared with a squeegee (of the kind you might use to scrape ice from a windscreen). This simple-sounding technique often achieves the hat-trick of creating a work that is innovative, dynamic, and pleasant to look at.

As if to prove he could do it, Richter is also known for realistic paintings involving skulls and lighted candles, in the style of Georges de La Tour. For an example, see his cover design for 1988's *Daydream Nation* album by the American rock band Sonic Youth. His reputation as a Picasso-like genius rests partly on the wide range of styles in which he has worked. His back catalogue also includes works inspired by the op art of the 1960s, and his beautiful stained-glass window in Cologne Cathedral, which consists of small squares, their colours chosen randomly by a computer.

Richter was born in Dresden. His father was a member of the Nazi party. His maternal aunt, a schizophrenic, was killed by the Nazis as part of their programme of euthanasia for the sick. In person, the artist combines the gravity of his traumatic background with a wry sense of humour and an air of courteous surprise, as if he's startled to find himself still around. Painting, he says, is something to be taken seriously, a fundamental human capacity, like dancing or singing. At the same time, he dismisses the astronomical prices his works now command as 'daft'.

Andy Warhol, artist (1928–87)

USAGE: These days Andy Warhol is most often name-checked in reference to his 'fifteen minutes of fame' concept.

To some, the contemporary art world seems shallow. Yes, Andy Warhol would say. Isn't it beautiful! (Beautiful was one of his favourite words.) More interested in fame than talent, in his lurid silkscreen prints the artist chose as his subjects actors and pop stars such as Marilyn and Elvis. 'In the future,' Warhol memorably declared, 'everyone will be world-famous for fifteen minutes.' In one sense, this was wilfully contro-versial; in another, though, it has arguably come true. The internet now allows anyone to shout their opinions to the world. Who knows? Your Tweet may go viral.

As with many great artists, his achievement is to some extent a marketing ploy, but only to some extent. Part of the challenge is to establish new territory: for the visual artist, this means creating a kind of work that is so associated with you that ever afterwards, if anyone does anything similar, they will be said to be ripping you off. Warhol certainly achieved this with his screen prints, which fetishised the faces of the famous, along with commercial household objects such as a can of soup, say, or (as in his sleeve design for the debut album by rock band The Velvet Underground) a banana. Somewhat less impressive, perhaps, were the avant-garde films he made, with thumpingly explicit titles. *Sleep* (1963) consisted of footage of one of his friends sleeping. *Blowjob* (1964) largely focused on … well, you get the idea.

Warhol believed that if you want to be a celebrity, you need only look like one. Accordingly he wore silver wigs, which he changed regularly, so it looked as if his hair was growing. At his New York studio, The Factory, he attracted a gang of marginal characters: transvestites and drug-addled bohemians, whom he called his 'superstars'. One hanger-on, Valerie Solanas, got fed up and shot him in 1968. Warhol, however, survived. It's possible he felt a mere shooting was too conventional a method of assassination for an original such as himself. Not something that could be said of the bizarre way in which the Soviet Union tried to liquidate one of its greatest novelists …

Hard To Kill

Challenging the status quo will get you into hot water. The next three characters all had to remain on their guard, after narrowly escaping attempts on their lives.

Aleksandr Solzhenitsyn, novelist (1918–2008)

USAGE: Solzhenitsyn's name is often conjured as an example of a brave author writing about systematic state oppression while also stoically enduring it.

In 1971 the KGB tried to assassinate Aleksandr Solzhenitsyn (pronounced: SOL-juh-nit-suhn) by rubbing a poisonous gel into his skin while he was buying sweets. The result was a painful rash that confined him to bed, but didn't kill him. A few years later, the Soviet authorities had the novelist deported. He settled in the American state of Vermont, but remained on his guard against another attempt on his life. The KGB, it's said, resorted to sending him horrific photographs (of car accidents and brain surgery, for instance) in the hope of triggering a nervous breakdown. This too proved ineffective.

Solzhenitsyn has something of the status of a literary saint, for suffering the oppression of one of the worst dictatorial regimes in history, and, with a rare obstinacy of spirit, continuing writing, and writing well, about the injustices being carried out. He knew what he was talking about. Having served with distinction in the Second World War, he was tried for subversion after he wrote a letter to a friend that hinted at criticism of Stalin. The author then served eight years in the gulags (forced labour camps), enduring horrific conditions. After Josef Stalin's death, his successor Nikita Khrushchev permitted the publication of Solzhenitsyn's *One Day in the Life of Ivan Denisovich*, a novel describing a day in the life of a man in a gulag. The book made Solzhenitsyn famous.

Then Khrushchev was ousted, and the author found himself back on the blacklist. Undaunted, he devoted himself to writing what some regard as his masterpiece, *The Gulag Archipelago*, a heavyweight tome describing the Soviet system of forced labour camps. It was this that prompted his exile – and the fact that, having won the Nobel Prize in Literature in 1970, he was becoming too influential. He hated living in America, proclaiming horror at the country's 'TV stupor and intolerable music'. As soon as he was able, after the fall of Communism, he returned to Russia.

Baruch Spinoza, philosopher (1632–77)

USAGE: To justify paying for expensive psychoanalysis, say that you're attempting to 'render my emotions active, in the Spinozan sense'.

One day, on the steps of his local synagogue, the Portuguese Jewish philosopher Baruch Spinoza (pronounced: ba-ROOKH spin-O-za) was attacked by a man who thought him a heretic. Ever afterwards, he kept (and occasionally wore) the knife-slashed cloak as a reminder to himself to live more cautiously. Although Spinoza, who lived in Amsterdam, was a mild-mannered fellow, his beliefs enraged people. For he argued that the soul was not immortal, and there was no point praying to God, since He took no hand in affairs. God, Spinoza said, was essentially the sum of all the things in the universe. God was Nature.

As he explained in his masterpiece, *Ethics* (published posthumously), Spinoza believed there was no such thing as free will. All our actions, if we knew enough, could be predicted. The only way to have anything like free will is to have understanding, which renders our dictatorial emotions 'active', as he put it, instead of 'passive'. 'To understand,' Spinoza declared, 'is to be free.'

Spinoza devoted himself with astonishing purpose to these goals of freedom and understanding. He lived very frugally, ate little, abstained from sex, and often spent days on end working, without leaving the house. His only vice, it's said, is that he sometimes enjoyed watching spiders chase flies. Academic honours were offered him and rejected. Instead, he earned a meagre income by making lenses for microscopes and telescopes. The dust from the grinding of the required powders is thought to have exacerbated the lung condition that killed him aged 44. However, Spinoza's impact as a man of fearless rationality – one of the exemplary forefathers of the Enlightenment – is incalculable.

Leon Trotsky, revolutionary (1879–1940)

USAGE: If someone is described as a Trotskyist, or a Trotskyist Marxist, it often means they subscribe to Trotsky's belief that the revolution has to be carried out all over the globe simultaneously: a concept sometimes expressed by the phrase 'permanent revolution'. This is in contrast to Stalin's belief that you should first concentrate on your own country.

Not content with banishing his former revolutionary colleague Leon Trotsky from Russia, the dictator Josef Stalin ordered his assassination. Despite the fact that Trotsky had taken refuge on the other side of the planet, in Mexico, he was tracked down. In a first attempt, killers entered his house but were fought off by bodyguards. Then, in a later incident, an assassin stole up on Trotsky while he was reading and struck him in the back of the head with an ice axe. He was clumsy and missed his mark. Trotsky spat on and wrestled with his assailant. But he died a day later from blood loss.

It goes without saying that Trotsky is in some ways a more attractive figure than Stalin. In addition to having a funky beard and moustache, he was a brilliant military leader, orchestrating the Red Army's successful victory in the civil war that followed the 1917 revolution. But in doing so, he was clinically brutal. Consider this representative sentence from his memoirs, which is finely expressed but at the same time chilling: 'So long as those malicious tailless apes that are so proud of their technical achievements – the animals that are called men – will build armies and wage wars, the command will always be obliged to place the soldiers between the possible death in the front and the inevitable one in the rear.' This was Trotsky's way of saying deserters would be shot.

He was a compelling speaker, and this, perhaps, contributed to his downfall. After the extremities of the previous years, in the 1920s many Russians longed for a return to a calmer life, and in this respect the boring-seeming Stalin seemed a safer bet. When Lenin died, Trotsky was away. Don't hurry back, Stalin told him. Trotsky didn't, and by the time he returned Stalin had taken control. In exile, first in Turkey and later in Mexico, he was consoled by the companionship of his wife, Natalia. But he couldn't quite resist having an affair with a certain dashing painter ...

Sapiosexuals

They say that like attracts like. So when important cultural figures sleep with important cultural figures, it's no more surprising than when, say, Brad Pitt ends up with Angelina Jolie.

Frida Kahlo, artist (1907–54)

USAGE: Cite Kahlo as an example of an artist who was inspired by the experience of extreme physical trauma.

The art of Frida Kahlo is inextricably linked to pain. When she was just eighteen years old, she was involved in a horrific accident in Mexico City when the bus she was travelling in collided with a tram. Kahlo suffered a broken spine, collarbone, ribs, pelvis, leg and foot. An iron handrail that detached from the wreckage pierced her womb. It was while she was recuperating from these injuries, which prevented her from having children, that she resolved to be an artist, going on to create vibrant personal paintings that would ultimately make her the most successful female painter in Mexico.

During her lifetime, she was better known for being married to another Mexican artist, Diego Rivera. Their relationship was volatile, to say the least. Neither was faithful. Kahlo had affairs with women as well as men. Apparently Rivera didn't mind about the women. Kahlo, however, drew the line when she discovered her husband had been sleeping with her younger sister, Christina. In retaliation she went to bed with the exiled Communist leader Leon Trotsky*. As responses to romantic betrayal go, that's pretty hard to beat.

The Surrealists claimed her as their own for the naive, dreamlike quality of her art, which she filled with symbols from Mexican mythology. Kahlo has also been hailed as a feminist icon for the bold independence not only of her private life but also of her art. Its subject matter is often visceral (in one picture, she portrays herself emerging from her mother's womb). In her many self-portraits, her gaze is direct, and she refuses to prettify herself. A handsome woman, she invariably depicts the way her eyebrows met in the middle and the downy moustache on her upper lip.

Hannah Arendt, philosopher (1906—75)

USAGE: If reading a profile of a murderer who, apart from their penchant for killing people, seems quite normal, you could exclaim: 'Another example of Arendt's banality of evil.'

When the German philosopher Hannah Arendt embarked on an affair with her university professor, Martin Heidegger*, it was a rather unlikely union. Arendt was a Jewish anti-fascist, while Heidegger was, at least for a time, a supporter of Nazism. (For example, it was he who instituted the Hitler salute at the university where he worked.) Much later, long after the relationship was over, Arendt defended her ex-lover against Allied charges, claiming that he had been at worst naive. Her words carried a certain weight, coming from someone who had at one point been incarcerated in a concentration camp. On top of which, she was by then a literary star, particularly renowned for her analysis of dictatorial regimes.

In her most famous work, *The Origins of Totalitarianism*, Arendt pointed to similarities between Stalinism and Nazism, which had in common not only their rampant anti-Semitism, but also their respective nostalgia for lost empires. Russia and Germany had both at one stage controlled colonies around the world, which they had been forced to give up.

During her research into Nazism, Arendt coined the phrase 'the banality of evil', to make the point that atrocious acts are often carried out by characters who are apparently not possessed by demons or just purely evil. She used it to describe Adolf Eichmann, one of the architects of the Holocaust. Arendt believed that Eichmann had been able to send countless Jews to their deaths not because he hated Jews or was a sadist, but for the tragically banal reason that he was ambitious. He knew that killing Jews would help him advance up the Nazi party ranks, and so had simply turned a blind eye to the horrors it entailed.

Martin Heidegger, philosopher (1889–1976)

USAGE: Next time you go for a walk, claim to be doing it not only for the exercise, but also in the hope of escaping from your Heideggerian 'thrown-ness' or *Geworfenheit*.

The German philosopher Martin Heidegger was once asked what people might do to lead better lives. He replied that we should all 'spend more time in graveyards'. As advice goes, this may sound a little morbid, but Heidegger's overarching philosophy, of which the acceptance of our mortality is an integral part, is surprisingly practical and positive.

In his work *Being and Time* (1927), Heidegger argued that it is only by confronting the fact we are going to die that we can start to live. Or to use his terminology, it is only by embracing *Das Nichts* (non-existence) that we can get to grips with *Das Sein* (existence). Most of us spend most of our time living 'inauthentic' lives: worried about the opinions of people who don't really care for us, and who in any case cannot save us from death – so why are we striving to impress them? Secondly, he wrote that we are all 'thrown' into this world. By this he meant that we don't choose to be born, or where we are born, or who our parents are, or what our education should be. As a result, our early experiences and beliefs are 'thrown' upon us. This 'thrown-ness' (*Geworfenheit*), like our inauthenticity, is something we must transcend. How? Heidegger recommended long walks in the countryside, pondering the miracle of existence.

If this all makes Heidegger sound relatively easy to understand, don't be misled. One of the most important, and complicated, philosophers of the 20th century, he took his place in a tradition of German philosophical incomprehensibility, along with the likes of Immanuel Kant*. (This of course makes him a particularly impressive name to drop into conversation.) Which means that one can't say with total certainty what he believed about anything.

Man Ray, artist and photographer (1890–1976)

USAGE: Any photograph that contains a surreal element – something absurdly out of context – may be said to owe something to the influence of Man Ray.

Like a lot of creative types, the American artist Man Ray liked to go to bed with other creative types. One example was the Belgian poet Adon Lacroix, who became his first wife in 1914. When they separated in 1919, she told him bitterly: 'You'll never amount to anything without me!' His reply was understated: 'We'll see.' Yet it must have seemed an increasingly crushing riposte as time went by. Soon afterwards, Man Ray moved to Paris and embarked on the most fertile phase of a career that would see him hailed as one of the most important artists of the 20th century.

'There is no progress in art,' Man Ray once remarked, 'any more than there is progress in making love. There are simply different ways of doing it.' It was a nice line, but there was definitely progress in his own artistic development. Born Emmanuel Radnitzky, the son of a tailor, he started out painting in a rather conventional style, but later, inspired by

Marcel Duchamp*, he became a key member of the Surrealist movement. One of his signature works was *Enigma of Isidore Ducasse*: it consisted of a sewing machine (a nod to his father's profession) draped in a piece of cloth.

Man Ray knew everyone who was anyone, and moved from style to style with effortless energy. He is perhaps best remembered these days for his experiments in photography. A characteristic example of his visual wit was *Violon d'Ingres*, a black and white photograph of his lover, the splendidly named Kiki de Montparnasse, whose naked back, seen from behind, suggests the curves of a violin. He also cannily took photographs of many of the brilliant people of his time, including James Joyce*, Gertrude Stein*, and a certain gifted and extremely beautiful protégée …

Lee Miller, photographer and muse (1907–77)

USAGE: To endear yourself to a precocious young woman, try declaring admiration for the work of Lee Miller.

It's easy to think of men who were good-looking, lived and loved with style, and occasionally produced great art or literature, but the female examples are relatively few. One is the American photographer Lee Miller. Preternaturally beautiful, she started out as a fashion model for *Vogue*; then ran off to Paris to become the muse and lover of the Surrealist photographer Man Ray (among others); and later reinvented herself as a war photographer, being among the first to take pictures of the horrors of the Nazi death camps.

21

As a rule, her style behind the camera combined the wit of the Surrealists with the savoir faire of glossy magazines. Yet she's more likely to be remembered for the pictures taken of her than for those she took herself (always a danger when you're preternaturally beautiful). Perhaps the most extraordinary is an image of her, naked, in Adolf Hitler's bathtub in Munich, taken a few days before the Führer killed himself in his Berlin bunker. In front, we can see Miller's boots, still caked in mud from the concentration camps.

In later life, she became an alcoholic, haunted by the horrors she had seen. Some critics speak of her slightingly as a flibbertigibbet or egomaniac or both: men are always troubled by women who do as they like. After marrying the artist Roland Penrose (who was eventually knighted, meaning she became Lady Penrose), Miller settled in a farmhouse in the English countryside. She devoted herself to creating Surrealist culinary dishes such as blue spaghetti and cauliflowers made to resemble breasts, and rarely spoke of her former life – though anyone in any doubt can peruse her historic photographs, or look out for her appearance in Jean Cocteau's* 1929 movie *The Blood of a Poet*. With her sleek beauty, she confirmed cinema as what a certain Canadian cultural theorist would term 'a hot medium'. The latter would himself pop up on screen from time to time …

The Silver Screen

*You know you've made it when you get
name-checked in a movie. Better still
if you actually appear on screen.*

Marshall McLuhan, philosopher
and media theorist (1911–80)

USAGE: A nice way to put down someone who accuses
you of talking nonsense – turn to them and murmur, '
As Marshall McLuhan used to say, "You know nothing
of my work."'

It's such a great scene. In 1977's *Annie Hall*, Woody Allen
is annoyed by a self-important man in a movie queue, who
keeps droning on about the theories of Marshall McLuhan.
To prove him wrong, Allen produces McLuhan himself, who
declares, 'You know nothing of my work.' Then, turning to
the camera, Allen observes, 'Boy, if only life were like this!'
In a sense, though, it was like life. 'You know nothing of my
work,' was one of McLuhan's favourite phrases. It was a postmodern scene (in that it drew attention to its own unreality)
and McLuhan was a postmodern theorist.

'The medium is the message' is a key quote used to sum
up his central idea. McLuhan, a Canadian academic who
practically invented media studies, believed it was more

interesting to consider the medium of books and films in isolation from their content. What effect does it have on us, the fact that we're readers and film-goers? Until relatively recently, most people didn't read. Now it looks as if few will continue to do so. Until the 1950s, most people didn't have a TV. Now we all watch films on our laptops. According to McLuhan, these changes in the medium (regardless of whether books and films have a moral or immoral content) have a huge impact on the very structure of our thought processes, defining who we are as people. He set out his ideas in *The Gutenberg Galaxy* (1951) and *Understanding Media* (1964), which made him a huge intellectual celebrity in the 1960s. McLuhan also seems to have predicted the internet about 30 years before it was invented.

One key distinction he made was between 'hot' and 'cool' media. The way McLuhan used these terms was a bit confusing, but he would probably have regarded the modern blockbuster as hot, since it blasts out at you and you lie back and let it hit you. By contrast, a complicated book – such as one by McLuhan himself – is 'cool'. The reader has to work hard to understand it.

Pina Bausch, choreographer (1940–2009)

USAGE: If you're clumsy on the dance floor, suggest to your partner, 'Let's don blindfolds and pretend we're taking part in a sight-impaired performance of Pina Bausch's *Café Muller*.'

Pina Bausch grew up in the German town of Solingen, where her parents ran a hotel. As a girl – the name Pina is short for Philippina – she would watch couples fall in love or break up in the restaurant, and this prompted her obsession with the intricacies of human relationships. Violence and tenderness, she saw, could be two halves of the same coin. Always resistant to categories, in her work she concentrated on so-called Tanztheater, also known as dance-theatre. As the name suggests, it refers to something halfway between dance and theatre.

This blurring of boundaries characterised her career. A dancer herself, who had trained at the renowned Juilliard School in New York, in her choreography Bausch blended tradition with improvisation. She cut an androgynous figure, with sharp, strong, almost manly features; in several of her works, she would dress her male dancers in drag. Her vision could seem bleak – to some, it seemed exhaustingly so – its emphasis on strife and a search for meaning that is doomed to failure. In her most famous work, *Café Muller* (a direct homage to her upbringing in Solingen), many of the dancers performed with their eyes closed, knocking over chairs and tables.

Her influence, like her choreography, crossed boundaries. She has been revered and imitated by everyone from the rock

25

star David Bowie to the film-maker Pedro Almodóvar, who incorporated her techniques into his 2001 film *Talk to Her*. Her ambition was never in doubt – evidenced, for instance, in her 1975 version of Stravinsky's *The Rite of Spring*, which involved a stage covered in soil, and ended with the dancers exhausted, covered in sweat and dirt.

Jean Baudrillard, philosopher (1929–2007)

USAGE: You can name-drop Baudrillard whenever you see someone purchasing a luxury item: 'Do you really want it? Or, to paraphrase Baudrillard, do you just crave the status it denotes?'

In the sci-fi thriller *The Matrix*, a character is seen reading a copy of *Simulacra and Simulation* by the French philosopher Jean Baudrillard (pronounced: BOE-dree-ar). Fittingly so. For the film questions the nature of reality, and Baudrillard's big idea was that images of reality have become more 'real' than reality. For instance, pornographic images dominate the way we think of sex more than the experience of sex itself. (To which one is tempted to say: speak for yourself, Baudrillard!) Or when we think of love, we don't think of love as it is, but as we have seen it portrayed in movies such as *Titanic* or *Brief Encounter*, or in advertisements for after-shave or washing powder. Ditto cars, dogs, packets of biscuits – pretty much everything, in fact. To make his theory sound more impressive, the author referred to each of these received and influential images as a 'simulacrum' (plural: simulacra).

Taking the argument further, he pointed out that an object was never merely an object, but always came with certain ideas and values attached. For example, a BMW is not only a car but also a proof that you are well off. He got into trouble when he claimed that the Gulf War didn't exist; it was just TV images of it that existed. Not a very tactful observation. His critics say that when you decode Baudrillard's theories, it turns out he's just stating the obvious. More than that, he's overstating it. For while it might be true that we send more emails than we have conversations over the course of an average day, that doesn't mean the internet is more real for us than the real world. It merely means we're making use of technology.

Some have also suggested that Baudrillard may have taken himself too seriously. He was never entirely comfortable with the idea of being associated with *The Matrix*, and tried to distance himself from the movie, claiming that the brothers who had directed it had misunderstood his *oeuvre*.

F.R. Leavis, literary critic (1895–1978)

USAGE: If spotted reading a serious novel, explain that you're trying to be more of a 'Leavisite' in your literary tastes.

In a scene in the 2001 romantic comedy *Bridget Jones's Diary*, the heroine, who works in publishing, pretends to be on the phone to the literary critic F.R. Leavis. Her bluff is called by her boss, who points out that Leavis died in the 1970s. Why did Bridget pick Leavis? Presumably because he was the only critic she could think of. People who write about books don't tend to become household names, but the Cambridge English literature professor was an exception.

One way he achieved his fame was by the startling severity of his literary judgements, which jolted readers into fearing that perhaps he might know something they didn't. T.S. Eliot*, W.B. Yeats and D.H. Lawrence* were all geniuses, in Leavis's eyes. By contrast, in *The Great Tradition* (1948) he pointedly ignored the works of Charles Dickens*, Thomas Hardy and Laurence Sterne*, though he later changed his mind about Dickens.

Leavis didn't always get it right. He was a fanatical admirer of the works of one Ronald Bottrall: a judgement that has not been borne out by posterity. What he did succeed in doing was in persuading the lazy English to take the business of literature a bit more seriously. He is now generally thought to have been a sounder critic of poetry than of novels: in the case of the latter, he tended to get carried away with his insistence that a book could only be 'good' if it engaged with the moral complexities of the age in which it was written. Looking at the list of the authors Leavis admired, one is tempted to suggest he may have favoured ones who used double initials. His own initials, incidentally, stood for Frank Raymond.

Thomas Pynchon, novelist (b. 1937)

USAGE: Any novel that's sprawlingly long, and mixes references to high and low culture, may be described as Pynchon-esque.

In the recent film of his novel *Inherent Vice*, it's rumoured Thomas Pynchon has a cameo. Hard to be sure, since he's such a recluse that no one knows what he looks like. If you scan images online, there are a few of a lazy-eyed, un-beautiful young man with severely protruding teeth. There's a rumour that embarrassment about his teeth may be one reason the author shuns the limelight. He did, though, once provide the voice for a cartoon version of himself (with a paper bag on its head) in the animated TV show *The Simpsons*.

We know he studied at Cornell University in New York and attended lectures by Vladimir Nabokov*, despite the fact that Nabokov said he had no memory of Pynchon, and Pynchon has given out that he couldn't understand a word Nabokov said, owing to the latter's thick Russian accent. There are some who have found Pynchon's books similarly incomprehensible. Hefty volumes, many of them, they are definitively postmodern, bursting with humour, digression, and a signature blend of high and low culture. One critic likened the style to a combination of Hieronymus Bosch and Walt Disney. The big one is *Gravity's Rainbow* (1973), viewed by some as the greatest post-war American novel. What's it about? As Pynchon himself might put it, it's about 750 pages.

Other qualities of a novel that might earn the description Pynchon-esque are a mood of paranoia, and descriptions of drug use and bizarre sexual practices. The novelist

Salman Rushdie is one of the few who is known to have met the author. Asked to describe him, he said he was very 'Pynchon-esque'. The recluse tag has got people so excited, crazy theories abound as to his true identity. There's a theory that he is really a woman named Wanda. Few have made such a virtue of shunning the limelight as Pynchon, though there are one or two who have tried. Consider the case of a certain South African novelist, who rarely even deigns to turn up in person to receive prestigious literary awards …

Hermits

You don't have to live in a cave to write a good
book, but it helps if you're not especially sociable.

J.M. Coetzee, novelist (b. 1940)

USAGE: There doesn't seem to be one accepted correct
pronunciation of Coetzee's name. Be confident and pronounce
it as eccentrically as possible. Perhaps Cut-say-yah!

The South African novelist J.M. Coetzee is so reclusive that,
on the two occasions when he won the Booker prize, he didn't
bother turning up to receive it. But when he was awarded
the Nobel Prize in Literature in 2003, he deigned to attend
the ceremony, where he heard himself praised for novels
that explore 'the surprising involvement of the outsider', and
which display 'well-crafted composition, pregnant dialogue
and analytical brilliance'. A shy, gentle, softly spoken, lightly
bearded man, Coetzee is reported to have a habit of attending dinner parties but not uttering a single word. A colleague
who knew him for years claimed to have heard him laugh on
only one occasion. Sadly, history doesn't relate the nature of
the joke that prompted this outburst.

Along with Nadine Gordimer, Coetzee is an example of
a South African author who has dared to analyse his country's troubled politics, and done so with such a measured

intelligence that he has for the most part escaped censure. There are no quick or clumsy allocations of blame in Coetzee's books. *Disgrace* – perhaps his best-known novel internationally – tells the story of a white South African literature professor who takes sexual advantage of one of his students (in a way that falls just short of rape). Sacked from his job, he moves to live with his daughter on her farm. Some black thugs break in, and rape and impregnate his daughter. Coetzee doesn't assign a moral equivalence to the crimes. By juxtaposing them, he encourages a more thoughtful response to each.

Arthur Schopenhauer, philosopher (1788–1860)

USAGE: In a conversation about retirement plans, you might reveal your intention to 'withdraw from society, and cultivate a Schopenhauerian detachment from the common struggle'.

One difficulty with understanding philosophers is that they're nearly always responding to other philosophers. To understand philosopher A, you need to know something about philosopher B. So it was with Arthur Schopenhauer, whose masterwork *The World As Will And Representation* commented on the theories of his fellow German Immanuel Kant*.

Kant had claimed it was impossible to penetrate our veil of perception and grasp anything about the real or 'noumenal' world. Not so, Schopenhauer retorted. We can sense within our every mental action the workings of our will, which he termed 'the will to live', and conceived as a constant struggle to survive and reproduce. The original bleak existential philosopher, he was extraordinarily (one might say 'wilfully') pessimistic. For Schopenhauer, life was 'a constantly prevented dying', just as walking is 'a constantly prevented falling'.

The will that drives us makes us unhappy. The good news is we can escape. A respite is possible in aesthetic contemplation: as we gaze at a painting, we forget ourselves and are briefly happy (or at least not unhappy). A more permanent solution is a quasi-Buddhist withdrawal from the daily struggle, living like a hermit. Schopenhauer was one of the first Western philosophers to pay attention to the traditions of Eastern religions. Bizarre-looking, with a huge domed forehead and crazy clown hair, he was objectionable in person, despising women and Jews. In later life, he increasingly practised what he preached and kept himself to himself, rarely venturing out of doors and devoting himself to his studies. Almost the only company he could tolerate was that of his beloved pet poodles, to each of whom he gave the same name, Atma: the Hindu word for the universal soul.

More on 'Hermits' overleaf

Nathaniel Hawthorne, novelist (1804–64)

> **USAGE:** If you've behaved in a way that society is likely to condemn, you could wryly remark that you're considering embroidering the letter A on your chest, like in Hawthorne's *The Scarlet Letter*.

Pathologically shy, Nathaniel Hawthorne – regarded as one of the greatest American novelists – was appalled at the idea of literary celebrity. It wasn't just that he dreaded the attention. He also feared that public scrutiny would reveal one of his ancestors had been a judge who had notoriously sentenced innocent women to death at the Salem witch trials. To conceal the connection, the author, who had been born Nathaniel Hathorne, added a W to his surname – a single letter designed to conceal a crime, just as, in his most famous work, a single letter would proclaim one.

The Scarlet Letter (1850) tells the story of a woman, Hester Prynne, who has a child by a married man, and is then forced by her shocked community to wear a capital A (for Adultery) embroidered on the front of her dress. The heroine shows more strength and serenity than any of the flaky male characters surrounding her, including the guilt-stricken father of her child, whose identity she refuses to divulge. For this reason – and for the strong female characters in his other books, such as *The House of the Seven Gables* (1851) – Hawthorne is hailed as a proto-feminist. He's also classed as a Dark Romantic, along with the likes of Edgar Allan Poe, because he described intense passions leading to gloomy consequences of a generally grim and bloody nature.

Hawthorne's admiration for women was fuelled by his close relationship with his mother, and his long, happy marriage to a woman who was almost as shy as himself. For such a recluse, he had a large number of distinguished friends. The pallbearers at his funeral included the poet Henry Wadsworth Longfellow and the Transcendentalist philosopher Ralph Waldo Emerson*.

Michel de Montaigne, essayist (1533–92)

USAGE: If you revere a journalist who writes in a way that is both personal and universal, witty and wise, you might say that his writing is imbued with the spirit of Michel de Montaigne.

When Michel de Montaigne (pronounced: mon-TEN-yh) was 38, his best friend Étienne died, and, racked by grief, he shut himself away in a tower on the family estate, surrounded by books. He stayed there for a decade, seeing no one and devoting himself to writing a huge volume of *Essays*. These were remarkably ahead of their time. No one had thought of combining intellectual arguments with personal anecdotes in the way Montaigne did, though the style is now copied by countless journalists the world over. Not that, on the whole, they manage it with quite the eloquence and wisdom of Montaigne.

One who came close was the English journalist William Hazlitt, who summed up the admiration in which the French author is universally held by describing him as 'the first who had the courage to say as an author what he felt as a man'.

For Montaigne didn't kowtow to the religious orthodoxies or conventional views of his day. He wrote, simply and succinctly, what he personally felt on an amazing range of topics – and wrote so well that he's extremely readable even five centuries on, whether he's musing about the trouble with religions (that they lead to wars) or expounding his theories of education. The best method for teaching children, he argued, was to give them the space to teach themselves. That's the only way anyone ever really remembers anything.

He'd had a pretty strange education himself. His father had insisted that he should be spoken to only in Latin, so Latin would be his first language. Then he was assigned a German tutor who couldn't even speak French. In the event, it all seemed to work, for the eccentric upbringing produced one of the most enlightened and delightful writers of all time. But don't take our word for it. According to Friedrich Nietzsche*, Montaigne 'truly augmented the joy of living on this Earth', while French literary critic Charles Augustin Sainte-Beuve recommended reading at least a page of his writing every evening.

José Saramago, novelist (1922–2010)

USAGE: Borrow a line of Saramago's, and if you're ever criticised for showing disrespect towards the devout, murmur: 'They should just focus on their prayers.'

Any struggling author who has yet to hit the big time can take comfort from the thought that Saramago didn't manage it until his sixties. That was when the novelist – who was born of sturdy Portuguese peasant stock (his surname means 'radish') – finally earned a name for himself with the novel *Baltasar and Blimunda*. His typical style was to write very long sentences, sometimes going on for pages at a time. He rarely bothered with quotation marks to indicate dialogue. Many of his books were allegories involving fantastical events. For instance, in *The Stone Raft* (1986), the Iberian peninsula breaks off from the rest of Europe and goes sailing around the Atlantic. In *Blindness* (1995) a country is inexplicably afflicted by a plague that makes everyone go blind: a metaphor, the author said, for the way people turn a blind eye to the rise of right-wing dictatorships, such as those that had run the show in Portugal over the years.

A dedicated communist, Saramago never lost his ability to annoy people, whether it was religious conservatives ('I respect those who believe,' he once said, 'but I have no respect for the institution') or Israelis, who were incensed in 2002 when the novelist declared: 'What is happening in Palestine is a crime we can put on the same plane as what happened at Auschwitz.'

Of all his books perhaps the most controversial was *The Gospel According to Jesus Christ* (1991), which depicted Jesus living with Mary Magdalene and trying to back out of the crucifixion. (Little wonder the Vatican took exception when Saramago was awarded the Nobel Prize in Literature in 1998. On hearing of the Church's disapproval, he merely remarked: 'They should just focus on their prayers.') The furore stirred by the novel was so fierce that he no longer felt welcome in his home country. So he turned his back on Portuguese society and moved to Lanzarote in the Atlantic Ocean. So Saramago ended his life as an author who had *chosen* to become an islander – by contrast with a certain literary critic, who regarded it as a fate he was unable to escape ...

Islanders

From Robinson Crusoe *to Alex Garland's*
The Beach, *countless literary works have centred
on sea-girt rocks (sometimes complete with
coconut trees and welcoming maidens clad in
grass skirts). Islands have also provided many
authors with peaceful havens in which to write.*

Frank Kermode, literary critic (1919–2010)

USAGE: If anyone claims that things were better in the old days,
you can refer them to Frank Kermode's book *The Sense of an
Ending*, in which he argued that humans have always convinced
themselves that things were better in the past, are about to get
better in the future, but just at present are about as bad as they
could possibly be.

Brought up on the Isle of Man off the west coast of England,
Frank Kermode claimed that his background as an islander
left him feeling like an outsider in the metropolitan world
of literary criticism. He wrote like an outsider too – shunning the complex style of most critics, even after he became
Professor of English at Cambridge. He wanted the man in
the street to enjoy his books too. When he wrote his autobiography, he called it *Not Entitled*. The book did have a title,
of course – and so did he (he was knighted for services to

literature). What he meant was (tongue-in-cheek) that he was still an ordinary guy.

There are two keys to being a great literary critic. The first is that you have to write well about literature: that's to say, you must be a sensitive reader of literature, with the knack of communicating why what's good is good, and bad, bad. Preferably you should do so in prose that is itself so elegant and nuanced, it's almost worthy of literary study in itself. But that isn't enough. As well as writing well about writing well, you also need a 'big idea': some overarching theory that readers can use in ages to come when considering a particular aspect of literature.

Kermode set out his big idea in his 1967 book *The Sense of an Ending*. It was that we're all haunted by the insignificance of our little lives in the context of eternity. To make ourselves feel better, we convince ourselves that there was once a golden age when everything was okay, and even if things are terrible now, they're about to get better. We all persuade ourselves we're on the brink of a new golden age – because if we didn't, Kermode argued, we wouldn't be able to get up in the morning. It's not true, though. A new golden age never does dawn – which is depressing, on the face of it. But Kermode said we needn't be disheartened. It's thanks to this persistent optimism about the future that great writers have the energy to innovate. Embrace the lie, and as Winston Churchill put it, keep buggering on.

Sappho, poet (7th–6th centuries BC)

USAGE: If you really wanted to praise a brilliant singer-songwriter, you could describe them as 'the greatest lyric poet since Sappho'.

'Some say cavalry and others claim infantry or a fleet of long oars is the supreme sight on the black earth. I say it is the one you love.' So wrote Sappho at some point in the 7th or 6th century BC. She adds that for her the 'finest sight' is that of a certain Anaktoria: which is to say, another woman. Sappho – who wrote 'lyric' poetry, i.e. that which is performed to the accompaniment of a lyre – also expressed her passion for men, so was probably bisexual. Yet because she was apparently attracted to other women, she is widely perceived to have been a lesbian.

Indeed, the term 'lesbian' derives from her, since she lived on the island of Lesbos in the Aegean Sea. So does 'sapphic', an archaic expression used to mean the same thing. But actually, neither term is all that archaic. Both were invented by the Victorians in the late 19th century as politely classical ways to refer to women who sleep with other women. Before then, the idea of a lesbian barely seems to have existed. So what else do we need to know about Sappho? Not much, because not much is known by anyone. Details about her life are hazy, largely based on her poetry, which may or may not be autobiographical.

We don't even have much of that. What we do have, though, seems clear and graceful, like the following quotation. 'Sweet is the god, but still I am in agony and far from my strength.' I guess we've all had that feeling at one time or another. In her combination of literary talent and her passions for women as well as men, she has been a figure of inspiration ever since to intelligent, free-thinking women who find themselves attracted to others of their sex – a type resoundingly represented by the next in our catalogue of entries ...

Sapphic Love

*Intelligent women are likely to find most
men disgusting and pointless. Little wonder
that some are tempted to have affairs
with members of their own sex.*

Susan Sontag, critic (1933–2004)

USAGE: Anyone who posts too many pictures on Facebook may
be warned against a Sontagian erosion of memory.

Although she did date men, the most enduring relationship of the American cultural critic Susan Sontag was with
a woman, the photographer Annie Leibovitz. The liaison
wasn't without controversy. For Leibovitz recorded images
of Sontag's final months as she lay dying of cancer, which
some found distressing.

Photography and cancer were the subjects of two of
Sontag's best-known works. In *On Photography* (1977) she
argued that we rely too much on photos for our memory of
events (which seems particularly prescient in the light of
visually-oriented social media sites such as Facebook and
Instagram). In *Illness as Metaphor* (1978), she analysed
ways in which we talk of illnesses, particularly cancer,
and suggested that anything other than straightforward
language can belittle the experience of sufferers. Is it

judicious, for instance, to describe someone as 'battling' cancer?

Sontag does seem to have had a tendency to exaggerate or overstate her views. She notoriously described 'the white race' as 'the cancer of human history'. (This was before she became stricter about using metaphors to describe illnesses and illnesses as metaphors.) In the immediate aftermath of 9/11, she weighed in against those who viewed the plane strikes as 'a cowardly attack on civilisation or liberty', arguing that they were a response to 'specific American alliances and actions'. This caused outrage. As a rule, though, the loathing she stirs in right-wing, usually male, commentators is easily as hysterical as the hysteria of which they accuse her. Could it be that some of them feel threatened by an attractive woman who dared also to be left-wing and – let's face it – clever?

Mary Wollstonecraft, author and campaigner for women's rights (1759–97)

USAGE: Some of the fundamental tenets of feminist belief may be attributed to the influence of Mary Wollstonecraft's writings, and to the personal example she set.

It would be misleading to say the women's rights campaigner Mary Wollstonecraft was a lesbian, but she was attracted to women, in particular a close friend of hers named Fanny Blood. And she was unconventional: after falling in love with the married painter Henry Fuseli, she suggested living with him and his wife in a *ménage à trois*. Unconvinced, Fuseli ended the affair.

Soon afterwards, Wollstonecraft wrote what is sometimes called the first lesbian novel by a woman, *Mary: A Fiction*. Then in 1790, she penned *A Vindication of the Rights of Men* in support of the French Revolution. Emboldened by success, she went on produce her most famous work, 1792's *A Vindication of the Rights of Woman*. Regarded as a founding text of feminism, it argued not that women and men were equal, but that they should have equal rights. Crucially, it made the case that if women seemed intellectually inferior – 'spaniels' or 'toys', to use her terms – this was because men had decreed that they should have next to no education, and drummed it into them from infancy that the most important thing was that they should be sexually attractive.

Wollstonecraft was a scandalous figure in her lifetime, bearing a child to a man named Gilbert Imlay, then twice attempting suicide when the relationship turned sour. She finally found love with the philosopher William Godwin, only to die a few days after giving birth to their daughter, Mary (who would write the novel *Frankenstein*). In the agony of his grief, Godwin wrote: 'I firmly believe there does not exist her equal in the world. I know from experience we were formed to make each other happy. I have not the least expectation that I can now ever know happiness again.'

Margaret Mead, anthropologist (1901–78)

USAGE: To justify an old-fashioned approach to relationships – being a monogamous heterosexual, for instance – you might say, 'I'm not a subscriber to Margaret Mead's idea of sexual liberation.'

The American anthropologist Margaret Mead was fascinated by all human life and she extended this impartiality to her romantic interests. As well as three husbands, she had long affairs with two female anthropological colleagues, with one of whom, a woman named Rhoda, she spent her last twenty years. If she felt any guilt, as an Anglican Christian, about flouting social conventions in this way, Mead may have consoled herself with her research, from which she concluded that in some primitive societies, when it came to sex and romance, pretty much anything went.

That was the message a lot of readers took away from her two key works, 1928's *Coming of Age in Samoa*, and 1935's *Sex and Temperament in Three Primitive Societies*. They made Mead an inspirational figure for feminists in the sexual revolution of the 1960s, despite the fact that by then her work had come in for severe academic criticism. Particularly controversial was her claim that in Papua New Guinea there was a community living by Lake Tchambuli (now Chambri) that was ruled by women. Some argued that this was probably an aberration brought on by the ban on local warfare imposed by Australia, which controlled the country (this meant that men could not seize control in their usual manner – by force). Moreover, later research found no evidence for a society of the kind described by Mead as ever having existed in the area.

Once a name to conjure with, she is regarded now as more of a footnote in intellectual history. As a footnote to that footnote, Mead is also sometimes cited for her new-fangled theories about childcare. Among other ideas inspired by her work, she suggested – along with her friend Benjamin Spock – that mothers should feed babies not only at set times of day, but also whenever they cried.

Simone de Beauvoir, philosopher (1908–86)

USAGE: In any discussion of the systematic ways in which men have oppressed women through the ages, a name-check of de Beauvoir's *The Second Sex* would be appropriate.

At a glance, Simone de Beauvoir's love life seems in keeping with her vocation as an intellectual and a leader of the women's rights movement. She refused to be confined by convention and enjoyed affairs with lovers of both sexes. However, there was an exploitative side to her 'liberated' shenanigans. It seems that, as a teacher in her thirties, she used to seduce her female pupils and then pass them on to her long-term lover, the swivel-eyed midget Jean-Paul Sartre*, who had a penchant for deflowering virgins. The two of them referred to these arrangements as 'trios'.

But let's move on. De Beauvoir denied that she was a philosopher, but her 1944 essay *Pyrrhus and Cineas* forms a nice counterpoint to Albert Camus'* *The Myth of Sisyphus*: de Beauvoir too takes a classical story as a starting point for a consideration of existentialist philosophy (asking, basically:

what's the bloody point?). She also wrote novels, usually auto-biographical, one of which, *The Mandarins* (1954), won the Prix Goncourt. Yet it's for her feminist call to arms *The Second Sex* (1949) that she is best remembered. The book's title sums up the central argument. Women, de Beauvoir argues, have been habitually presented by men as secondary, an after-thought, as if they were, so to speak, men without penises (to give just one example, the Bible states that God made Adam first).

More broadly, she considers how men, under the guise of gallantry, entrap women in roles that are convenient to men. For example, some husbands will praise their wife as a 'domestic goddess'. Don't be fooled into thinking this is a compliment, said de Beauvoir. No, these husbands ascribe this label to ensure their wife is forever saddled with the role of cleaning the house. Expressing the idea in the terminol-ogy of existentialism, the author wrote: 'One is not born, but rather becomes, a woman.' This means you're born a human. It is male conditioning that will make you 'a woman'.

Virginia Woolf, novelist (1882–1941)

USAGE: If someone is being long-winded in a business meeting, you could say, 'Can we keep it short? This isn't a Virginia Woolf novel.'

Virginia Woolf. Lesbian. Feminist. Killed herself. Who's afraid of her?, as Edward Albee* famously asked. Pretty much everyone, right?

Woolf was, of course, a far more sympathetic and interesting figure than this summary implies. She may have had lesbian affairs, for example with the garden designer Vita Sackville-West, but she also loved and made love to her husband, the author Leonard Woolf. As a novelist, she contributed to the development of the ground-breaking stream-of-consciousness technique (getting inside a character's head and writing down all their thoughts). At its best, it can seem very real and interesting. At its worst, it's a case of 'too much information'. For those who aren't tuned in, *Mrs Dalloway*, in which a middle-aged woman plans a party, seems dull. Ditto *To the Lighthouse*, describing a family outing (to the eponymous beacon). Such readers may prefer *Orlando*, a lighter tale, ranging across the centuries, about an immortal character who changes gender from male to female (it was inspired by Woolf's admiration for Sackville-West).

Woolf committed suicide at the age of 59 after decades of struggling with what would now be diagnosed as bipolar depression. She put stones in her coat pockets and walked into the River Ouse. 'Everything has gone from me but the certainty of your goodness,' she wrote in a last message to Leonard. 'I can't go on spoiling your life any longer.' As suicide notes go, hers was heartbreaking, so honest and kind it could move almost anyone to tears. Quite a contrast, then, with the final message of a certain Austrian novelist, which has been rather harshly criticised by at least one critic on the grounds of its prose style ...

Self-Slaughter

With great talent comes, all too often, great internal angst. The following are just some of those who have finally taken matters into their own hands.

Stefan Zweig, novelist (1881–1942)

USAGE: A story set in middle Europe, rich in nostalgia for the past and apparently designed to make you sob, may be described as Zweigian.

His surname means 'branch', and that was the name – Stephen Branch – under which bootlegged copies of Stefan Zweig's novels were once sold in England. Those novels were (to extend a metaphor) rooted in his Austrian upbringing, formal, nostalgic and sentimental. Too sentimental, some said. *Letter from an Unknown Woman* was an exploration of the consequences of a lack of feeling: a smugly successful author receives a posthumous letter from a woman he knew as a girl, and later twice slept with, neither time remembering her. *Beware of Pity* considers the opposite. A man pities a paralysed girl, and to persuade her to take a treatment that could cure her, tells her he'll marry her when she recovers. She discovers he's been denying this to friends, and kills herself.

Hugely successful in his day, Zweig was oppressed by the fear that civilisation was about to end. When the Nazis came to power, he fled to England, and then, in case England fell, carried on to New York and later, to be on the safe side, Brazil. But the news from home continued to depress him and in 1942, when Hitler seemed likely to triumph, he and his wife Lotte killed themselves in a suicide pact. One critic has harshly commented that his suicide note was as fake and sentimental as all his novels. But after his popularity in his lifetime – to the point where he was deemed distinguished enough to deliver one of the eulogies at the funeral of Sigmund Freud* – and the decline in his reputation following his death, Zweig is on the up. Several of his books were recently reissued by the Pushkin Press. And the filmmaker Wes Anderson has admitted that his acclaimed film *The Grand Budapest Hotel* was inspired by *Beware of Pity* and other books by Zweig.

Heinrich von Kleist, playwright
and short-story writer (1777–1811)

USAGE: To help someone who's feeling miserable, you might recommend the Von Kleist approach of forming a clear plan for achieving one's goals in life.

The German author Heinrich von Kleist was convinced that the surest route to happiness was to have a plan. This alone, he believed, could bring you peace of mind. And he had one himself – namely to be a great author – in which he undoubtedly succeeded. He's generally regarded as one of the most important German Romantic playwrights, and as having made a significant contribution to the development of the short story, with his deadpan, almost forensic writing style. Nevertheless, despite the fact that he had achieved everything he could have hoped for at a relatively early age, or perhaps because of this, he fell into a deep gloom and killed himself. He chose a nice spot for it: on the lakeshore of the Kleiner Wannsee. Before he did the deed, he first, at her request, shot dead his terminally ill lover, Henriette.

Not a barrel of laughs, then, Von Kleist, by all accounts. Yet when a friend challenged him to write a comedy, on the assumption that it would be beyond him, he stirred himself to the task and produced one of his best-known plays, *The Broken Jug*. The story concerns a judge named Adam who is trying to find out who broke a certain jug. As he investigates the crime, it gradually becomes clear, to him as well as to us, that it was he who inadvertently did it. When the truth comes out, Adam makes a run for it. As well as his plays and short stories, Von Kleist wrote poetry, and essays analysing human psychology that are thought to have pre-empted Freudian ideas of the subconscious. Because of the patriotic fervour in some of his works, he was later adopted and praised by the Nazis as a fine Germanic author.

Diane Arbus, photographer (1923–71)

USAGE: On examining a friend's unflattering passport photograph, you might observe, 'It wouldn't look out of place in an exhibition of portraits by Diane Arbus.'

Most portraitists have been drawn towards the convention-ally beautiful. Diane Arbus was one of the exceptions. She started out, in collaboration with her husband Allan, as a magazine photographer, contributing images to publications such as *Vogue* and *Harper's Bazaar*. Later, she was awarded a grant for a project on 'American rites, manners and cus-toms'. Encouraged to explore less traditional subject matter, she began photographing people on the margins of society: dwarfs, giants, circus performers, transvestites.

From a comfortable background – her Jewish parents owned Russek's, a New York department store – Arbus felt guilty about her privileged upbringing. Sometimes dubbed 'the photographer of freaks', she has been accused of holding her subjects up for mockery. Equally it could be said that she paid them the compliment of drawing them out of the shadows into which they had been shunted by society. 'Most people go through life dreading they'll have a traumatic experience,' Arbus once declared in a lecture. 'Freaks were born with their trauma. They've already passed their test in life. They're aristocrats.' In many cases, she spent years getting to know her subjects before she photographed them. This, she said, was the real adventure.

A sufferer from depression, Arbus killed herself in 1971. The following year, she became the first American photographer to have a show dedicated to her work at the Venice Biennale. She now holds a hallowed position in the American cultural firmament.

Hunter S. Thompson, journalist and writer (1937–2005)

USAGE: Since few people know what his middle initial stands for, you can impress your friends by referring to him as Hunter Stockton Thompson.

'I hate to advocate drugs, alcohol, violence, or insanity to anyone, but they've always worked for me.' So wrote the journalist Hunter S. Thompson, handily summarising his favourite themes: namely, drugs, alcohol, violence, insanity … and himself. In theory, journalism is all about dispassionate reporting in which the reporter removes him or herself from the story. But in the 1960s a style arose known as the 'New Journalism': long, personal articles, which used techniques more commonly found in novels, such as extensive dialogue and a flowery style.

Then along came Thompson with his own brand – published in magazines such as *Playboy* and *Rolling Stone* – which he called 'Gonzo Journalism'. It was crazier and more surreal, leaving it unclear what was true and what was a flight of fancy, and invariably involving Thompson himself as one of the characters. The author was disgusted by corrupt politicians and bourgeois fakery of all kinds and he strove to embody the values he believed in. For him, journalism – as exemplified in his book *Fear and Loathing in Las Vegas* – was all about getting loaded on drugs and booze and waking up a week later to try to piece together what the hell had happened in the interval.

Exhausted, and aware it had been years since he'd written a really good book, Thompson finally killed himself at his home in Aspen, Colorado, by a gunshot wound to the head. His son and daughter-in-law, who were in the next room, didn't react. They thought the bang had been the sound of a heavy book falling from a shelf.

Arthur Koestler, writer (1905–83)

USAGE: Discussing the history of Soviet communism, mention Koestler's novel *Darkness at Noon* as an early example of someone calling time on that whole sorry experiment.

The last thing Arthur Koestler (pronounced: KESS-ler) published was a pamphlet about suicide. He set out the reasons for and against, and analysed the pros and cons of the various ways of doing it. Then he did it, taking his own life by a mixture of barbiturates and booze at the age of 78. People who knew him weren't surprised, given the extremity of his opinions and the life he'd led. What was more controversial was the fact that his wife Cynthia killed herself with him, despite the fact that she was only 55 and in perfect health. Why, critics asked, hadn't he talked her out of it?

A Hungarian Jew, he had been brought up in Budapest, then moved to Israel where he worked in a kibbutz. As a journalist, he covered the Spanish Civil War, only to be captured and sentenced to death by Franco's forces. Released as part of a prisoner exchange, he lived in Paris, where, a onetime communist, he became disillusioned by the horrors of Stalin's regime – long before these were widely known about – and wrote the definitive anti-communist novel, *Darkness at Noon*. His English girlfriend Daphne translated it for him and was taking it to England when they were separated. He heard she'd been killed, and attempted suicide. Fortunately he failed, for he'd been misinformed. He and Daphne were reunited and the novel was published in English and hailed as a masterpiece.

As well as other novels, Koestler, who settled in London, went on to write non-fiction books, his interests increasingly focusing on the paranormal. He was fascinated by the possibilities of ESP and levitation. In his will he decreed that most of his fortune should go to set up a department for research into these subjects at a British university. Edinburgh University accepted the bequest, and commissioned a bust of Koestler to commemorate his generosity. However, the bust was later removed, after a posthumous rumour arose that he had been a serial sexual offender. Koestler, it seemed, had never experienced an Augustinian conversion …

Highly Sexed

Writers and artists are widely thought to be highly sexed. Quite often the perception is simply true.

St Augustine, theologian
and philosopher (354–430)

USAGE: Why speak of 'the idea of original sin' when you can instead refer to it as 'the Augustinian idea of original sin'? Which sounds so much more impressive.

'Lord, grant me chastity and continence, but not yet!' That was the famous prayer of St Augustine, which he uttered during his dissolute youth. Brought up in the Roman-controlled town of Hippo in northern Africa, he detailed in his autobiographical *Confessions* (an early example of a tell-all memoir) how he had once been a slave to lust and general depravity. He had mistresses and an illegitimate son, and consorted with a dodgy crowd.

Then, in his thirties, while pursuing an academic career in Italy, he seemed to hear a child's voice telling him repeatedly to 'Take up and read!' (in Latin, 'Tolle! Lege!'). Augustine snatched up a copy of the Bible, which happened to be to hand. It fell open at a passage in Paul's Letters to the Romans: 'Not in rioting and drunkenness, not in chambering and wantonness, not in strife and envying, but put on the Lord Jesus

Christ, and make no provision for the flesh to fulfil the lusts thereof.' He did as he was instructed. He turned over a new leaf, shunned sex, and ultimately became Bishop of Hippo.

In his writings, Augustine did much to develop Christian ideas of the eternal struggle between body and soul, and of original sin – the idea that we're all basically evil, and that unless we try really hard to be good, we're going to burn in hell. Depending on which way you look at it, this can either seem like a joyless vision of humanity or an inspiration to lead a more moral, civilised life. Of the influence of St Augustine (or Augustine of Hippo, as he's sometimes known, to distinguish him from other, less important Augustines) there is no doubt. He's generally regarded as one of the founding fathers of the Christian Church. And in the story of his own life, he provides a useful symbol of the battle for self-mastery that is central to Christian teaching.

Sarah Bernhardt, actress (1884–1923)

USAGE: To convey the idea that a woman isn't conventionally beautiful, but has definite 'star quality', compare her to Sarah Bernhardt.

Sarah Bernhardt was a famous French actress. But she is arguably best remembered for her scandalous private life. Her numerous lovers included the Prince of Wales; Nikola Tesla, the fabulously wealthy inventor behind the AC power supply (who eventually dumped her because she was distracting him from his electricity); a Belgian nobleman (with whom she had a son, who ultimately became her manager); and a female painter. This isn't to mention the many sexual partners she accumulated during her stints as a courtesan. She inherited the profession from her mother, and returned to it from time to time when she needed to make a quick franc.

As an actress, Bernhardt wasn't staggeringly gifted. Her voice was breathy, not powerful, and she was striking-looking rather than beautiful. But she had undoubted star quality (for which read sex appeal). Her most notable performance was as Hamlet: not a walk in the park, as dramatic roles go, but in Bernhardt's case the feat was especially impressive, since – although in Shakespeare's day boys had played the female parts – it was unusual to see a woman playing a man. For a woman to take on what is probably the best-known male dramatic role of them all was a feminist coup in an era when, in most countries, women weren't even permitted to vote.

Bernhardt also scandalised public opinion by appearing in Biblical roles. Oscar Wilde* wrote his play *Salome* with her in mind. And she appeared as the lead in a tragedy called *Judas* in which Judas Iscariot (played by Bernhardt) betrays Jesus not for money but revenge: Jesus has stolen Judas' girlfriend, Mary Magdalene. A notorious self-professed atheist, the great actress lost her nerve on her death bed, and demanded the Catholic Last Rites.

More on 'Highly Sexed' overleaf

Michel Foucault, philosopher (1926–84)

USAGE: 'Foucauldian' is the adjective you want (note that devilish 'd'). It may be used to bolster the argument that 'there's no such thing as normal', or that scientific theories may be being engineered by the government as a means to control people.

Michel Foucault (pronounced: foo-COE) was an extremely weird Frenchman who argued that there was no such thing as normal. It wasn't just his shaven head and penchant for wearing turtleneck sweaters, though these were striking enough. Foucault was also prone to violence when young. He self-harmed and at university chased one of his fellow students, brandishing a knife. In later life he was highly promiscuous, and enjoyed hanging out in gay bars and engaging in sado-masochistic activities with strangers. Yet he himself would have argued – indeed this was the central argument of his life's work – that there was nothing especially unusual about all this. For the very ideas of usual and unusual were (and had always been) artificial constructs invented by the few who had power to control the many who had none.

He backed up his theories in tomes such as *Madness and Civilisation* (1960), *Discipline and Punish* (1975) and his unfinished *History of Sexuality*, in which he highlighted fascinating examples that supported his cultural relativism: instances where the pronouncements of science or medicine were designed to oppress a particular class of people. Anti-authoritarian Foucauldianism was trendy in the 1960s and still appeals to many who feel excluded or pigeonholed. Clearly, he had a point, but there were limits. It's hard, for example, to make the case that the concept of mental illness is entirely a social construct designed to oppress certain social groups, as some have done, quoting Foucault. Sometimes these attractive near-conspiracy theories came up hard against the brick wall of reality. For instance, when Foucault first heard about Aids, he declared it to be a lie devised by the government in order to persecute the homosexual community. In due course, however, he contracted the disease, which ultimately killed him.

Pablo Picasso, artist (1881–1973)

USAGE: If someone compliments you on a blue item of clothing you're wearing, you might reply, 'I'm going through my Blue Period.'

A little man, Pablo Picasso had a lot of lovers. As he got older, his girlfriends stayed young. In the last decades of his life, he had a string of affairs with women at least 40 years his junior. By all accounts, he didn't treat them well. (The 1996 film *Surviving Picasso* focuses on this theme.) It was as if he thought, because he was an artistic genius, he could do whatever he wanted.

There aren't many who dispute that a genius was what he was. The proof lay in his vast output over the course of his long career, the sheer range of styles in which he excelled, his apparent effortlessness. When he was a boy, he was so good at drawing that his father, a professional artist, retired in despair. The key phases of the career that ensued – once young Pablo had made the journey from his native Spain to

Paris, where he spent the rest of his life – included his Blue Period (in which his paintings used a lot of blue and were depressing) and his Rose Period (in which the colours were rosier and more cheerful). Picking up where Paul Cézanne had left off, Picasso painted *Les Demoiselles d'Avignon* in 1907, in which the view of a group of posing prostitutes is weirdly fragmented. From here it was a short step to Cubism, which he developed with Georges Braque. This involved taking as subject matter a familiar object or human being, then drawing this object, viewed from many different angles, onto the canvas. Cynics said that, by the end, there were so many overlapping images that the original object was impossible to make out. (Incidentally, it was called Cubism because one critic observed that the final painting looked like it was composed of many different cubes.)

Picasso never went fully abstract. His paintings always represented something. In the large-scale mayhem of his 1937 canvas *Guernica*, a horse's head emerges, screaming. It was the artist's response to the Nazi bombing of the eponymous Spanish town. After the occupation of Paris, some Gestapo officers came to his apartment. Spotting a photograph of his Guernica painting, one of them asked, 'Did you do that?' 'No,' Picasso replied drily. 'You did.'

Internationally famous, universally acclaimed, he died in the midst of dinner, while he and his wife Jacqueline were entertaining guests. It was a fate shared by another man who is also routinely described as one of the most influential artists of the 20th century ...

Slumped Over the Soup

*For many, Picasso would be high on their list
of people they would most like to have dinner
with – they'd just have to hope they didn't catch
him on the occasion when he expired. And the
same could be said about the next two names.*

Marcel Duchamp, artist (1887–1968)

USAGE: Faced by any incomprehensible work of art, observe
sagely: 'It's another contribution to Marcel Duchamp's debate
about the nature of art itself.'

What a nice way to go. The French artist Marcel Duchamp
(pronounced: doo-SHOM, though the M is almost silent) had
enjoyed a wonderful dinner at his home in Paris, along with
friends including fellow artist Man Ray*. In the early hours of
the morning, he bade them good night and retired. It seems
he then expired suddenly while chuckling over an amusing
passage in a book by the comic author Alphonse Allais.

Humour had always played a role in Duchamp's career.
One of his best-known works was a postcard of Leonardo
Da Vinci's *Mona Lisa* on which he had drawn a beard and
moustache. Could this be considered art? That was the question Duchamp wanted us to ask. He was bored by paintings
that were merely pleasing to the eye, dismissing them as

'retinal' art. Instead he liked to try to startle people into engaging their brains. For example, his *Fountain* (1917) consisted of a urinal. That was it. Merely by presenting this utilitarian object as art (one example in a series of *objets trouvés* or 'ready-mades', as they were known), had Duchamp turned it into an artwork? If not, why not? The consensus seems to be that he had. For its shock value, for its implication that shock value was an artistic quality in itself, and for hugely broadening the public conception of what could constitute art, Duchamp's *Fountain* has been voted the most influential artwork of the 20th century.

While still in his thirties, the artist essentially stopped making art. Instead he devoted the remaining four decades of his life to playing chess. His obsession so annoyed his wife that on one occasion she glued his chess pieces to the board. 'While all artists are not chess players,' Duchamp once declared, 'all chess players are artists.' In 1968, he turned a game of chess into an artwork by playing an exhibition match against the modernist composer John Cage. Whenever one of them moved a piece, it triggered a note of music; so as the game went on, they composed a symphony.

John Cage, composer (1912–92)

USAGE: Next time there's an awkward silence during supper, when all you can hear is the scrape of cutlery on plate, murmur wryly, 'It's just like one of John Cage's silent symphonies.'

John Cage had had dinner with his boyfriend, the choreographer Merce Cunningham, and just fixed himself a soothing cup of peppermint tea, when he suffered a fatal stroke. Thus departed the most exciting composer of his generation. That was in the eyes of his fans, at least. To his detractors, Cage was a decidedly naked emperor. Who could take seriously a man whose most famous work consisted of four minutes and 33 seconds of near-total silence – and who was so shameless about it, he even named the piece 4′33″? In his defence, Cage was the first to produce silent symphonies, and being the first to do something always earns you a certain kudos. Secondly, any live recording of a piece of music will inevitably include the sound of the orchestra shifting in their seats, someone in the audience coughing, and so on. By producing a piece of music in which that was literally all you could hear, Cage was drawing attention to this fact.

The composer is also remembered for the symphonies he created randomly by reference to an ancient Chinese book. On every page there were instructions, which depending on circumstances (for instance, whether the sun was shining that day) would send you to another page in the book, where there would be further instructions. Cage assigned each page a musical note. Then he embarked on a trawl through the book, jotting down the notes it came up with. The end result was his symphony. Again, if you're inclined to scoff, bear in mind that he was at least an innovator.

It could all have been so different. The story goes that as a young man, Cage had been determined to be an artist. It was only while backpacking around Europe that he was struck by a sudden realisation: he had no artistic talent. At first this threw him into despair, but something good came out of it, for it sent Cage off on a new career path, which led to fame and fortune. In the process, it saw him take his place in a fine tradition of Americans going to Europe and finding themselves – whether by bohemian living or through the experience of war, as in the case of the next, syntactically challenged poet …

Creative Traumas

*Sometimes the worst thing that happens to you
turns out to be the best. Grief leads to knowledge
and trauma inspires great works of art. So, at
least, it proved in the cases of these three.*

e.e. cummings, poet (1894–1962)

USAGE: For an example of something relatively low-brow masquerading as something relatively high-brow, mention Cummings' poetry.

One of the few advantages enjoyed by writers is that, when something awful happens, they can console themselves by writing about it. A case in point is the American poet E.E. Cummings, who enlisted in the ambulance service during the First World War. His pacifist instincts were confirmed by the carnage he witnessed on the Western front, and he became so anti-war he was arrested by the French military and imprisoned for months on suspicion of espionage. After his release, Cummings used the experience as the basis for his acclaimed novel *The Enormous Room*. In 1926, he suffered a further trauma when his father was killed (and his mother injured) in a horrific car accident. The grief is thought to have ushered in a new phase of maturity in Cummings' work.

Although he wrote plays and novels, it is as a poet that he is best remembered – above all, one with an extremely unusual approach to punctuation and syntax. You can tell a Cummings poem at a glance because he rarely uses capital letters (even sometimes styling his name e.e. cummings). He also uses language in an odd way, avoiding natural word order, using verbs as nouns, etc. As a result, you may feel you're reading some work of high modernism, but Cummings cannily made sure his actual meaning was actually quite straightforward, even rather sentimental.

In his poetry, he often addressed erotic themes (which always go down well). Sometimes, he expressed his joy at being alive. It was all rather endearing.

Rumi, poet (1207–73)

USAGE: It's possible to argue that the British have produced greater poetry than any other nation. Another contender, you might observe, is Persia, whose poetic geniuses include Rumi.

The 13th-century Persian poet Rumi (pronounced: ROOM-ee) is said to be the bestselling poet in the US. Heaven knows how they measure such things. Yet the very fact that such a claim is made is pretty striking.

Born in a region of what is now Afghanistan, Rumi and his family later settled in the town of Konya in Turkey. He grew up to be an Islamic teacher whose life was transformed when he met a mystic named Shams of Tabriz. There followed a profound spiritual friendship that ended abruptly when Shams disappeared, possibly murdered by Rumi's jealous pupils. In his grief, Rumi began walking round and round a pole in his back yard and reciting poetry off the top of his head (his circling of the pole inspired the Whirling Dervishes). Those who heard what he was saying were astounded and began writing it down, for the verse he was declaiming was perfectly formed in its metre and rhyme – and, many have found, deeply consoling in its spiritual wisdom.

This may sound like New Age nonsense, but Rumi's poetry is worth taking for a spin, combining – at least in Coleman Barks' loosely freewheeling translation – a simplicity of expression with a sensual appreciation of the good things in life. A Muslim who preached love, Rumi believed that God was found in ecstatic communion, in experience not scripture. Theologians who bicker over doctrine are like fish, he said, arguing about the existence of the ocean. It was grief that had made Rumi a poet. 'Hold on to your particular pain,' he advised. 'That too can take you to God.'

Paul Auster, novelist (b. 1947)

USAGE: You can use Auster's name to evoke a sense of unease and bewilderment, when there seems to be little rhyme or reason in anything taking place. 'After trying, and failing, to pay my utility bill over the automated telephone system, I felt I was trapped in some endless Paul Auster novel.'

In the work of Paul Auster, things frequently seem to happen at random: a mood that stems from a disturbing real-life incident, the writer has claimed. When he was a child, out playing during a storm, he saw a thunderbolt strike the boy next to him, killing him instantly. 'I remember holding his tongue so he wouldn't swallow it,' the author later recalled, 'and watching his skin turn blue. If you see that when you are fourteen years old, you begin to sense that the world is a lot less stable than you thought it was.' The incident must have been awful to witness, but it gave Auster's work one of the serious themes – the randomness of the world – that has led to his being one of the few thriller-writers to enjoy high-brow literary acclaim.

His most lauded work, the three novels known as *The New York Trilogy*, deploys the mood and techniques of thrillers – for example, a growing sense of unease – but focuses on the search not for a killer but rather for the meaning of life (which the characters, in the end, predictably do not find). Some critics have said that this concept of the existential thriller (less interested in the who-done-it than in the why-does-it-matter) is a little contrived. Auster disagrees. 'I believe the world is filled with strange events,' he has remarked. 'Reality is a great deal more mysterious than we ever give it credit for.' His books tend to depict America as an incoherent, confusing place, which partly explains why they are so popular in France. In recent years, he has complained he has run out of ideas, confessing: 'I used to have a backlog of stories, but a few years ago I found the drawers were empty.'

Auster is a self-deprecating sort – though his modesty has never stretched quite as far as one novelist, who on being told she had won the highest award in literature, remarked that it was probably because she wasn't going to be around for much longer …

Who, Little Ol' Me?

Real or false modesty? It's sometimes hard to say, but the following figures seem genuinely humble about their achievements.

Doris Lessing, novelist (1919–2013)

> **USAGE:** Cite Lessing as the best sort of feminist, i.e. one who didn't toe the party line of the sisterhood, but always said exactly what she thought.

When the 89-year-old Doris Lessing came home to find a lot of people with TV cameras milling about in her street, it didn't occur to her that they were waiting for her. She assumed they were filming a soap. But then one of them informed her that she had been awarded the Nobel Prize in Literature. 'Oh Christ!' she exclaimed; then added that she supposed they expected her to make some 'uplifting remarks'. She later observed that the judges had probably given her the prize because they assumed she would soon 'pop off' – which, a few years later, she did.

Lessing is generally regarded as a feminist author, but it's a bit more complicated than that. When her most famous book, *The Golden Notebook* (1962), was hailed as a feminist masterpiece, she professed herself surprised. She had intended the novel – an elaborate account of a woman's descent into madness – to explore the psychological wounds created by a loss of faith in communism: an experience Lessing had had herself, growing up in Rhodesia. (She moved to London in 1949.) One thing that made the book seem feminist, perhaps, was that it was unflinchingly direct about sex. Most Englishmen were unfaithful, according to Lessing, and those who weren't tended to ejaculate prematurely. The only thing that stopped young mothers from killing themselves was a sense of loyalty towards their babies. Vaginal orgasms were superior to clitoral ones.

Nothing was off-limits for Lessing, who delighted in confounding expectations. In her later career, she startled her fans by turning her talents to writing science fiction (for example, 1982's *The Making of the Representative for Planet 8*). Eternally mischievous, she once sent her latest novel to her publisher with a different name attached, to see if they would accept it. They didn't. Lessing claimed this proved how hard it was for unknown authors to get published, although after the book eventually appeared, some suggested it may also have been because it wasn't very good.

Frank Gehry, architect (b. 1929)

USAGE: If you're building a garden shed, and it ends up leaning at a dangerous angle, say you were aiming for a kind of Frank Gehry effect.

If architecture bores you, read on. Because the works of Frank Gehry may well be the exception. Many of his buildings are breathtaking, like Surrealist sculptures, but with higher stakes. Are they safe? Taking the principles of 'deconstructivism' to extremes (don't worry about what this means; just say it), the cumbersomely named New York by Gehry at Eight Spruce Street (2011) is a skyscraper displaying crooked fault lines in its facade that look like cracks in a structure about to collapse (a daring implication in post-9/11 New York). Equally, they could be the tendrils of a plant, thrusting upwards into the sky.

The Jewish American architect first attracted attention with his remodelling of his own home in California in the late 1970s. Gehry set up a metallic screen around the house, leaving gaps to reveal some of the more traditional features of the building within. He has come a long way since then. The most successful of his creations maintain a harmonious tension between order and chaos, the natural and artificial worlds, the past and the future. His Jay Pritzker Pavilion (2004), an outdoor auditorium in Chicago, resembles the vast fossilised skeleton of a dinosaur. Probably his most famous work, the Guggenheim Museum Bilbao (1997), looks like a sturdy ship being swamped by waves: again, there's a blend of progress and potential destruction within the same frame.

'You've got to bumble forward into the unknown,' Gehry has observed of his method, with disarming, possibly Socratic modesty. If he's a bumbler, he's a lucky one. He received the Pritzker Prize (the architectural equivalent of a Nobel) in 1989. His Bilbao museum, meanwhile, is widely agreed to be one of the most important works of architecture completed in the past few decades.

Enrico Fermi, physicist (1901–54)

USAGE: To praise someone who excels both in theory and in practice, compare them to Enrico Fermi.

It is one of the ironies of the Second World War that some of those who most contributed to the ultimate victory of the Allies had originally been citizens of Axis countries, driven out by racial prejudice. Enrico Fermi was a case in point. Born in Italy, he emigrated to the US in 1938, after anti-Semitic laws imposed by Benito Mussolini made life uncomfortable for his wife Laura, who was Jewish. The loss to Italy couldn't have been clearer. In that same year, Fermi was awarded the Nobel Prize in Physics for his work on inducing radioactivity by neutron bombardment.

Fermi is revered as one of the very few scientists who excelled as much in carrying out experiments as he did in developing ground-breaking theories. Although he made contributions to almost every field of physics, he will best be remembered by the non-specialist for presiding over the first-ever controlled nuclear reaction. The great event took place in Chicago in a racquets court, whose spacious 30ft by 60ft dimensions were suitable for the purpose. There, on 2 December 1942, under Fermi's guidance, a new form of energy was harnessed. Later developments in the destructive use of nuclear power, in which he also played a role, led to the creation of the atomic bomb, of which, along with Robert Oppenheimer and Albert Einstein*, he is regarded as one of the fathers.

For all his achievements, Fermi was a self-effacing, softly-spoken man. His colleagues used to say that his pragmatism – and, perhaps, his modesty – was clear from the stubby three-inch slide rule he carried with him everywhere. It was this that he whipped out in the racquets court in Chicago on that day in 1942, to take the final measurements. Then, with quiet assurance, he declared: 'The reaction is self-sustaining.' No grand speeches were delivered to mark the occasion. He and his team celebrated with a few mouthfuls of Chianti, drunk from paper cups.

Don DeLillo, novelist (b. 1936)

USAGE: In a conversation about the greatest living novelist, DeLillo's is a name you could reasonably toss into the mix.

Don DeLillo is often named as a Great American Novelist, along with the likes of John Updike* and Philip Roth*. But if you listen to DeLillo, he just got lucky. For the author plies a fine line in humorous self-deprecation. When his eighth novel *White Noise* received a prestigious prize, he stood up at the awards ceremony and declared: 'I'm sorry I couldn't be here tonight, but I thank you all for coming.' Then he sat down again. And he has been known to use a business card that simply displays his name, and underneath, the message, 'I don't want to talk about it.'

In general, though, it seems DeLillo *does* want to talk about it. His most acclaimed books – *White Noise* (1985), *Libra* (1988) and *Underworld* (1998) – are hefty tomes that tackle hefty subjects: the cost of consumerism, the assassination of JFK, and the psychological fall-out from the end of the Soviet experiment. A DeLillo book will characteristically mock the absurdities of academia, be anti-capitalist in its preoccupations, and involve a mood of paranoia punctuated by acts of violence. He's often described as a postmodernist, because his writing has questioned the assumptions of traditional fiction: for instance, the idea that words are an adequate medium for the expression of ideas. DeLillo himself denies being a postmodern author (which is rather postmodern of him).

In more recent years, he has produced shorter, slighter novels that have disappointed those who want all DeLillo's works to be monumental achievements. His self-deprecation has become more earnest. 'In the 1970s, when I started writing novels, I was a figure in the margins,' he has said. 'If I'm headed back that way, that's fine with me, because that's where I always felt I belonged.'

Katsushika Hokusai, artist (c. 1760–1849)

USAGE: Any image that combines strength and simplicity, with bright colours and clean, clear outlines, may be said to be Hokusai-esque.

For centuries Western art developed more or less independently from the art of the East. Then in the 19th century Impressionist painters discovered the virtues of Japanese *ukiyo-e*: images created by a technique of woodblock printmaking, each of which could be sold to the public for about the price of a double-helping of noodles. The best of these exhibited a grace of line and strength of composition that stood comparison with the masterpieces of any era. And of these *ukiyo-e* artists, none was better than Katsushika Hokusai.

Hokusai broke with tradition by portraying landscapes and scenes of ordinary life (most of his peers were portraying artists and courtesans). Once, in a contest with a rival, he painted a blue curve on a huge sheet of paper. Then he dipped the feet of a chicken in red paint and persuaded the bird to walk all over the paper. The resulting image, he said, represented the Tatsuta river with red maple leaves floating in it. The judge gave him the prize.

The artist's greatest success came late in life, after he'd been forced out of retirement owing to the financial recklessness of his grandson. It was around then that Hokusai, who would claim to have produced nothing that was any good before the age of 70, created *The Great Wave off Kanagawa*, which shows two boatloads of oarsmen at the mercy of a huge overarching wave, which seems on the point of crashing down on them. It's an image that is now world-famous.

He was clearly inspired by disasters, whether it was huge waves, financial setbacks, or warehouse fires. When he was 79, a fire broke out in his studio, destroying many of his prints. But at least, as far as we know, it wasn't a deliberate case of arson – unlike the fire that destroyed the home of one of America's greatest architects …

Consumed by Flames

Paper, scissors, stone? Fire beats all of these,
as the next two names also discovered.

Frank Lloyd Wright, architect (1867–1959)

USAGE: Admiring the open-plan design of a friend's home, mention
that this was an invention of Frank Lloyd Wright, in response to
the decline in the number of households that had servants.

In 1911, the architect Frank Lloyd Wright created Taliesin
in Wisconsin: a modernist masterpiece, and a home to shelter himself and his mistress Mamah (who, like Wright, was
already married) from the disapproval of the public. A few
years later, while he was away, a deranged servant set fire to
this house. The servant left only one escape route, through a
certain door, but anyone who emerged, he set upon with an
axe. Wright's lover was among those killed. Ten years later,
Taliesin suffered another fire: this time the result of an electri-
cal fault. Wearily, Wright re-rebuilt it. Taliesin III.

The name derives from a bard in Welsh mythology, who
was blessed with magical powers. This perhaps was how the
architect saw himself, a druidical figure, conjuring beauty
from mundane materials. Wright – who has some claim to
be the founder of modernist architecture – broke from prece-
dent by building in concrete. He often employed bold (some

would say blunt) geometric shapes, inspired by the building blocks his mother had given him as a toddler. He pioneered open-plan designs, partly so that housewives (who increasingly had to make do without servants) could see through from the kitchen to the nursery. And he tried to incorporate an 'organic' element to his architecture, meaning either that his houses blended in with the landscape, as at Fallingwater (constructed over a waterfall), or that they evoked natural organisms, as in the case of the Solomon R. Guggenheim Museum in New York, which rises up in a spiral shape like that of a seashell.

For all his success, and the admiration in which he's held (he has been voted the greatest American architect of all time), Wright was notoriously impractical. The roofs of some of his buildings leaked. His engineers often had to correct his designs. And he was hopeless with money, relying on his skills as a dealer in Japanese prints to keep himself solvent in times of crisis.

Heinrich Heine, poet and dramatist (1797–1856)

USAGE: In a conversation about the policy of appeasement that permitted the Nazis to strengthen their hold on central Europe in the 1930s, point out that Heinrich Heine had predicted the atrocities of the Third Reich a hundred years earlier.

In Bebenplatz square in Berlin, you can find a plaque on which these words appear: 'That was the only the beginning. Where they burn books, they will also, in the end, burn people.' The quotation is from a play by the German

Jewish author Heinrich Heine, who was writing in the early 19th century. And his words came to seem grimly prophetic a century later, when Heine's books – along with countless others deemed to be 'degenerate' – were publicly set alight in the Bebenplatz and other places, as part of the Nazi campaign to 'purify' German culture.

Like Lord Byron before him, Heine started out a Romantic, possessed by semi-incestuous passions. In his case, he yearned for his cousin. Later, after she had rejected him, he turned his attentions to her sister, who also gave him the cold shoulder. Embittered, he increasingly employed irony and preferred to write satire than love poems. In one genuinely funny criticism of the extreme levels of censorship that existed in Germany, Heine composed a passage consisting entirely of words that had been blotted out, with only the phrases 'the German censors' and 'idiots' left visible.

Another famous example of his satire, the poem 'Atta Troll', is about a bear who believes God must also be a bear; and his cubs all hold absurdly nationalistic views. Heine professed to love his country, but to hate those who loved it too much. He predicted that German nationalism would ultimately lead to a tragedy that would 'make the French Revolution look like an innocent idyll'. So apart from the fact that he was brought up a Jew (though he converted to Christianity), the Nazis condemned him for being anti-German. Other evidence produced against him included the fact that he spent much of his adult life in Paris, married a Parisian (an illiterate shopgirl named Mathilde), and even spoke French well enough to write translations of his own works for a French readership. He didn't, though, go the whole hog and adopt French as the first language in which he wrote, like the following lugubrious playwright ...

Cunning Linguists

If you're English or American, you can get by pretty much anywhere in the world without bothering to learn another language. Kudos, then, to those who have been so linguistically talented they could write in a language that wasn't their first.

Eugene Ionesco, playwright (1909–94)

USAGE: If a friend has taken a swerve to the right politically, you might observe, 'I'm a bit worried he's going to go the whole way and turn into a rhinoceros.'

One of the big ideas of the 20th century was that everything is completely meaningless. We're all going to die and there's nothing after death. While we're alive, most activities are ridiculous, from wearing silly clothes to trying to communicate via a range of more or less arbitrary noises. See Albert Camus*. See Samuel Beckett*. And see Eugene Ionesco.

The debut production of this Romanian playwright, who wrote in French, was inspired by his experience of learning English. His exercise book had presented scenes involving an English couple called the Smiths as a way of introducing the reader to new vocabulary. The whole thing was so absurd that Ionesco decided to write a play about the banal characters. With pointed arbitrariness, he called it *The Bald*

Soprano and it caused a sensation in Paris (where Ionesco lived) when it was first staged in 1950. It was at the same time a parody of Englishness, a mockery of the bourgeoisie, and a demonstration that everything is meaningless. The play can still be seen today at Paris's Théâtre de la Huchette, where it has been running meaninglessly for more than half a century.

In other works, Ionesco explored related themes. In *The Rhinoceros* (1959) the protagonist watches in bewilderment as everyone turns into rhinoceroses (a metaphor for fascism in 1930s Romania). It runs the risk of seeming a bit silly at times, but this short, bald, sad-eyed author believed silliness could be profound. At one point he belonged to a club of like-minded people, which awarded merit badges shaped like turds. He lived with his wife Rodika in their top-floor flat in Paris, on one wall of which hung a drawing of a rhinoceros by his friend Max Ernst*.

Milan Kundera, novelist (b. 1929)

USAGE: A culturally impressive way to say you're feeling under the weather would be to claim to be 'assailed by a sense of the unbearable lightness of being'.

At a certain point in the 1980s, the coolest book for any self-respecting young intellectual to be seen carrying around was *The Unbearable Lightness of Being* by Milan Kundera. Its combination of sexual kinkiness – there were some intriguing suggestions as to where you might want to put your thumb – and philosophical analyses were hard to resist. One moment you'd be reading about what Tomas did to Tereza in bed; the next, you'd be treated to a short essay on Nietzsche's* theory of eternal return. The idea was that, in an infinite universe, everything happens an infinite number of times, therefore nothing really matters. Life is appallingly 'light' or insignificant.

This theme of life's insignificance resounds in Kundera's *oeuvre* right through to his novel *The Festival of Insignificance* (2015). The title hints at its nihilism, and at its recommendation that our response should be a cheerful or ecstatic surrender. Like Camus'* Sisyphus we must be happy, despite everything. This wilful positivity seemed urgently heroic in the context of the Soviet oppression in Czechoslovakia, where Kundera grew up and began his career as a writer.

The novelist emigrated to Paris in 1975, a move some of his compatriots saw as betrayal. This was compounded when, as of the late 1980s, he began writing his books in French, rather than Czech. Kundera's critique of those who bent their knee to totalitarianism has laid his own past open to scrupulous – and sometimes not so scrupulous – judgement. (You might draw an analogy with the case of Günter Grass*.) In 2008, a newspaper unearthed a story that Kundera had informed on a political dissident in 1950, who had subsequently served eleven years in a labour camp. Fellow literary titans, including Carlos Fuentes*, Philip Roth* and J.M. Coetzee*, published an open letter defending the writer. He himself adamantly denied the truth of the story, which remains in doubt.

Vladimir Nabokov, novelist (1899–1977)

USAGE: Most English speakers pronounce the name Nabokov with the emphasis on the first syllable: NAB-okov. Score points by stressing the second syllable – Nab-O-kov – which is more correct.

On the whole, philosophers can be intimidating, but novelists seem friendlier, fluffier creatures. After all, they're just telling stories, right? Not entirely. Some novelists are so mind-bogglingly brainy that after reading them you're left feeling like an intellectual pygmy. Vladimir Nabokov, who tended to write in English, which was his third language (after Russian and French), is a case in point.

His best-known book, *Lolita*, is about a man successfully attempting to seduce a twelve-year-old girl, but don't let this deter you from reading it on public transport. The book is a masterpiece, with the author wringing extraordinary humour, and even pathos, from his literary tightrope act: taking the point of view of a manipulative and unrepentant paedophile (or strictly speaking, ephebophile, since the protagonist, Humbert Humbert, has an interest not in children but in adolescent girls). As with all his books (other key title drops include *Pale Fire* and *Speak, Memory*), the style is linguistically rich, filled with alliteration and word music, and a proliferation of plays-on-words. If you wanted to criticise the great man, you might murmur that for your taste, he includes too many puns.

It should be noted that Nabokov himself enjoyed a long and happy marriage to his wife Vera, who wasn't a twelve-year-old girl (although presumably she had been at some point). In his spare time, he was a distinguished lepidopterist who had several species of butterfly named after him. His eyesight was poor, exacerbated by long hours spent staring at the tiny genitals of insects (to identify their species). A man of peculiar, vivid perceptions, he's widely thought to have been a synaesthete – a condition that's also believed to have affected one of his fellow countrymen, and, just possibly, inspired him to invent abstract art …

Synaesthesia

*If you suffer from synaesthesia, then at least
two of your five senses are all jumbled up. For
example, some synaesthetes see colours when they
hear music. Pretty useful if you're an artist ...*

Wassily Kandinsky, artist (1866–1944)

USAGE: Obliged to comment on a work of abstract art, observe
that it might benefit from being rotated by 90 degrees, like
Kandinsky's *Composition IV*.

One day in 1911, the Russian artist Wassily Kandinsky's
winsome girlfriend Gabriele was tidying his studio and
inadvertently turned one of his experimental canvases,
Composition IV, on its side. The painter saw it, sank to his
knees and wept. It was, he said, the most beautiful painting
he had ever seen. For it had given him a vision of a kind of
art that could be truly abstract.

Did Kandinsky invent abstract art? You could say that.
If you think most art since Claude Monet is bunk, you
won't like Kandinsky (many of his works look as if someone
had tossed a grenade into an orchestra). Yet it was Monet's
Haystacks that made Kandinsky realise colour could be separated from reality and still move the viewer. He went on to
extend the theory to shapes and lines. As revered today for

his influential theories about art as for his artworks, he set out his views in *On the Spiritual in Art* (1910) and *Point and Line to Plane* (1926). They range from what now seem like obvious remarks about the temperature of colours (yellow is warm, blue is cold) to more dodgy claims about shapes (the circle, Kandinsky believed, represents the soul).

Yet in his central insight, he was clearly on to something: artworks could be entirely non-figurative and still have a strong emotional impact on the viewer. Like others before him (e.g. Plato*) he wrote about art as if it were music. 'Colour is the keyboard,' he once declared. 'The eye is the hammer. The soul is the piano with its many strings.' In fact, some believe that Kandinsky meant what he said on a deeper level, on the grounds that he had synaesthesia.

Arthur Rimbaud, poet (1854–91)

USAGE: Refer to Rimbaud scathingly if at all. And mention, if possible, that he had a few things in common with the movie character John Rambo.

Despite the slight similarity in the sound of their surnames, the French poet Arthur Rimbaud (pronounced: ram-BOE) has nothing whatsoever to do with the Vietnam veteran John Rambo as played by Sylvester Stallone in the 1982 film *First Blood*. However, they do have a few things in common. Both of them got shot at, suffered from anger issues, and were awkward company.

The French poet Arthur Rimbaud rejected his bourgeois background at the age of fifteen and ran away to Paris, where he threw himself into a life of decadent excess. He drank, did drugs, and had transgressive sex with the poet Paul Verlaine. Their tempestuous relationship ended when Verlaine shot him in the wrist and went to prison. Rimbaud probably had it coming: he seems to have been an absolute bastard. Once, when an artist was being boring about painting, he shat on a table to express his displeasure. On another occasion he put sulphuric acid in someone's drink as a prank. In his defence, he was very young, and believed that a 'deliberate derange-ment of the senses' was necessary to write good poetry. Which, incidentally, he did. One poem, 'Vowels', is a poetic description of synaesthesia, which Rimbaud suffered from. Another, 'The Sleeper of the Valley', describes a young man who seems to be peacefully asleep but is revealed in the chilling last line to have been shot dead. The prose work *Une Saison en enfer* (A Season in Hell) describes the author's life philosophy in feverish poetic terms. When the latter was panned by critics, Rimbaud gave up writing entirely. He was twenty.

He went on to serve as a soldier in the Dutch army in Indonesia, ran a quarry in Cyprus, and traded guns, coffee and possibly slaves in Ethiopia. He then developed bone can-cer, had a leg amputated and died at the age of 37. Because of his youth, talent, and dissolute character, Rimbaud has been revered as a great hero by pretentious bohemian types ever since. If you want to annoy them, just stubbornly pretend you think they're talking about Rambo. Then, to compound the crime, you might ask them if the jeans they're wearing were designed by Claude Lévi-Strauss …

Rambo/Rimbaud

Nothing's more annoying than being
continually mistaken for someone more
famous or glamorous. Sadly, if it happens,
there isn't much you can do about it.

Claude Lévi-Strauss, anthropologist (1908—2009)

USAGE: If you want to argue that people the world over have
more in common than you might think, you could cite the
arguments of Claude Lévi-Strauss.

Claude Lévi-Strauss (pronounced: LEV-ee STRAUSS) was
a 20th-century French anthropologist. He was in no way
related to Levi Strauss (pronounced: LEEV-eye STRAUSS),
who was a 19th-century German-American manufacturer
of jeans. But Lévi-Strauss was pretty important in his own
right: his books gave comfort to many with their argument
that there are structures of thought common to all humans,
from Wall Street bankers to the tribes of the Amazon.

The great professor first became famous when he published a non-academic book in 1955. *Tristes Tropiques* (Sad
Tropics) was a memoir of his time spent living among the
Amazons of Brazil. It was so beautifully written, the organisers of the Prix Goncourt lamented that they couldn't award it
a prize, as it wasn't a work of fiction. It might not be fiction,

his critics pointed out, but it contained distortions. For Lévi-Strauss hadn't actually spent that much time in any one place in Brazil, and in any case, he would never have been able to speak directly to the locals in their language.

No matter. In this and other books – most famously 1962's *The Savage Mind* and his four-volume *Mythologiques* – he set out his arguments concerning, firstly, the common structures to be found within family groups across all cultures, and secondly, the common structural elements to be found in people's stories and myths. (Because of these preoccupations, Lévi-Strauss was hailed as a leading figure in the movement known as structuralism, which teaches that all human culture has an overarching structure.) One example of his: ravens. Whatever the culture, the birds appear in myths as creatures of ill omen – whether it's the Greeks, who believed Apollo turned ravens black to punish them for feeding on the dead, or Shakespeare, who mentions the raven more than any other bird in his plays, and invariably to evoke a sense of dread.

Martin Luther, theologian and reformer (1483–1546)

USAGE: 'Not since the time of Martin Luther has the Catholic Church faced such a threat to its authority,' you might remark, when the Vatican comes in for heavy criticism.

You should on no account confuse the 16th-century Church reformer, Martin Luther, with his 20th-century near-namesake, the civil rights campaigner Martin Luther King. The latter was so named by his father, who on a visit to

Germany in 1934 had been profoundly inspired by Martin Luther's story. For this was a man who, throughout his life, committed to what he believed in, regardless of the personal cost.

As a young man Martin became a monk, throwing himself into practices of mortification (a kind of holy self-harm) that included going to sleep outside when it had been snowing. A trip to Rome changed his life. He was horrified by the corruption he saw among the clergy, and soon after penned his *Ninety-Five Theses*: a list of complaints directed at the Church. He is said to have nailed them to the door of a church in Wittenberg (in what is now central Germany), where he taught in the university. The document was printed and circulated, as were his later incendiary treatises, which so enraged Pope Leo X that he excommunicated him, essentially banishing Luther from the Church and condemning him to eternal damnation. At a trial misleadingly known as The Diet of Worms ('diet' here means 'assembly' and Worms is a town on the Rhine), Luther refused to recant. 'Here I stand,' he declared. 'I can do no other. God help me. Amen.'

His arguments – for instance, that good Christians should look to the Bible for instruction rather than to priests – would kick-start the Reformation: the split between the Catholic Church and Protestantism in its various forms, which persists to this day. Luther translated the Bible into German (from Hebrew and Greek) so it could be read by people who hadn't the benefit of an expensive education. He also believed that the clergy should be allowed to marry, and he put this theory into practice in 1525 when he wed a rather attractive former nun named Katharina von Brora, whom he had helped to escape from her nunnery concealed among some barrels of herring.

Georg Lukacs, philosopher (1885–1971)

USAGE: In any discussion of historical fiction, you could tentatively mention Georg Lukacs' theory that all such works are inherently Marxist.

It was fortunate for the Hungarian philosopher Georg Lukacs (pronounced: GYORG LOO-katch) that he died a few years before the release of *Star Wars*. For he would have been appalled to find he was now regularly confused with the similarly named director of that movie, George Lucas. The latter was an American, soon to become hugely wealthy. Moreover, he was a purveyor of what the austerely communist Lukacs would have regarded as Hollywood trash: just one of many devices by which capitalist states keep the people in a state of distracted apathy (cf. Theodor Adorno* and Guy Debord*).

Lukacs's detailed and devoted books on Marxist theory earned him such repute that he was invited to visit Russia in 1930. Once there, he learnt he wasn't allowed to leave but had to toil away in the Marx-Engels Institute for years, devising ingenious attacks on capitalist philosophy (e.g. his idea of 'reification', the belief that capitalism reduced people to the status of things or commodities). This ordeal did little to dampen Lukacs's revolutionary ardour. On his eventual return to his native Hungary, he's said to have collaborated in the imprisonment of anti-communist intellectuals.

His literary theories were a little less controversial, but only a little. Lukacs believed that the best novels were realist, while a focus on style over substance was a sign of capitalist decadence. He admired historical novels by the likes of Sir Walter Scott and Honoré de Balzac* on the grounds that by placing their stories in a historical setting, they reminded the reader of the possibility of social change. This was an inherently Marxist message (whatever the private political views of the authors might have been) and as such, was worthy of admiration, in Lukacs's eyes.

Given the intensity of his lifelong socialism, it may come as a surprise to learn that he himself was both rich and titled. He inherited the title of 'Baron' from his father, an investment banker. But at least he didn't write the world's most famous book on socialism while living off handouts from his uncle, who was also a banker …

Champagne Socialists

*It's a lot easier to write devastating diatribes
about social injustice if you have some
private wealth to support your lifestyle.*

Karl Marx, philosopher (1818–83)

USAGE: To offer a Marxist interpretation of something is to
view it through the prism of the belief that history is progressing
inevitably through stages of class struggle.

The German philosopher, economist and revolutionary
theorist Karl Marx came from a surprisingly comfortable
background. Indeed, while writing *The Communist Manifesto*
he was supported by his uncle, a banker. To be fair to young
Karl, he did spend most of his inheritance on the communist
cause. For example, he gave a third of it to revolutionaries
in Belgium, to help them buy guns. Then, after moving
to London (the only place in Europe that would put up
with his extreme political views), he lived in poverty with
his wife Jenny (a baroness) while composing his socialist
masterpieces.

Was he a crank? If so, he was a phenomenally influential one, his theories inspiring communist regimes across
the world (with varying degrees of tyranny, which hadn't
been part of his programme). You can't deny that Marx was

a biggie. He had a big beard to prove it. In his youth, he'd also been a big drinker and prankster, once waggishly riding a donkey through the streets of Bonn.

As he grew older, he got serious, devoting himself first to revolutionary journalism and later to his big idea. This was that, as Marx put it, all history has been 'the history of class struggles', and the working class was destined, in the end, to triumph. Hardly surprising that it has been a popular theory among the working class. More convincingly, he pointed out that what we think of as democracies are usually, in reality, run by the rich in order to benefit the rich. The answer was to abolish the class system and all live in a kind of enormous commune (hence commun-ism) in which the gap between rich and poor wouldn't exist. The problem, which Marx didn't foresee, was that to sustain this unnatural state of affairs would require a manic degree of authoritarian coercion.

Friedrich Engels, philosopher (1820–95)

USAGE: In a discussion of marriage, you might mention Engels' idea that it was an institution devised by men as a means of controlling women.

In theory, Friedrich Engels was a social reformer who believed in the redistribution of wealth. In practice, he was pretty well off. Having been born into a hugely wealthy German family, he decided against giving away all his money (as, for instance, Ludwig Wittgenstein* would do). When he died, he left his heirs a legacy valued at £3.4m in today's money.

These days, Engels is best remembered as the co-author with Karl Marx of *The Communist Manifesto* (1948), and it's true he rather lived in the older man's shadow. He first came across him in the city of Cologne in western Germany, where he wrote revolutionary articles for a newspaper of which Marx was editor. Soon the two were as thick as thieves. Engels even grew a huge bushy beard to rival Marx's. When his concerned parents sent him to England to work in a Manchester mill (one of several family businesses), Engels loathed the work, but still believed so much in the importance of his mentor's mission that he turned over a portion of his salary to support Marx as he was writing his masterpiece, *Das Kapital*.

Engels contributed a few ideas to Marxism, too. One was that it would be the workers who, having the most to gain from it, would bring about the revolution. Another was that marriage was just an idea that men had come up with as a means for controlling women. If these all seem like the products of a rather sombre mind, don't be fooled. In his personal life, Engels was known for his *joie de vivre*. He adored fox-hunting and throwing exuberant dinner parties. His personal motto, he said, was 'Take it easy'. And his love of champagne was such that his son-in-law dubbed him 'the great beheader of champagne bottles'. However, he didn't go so far as to present himself as an authority on booze, in the manner of the next author, who composed the magnificently titled essay *How to Drink Like a Gentleman: The Things to Do and the Things Not to Do, As Learned in 30 Years' Extensive Research …*

Champagne Drinkers

One tends to imagine writers getting sloshed on beer or spirits. But a few have had a taste for the more expensive stuff.

H.L. Mencken, journalist (1880–1956)

USAGE: These days, Mencken is celebrated for his one-liners, such as his quip that a misogynist is 'a man who hates women as much as women hate one another'.

The booze-loving American journalist H.L. Mencken was particularly partial to bubbly. Among his numerous publications was the long essay with the elaborate title mentioned in the previous entry. He recommended beer and wine over spirits, and observed that if you had work to do, it was better to stay sober until afterwards.

Like all good journalists, Mencken was ready to write on just about anything, and frequently did so. His keynote mode was witty belligerence, extending automatic respect to nothing and no one. Among his favourite targets for ridicule were religion, politicians and marriage. Then, aged 50, he fell in love with a woman eighteen years his junior, and married her. 'Like all other infidels,' he explained, 'I am superstitious and always follow hunches: this one seemed to be a superb one.' Alas, it was ill-fated, for his wife died of meningitis after five years, leaving Mencken heartbroken.

In his day, he was respected for his scholarly book *The American Language*, which analysed the way English was spoken in America. Now that's largely forgotten, and many of his opinions seem shockingly unreconstructed (he was quite happy to sound off against women, Jews, and black people). He's most often remembered for his aphorisms, for which he had a gift. The following give a taste. 'Democracy is the theory that the common people know what they want and deserve to get it good and hard.' 'The older I grow, the more I distrust the familiar doctrine that age brings wisdom.' 'Immorality: the morality of those who are having a better time.'

Charles Dickens, novelist (1812–70)

USAGE: As an adjective, 'Dickensian' normally refers to scenes of extreme poverty, or to characters who are amusingly grotesque.

He was the best of authors, he was the worst of authors. In what way the worst? For modern tastes, some of Charles Dickens' stories can seem extremely sentimental. As Oscar Wilde* snidely remarked, it's impossible to read the drawn-out description of the death of Dickens' Little Nell without laughing. His plots also depend on absurd coincidences. In *Bleak House*, one of the characters spontaneously combusts.

In what way was he the best of authors? He wrote with huge imagination and eloquence, inventing unforgettable personalities such as Uriah Heep, the oleaginous apprentice in David Copperfield, and Ebenezer Scrooge, the Christmas-hating businessman in *A Christmas Carol*. Dickens was a genius in his productivity, his originality and his humanity. He was the first to write novels with child protagonists (such as *Oliver Twist*), and the first to write for newspapers in instalments – for instance, his debut *The Pickwick Papers*. He was also one of the first to address contemporary social issues in his stories, such as the plight of the poor, which he had himself experienced.

When his father was imprisoned for debt, the twelve-year-old Dickens was plucked from school and forced to toil in a boot-blacking factory. The ordeal haunted him, and he later strove tirelessly, not only to help others, but also to sustain the security of his own private wealth. He became rich and famous, but continued working relentlessly, touring the country to deliver one-man performances of his books. On performance days, he would prepare for his exertions by drinking a pint of champagne at tea time.

More on 'Champagne Drinkers' overleaf

Brendan Behan, playwright (1923–64)

USAGE: Behan's alcoholic consumption was legendary. 'He'd drink Brendan Behan under the table' is a recherché way of referring to a big boozer.

The Irish playwright Brendan Behan's favourite tipple was a champagne and sherry cocktail. Unfortunately, it had a particularly high sugar content and Behan's drinking made him diabetic. He died aged 41 after collapsing at a bar in Dublin. In retrospect, his whole life seems to have been geared around alcohol. He used to rise at seven every morning so he could get a few decent hours' work in before the pubs opened at noon; which was when he would stop writing and start drinking. He was so committed to the latter that he once declared: 'I'm a drinker with a writing problem.'

At the age of sixteen, Behan joined the IRA and headed to England with the aim of blowing up the Liverpool docks. Instead he was arrested and spent the next three years behind bars. On his release, he tried to kill a couple of policemen and got imprisoned again, before being released under an IRA amnesty. He then lived in Paris for a while, writing porn to pay the bills. Finally it occurred to him that he should write about what he knew – which was mainly prison. The title of his first play, *The Quare Fellow*, referred to a term describing a man condemned to be hanged. His second play, *The Hostage*, also had a theme of imprisonment. It told the story of an English solider captured by the IRA, who falls in love with a young Irishwoman.

Although he received a certain amount of attention as a playwright, Behan didn't really become famous until he appeared, blind-drunk, on the TV show *Panorama* in 1956. Some say that this was the first-ever instance of a man swearing on British television, but the truth is it was difficult to tell what Behan was saying because his words were so slurred. That was why so many people rang up to complain: they couldn't understand him owing to a combination of how drunk he was and his already thick Dublin accent. Behan was a famously convivial drinker, liking to hit the hard stuff in company – unlike a certain American author, who tended to hole herself up in hotel rooms with a bottle of sherry …

Dipsomaniacs

Drinking too much is an occupational hazard for a writer. One thinks of Ernest Hemingway, Dorothy Parker, and Hunter S. Thompson. But the list goes on.

Maya Angelou, writer (1928–2014)

USAGE: If someone gives you grief for retiring for a snooze after lunch, you might claim that you're seeking inspiration, Angelou-style.

When Maya Angelou wrote, she invariably did so in a hotel room, in bed, with a bottle of sherry at her side. First she would get herself into a trance by playing solitaire. Then she would plunge back into her past, and plunder (taking occasional nips from that all-important bottle of sherry).

She had a lot to plunder. As one journalist put it, 'To know her life story is to simultaneously wonder what on earth you have been doing with your own life and feel glad that you didn't have to go through half the things she has.' After her parents divorced, Angelou was raped, aged eight, by her mother's new boyfriend. When she told her uncles what had happened, they murdered the culprit. Angelou became convinced that somehow her 'voice had killed him', and she didn't utter a word for the next five years. Instead, she buried herself in reading. She said that the stories of Edgar Allan Poe and

Charles Dickens comforted her and, eventually, gave her back the power of speech. After that, she worked as a prostitute, while experimenting with writing in her spare time.

It was a dinner party that kickstarted her career as an author. A fellow guest, who was an editor at Random House, dared her to write down her life story. The result was *I Know Why the Caged Bird Sings* (1969): the first, and best-known, of her seven volumes of autobiography. She wrote of her many relationships, but, more significantly, of the experience of being black, of being a journalist in newly de-colonised Ghana, and of marching with her close friend Martin Luther King (who was later shot dead on her birthday). She was one of the first black authors to place herself, as a black person, at the heart of her stories.

Sinclair Lewis, novelist (1885–1951)

USAGE: Sinclair Lewis is a good example, along with John Dos Passos*, of an American novelist feted in his day, whose reputation has since rather declined.

Sinclair Lewis was the first American author to be awarded the Nobel Prize in Literature. He earned it for his vivid portrayal of conflicted characters, the success with which he created stories that communicated his political fervour, and, perhaps above all, his penetrating insights into contemporary psyches. When it came to his own personality, however, he was less keen-sighted. For Lewis was an alcoholic who was informed by his doctor in 1937 that if he didn't quit boozing, it would kill him. Lewis thought he knew better, carried on drinking, and died of it in 1951.

His life hadn't had a promising beginning. His mother died when he was a boy, and his father didn't have much time for his sensitive, gawky-limbed son. Young Sinclair also had acne and rather bulging eyes. But he later became a big hit with the opposite sex – because of the sheer quality and success of his writing. His novel *Main Street* recounts the arrival of an intelligent, newly-married young woman in a small town in America. She tries to effect liberal change and is duly rejected by the local society. Accustomed to work extolling the virtues of small-town America, the public was shocked. The book made a massive impact when it appeared in 1920, and went on to become one of the publishing sensations of the century.

Among Sinclair's other acclaimed novels was *Elmer Gantry* (1927), about a hypocritical evangelical preacher. It was eventually made into a film that earned Burt Lancaster a Best Actor Oscar. For his liberal political leanings and his critique of contemporary America, Sinclair is regarded as hugely influential – even if not in quite the top league, perhaps, as a prose stylist.

Raymond Carver, short-story writer (1938–88)

USAGE: Helping yourself to another glass of wine, you might remark, 'I'm considering taking up drinking full-time, like Raymond Carver.'

The protagonist of the Oscar-winning 2014 film *Birdman* is a movie star who wants to be taken seriously as an actor. So what does he do? He puts on a theatrical adaptation of a short story by Raymond Carver entitled *What We Talk About When We Talk About Love*. Clearly, as far as this character is concerned, Carver's name is an impressive one to drop. The title of that short story also gives an idea of the author's style, and his interests. Short, simple words. And stripping away the surface of ordinary life to reveal what's really going on underneath. This, combined with the fact that Carver tended to focus on unsavoury characters or people engaged in unglamorous menial work, led to his being associated with a literary movement known as 'dirty realism'.

The other best-known fact about Carver is that he was a grade A, no-holds-barred (or perhaps that should be no-bars-withheld) alcoholic, as his father had been before him. So ferocious was his thirst that he would already be waiting outside liquor stores when they opened for the day. His other signature move was to get drunk over dinner in a restaurant, then run off without paying the bill. He seems to have felt constrained by a too-early marriage (he was nineteen, his wife Maryann sixteen, when they tied the knot) and getting drunk offered temporary relief. While holding down menial jobs in Washington state and later California, he began writing in his spare time – and drinking more heavily. At one stage, he famously claimed to have given up writing and taken up drinking full-time. But he managed to crank out some short stories during his periods of sobriety, and they were greeted with huge acclaim by critics, who hailed him as a late-20th-century Hemingway.

Charles Bukowski, writer (1920–94)

USAGE: If you fear you're losing an argument, quote Bukowski: 'The problem with the world is that the intelligent people are full of doubts, while the stupid ones are full of confidence.'

Whiskey was the poison of choice for the writer Charles Bukowski, a kind of literary bum who wrote almost exclusively about lowlifes in LA – of which he was one, as he was perfectly happy to admit. One of his best-known books is called *Ham on Rye*. It's a heavily autobiographical novel, set in LA, about an acne-ridden loner. The 'ham' part of the title refers to the fact that serious literary critics regarded Bukowski as a bit trashy and over the top (like a 'ham' actor). The 'rye' part alludes to his preferred type of whiskey.

Like all the best authors, Bukowski had a miserable childhood. His father used to thrash him regularly until he was eleven, and as if that wasn't enough, he then developed such bad acne it left his face permanently pockmarked. A series of dead-end jobs culminated in the most boring one of all, working in a post office. It was only at the age of 49 that in desperation he declared: 'I have one of two choices

– stay in the post office and go crazy … or play at writer and starve. I have decided to starve.' With that, he quit his job and embarked on the adventure of his literary career.

He wrote about women, whiskey, the drudgery of work and the problems of the poor. Perhaps his greatest achievement was a newspaper column entitled 'Notes of a Dirty Old Man', which was deemed so incendiary that the FBI opened a file on him. According to one critic, Bukowski's appeal is that he represents 'a certain taboo male fantasy: the uninhibited bachelor, slobby, anti-social, and utterly free'. He is generally perceived to have been the inspiration for the hit TV show – and subsequent box set – *Californication*, in which David Duchovny played just such a bachelor, slouching around in contemporary LA. This was TV, so naturally he had no pockmarks, and the beautiful Natascha McElhone was ever on hand to offer the promise of salvation. To its fans, *Californication* is one of the great achievements in TV of recent decades, on a par with the likes, say, of *Mad Men*, which was itself infused with the spirit of another maverick author …

Box Sets

In the first decade of the 21st century,
something happened to television. It became
the dominant narrative form, more exciting
than cinema, more articulate than novels. And
it got cleverer, paying homage in one way or
another to the cultural heroes of the past.

Ayn Rand, novelist and philosopher (1905–82)

USAGE: Of anyone who is clearly just out for themselves in the business world, you could wryly observe, 'Let's just say he'd get on well with Ayn Rand.'

In the TV series *Mad Men*, set in the world of strong-jawed, high-flying ad executives in 1960s New York, the hero Don Draper is advised by his boss to read a novel called *Atlas Shrugged*. It's a popular book with capitalists. Why? Because its underlying philosophy is that the most important person in your life is you, and if anyone tells you different, they're talking hogwash. No matter that it's very long and appallingly written (the sexy capitalists have such hefty jaws, it's a miracle they don't topple over). Since it appeared in the 1950s, the book has sold millions of copies.

Its author, Ayn Rand, literally turned selfishness into a philosophy. She called it 'objectivism' and she seemed pretty smug about it. She once declared herself 'the most creative thinker alive'. On another occasion, she declared that the only philosophers worth reading were 'the three As': Aristotle*, Aquinas*, and Ayn Rand. Her reason for including the first two (sometimes she left out Aquinas) was that they emphasised the importance of reason. Reason was her guiding light, for she argued that it led the unbiased thinker to embrace a total, lifelong egotism.

Although some find her message invigorating, to others it's hard to stomach. To put it in context, it was the philosophy of a woman who, born in Russia, had witnessed the excesses of the revolution. Escaping to New York, she went the other way, embracing a right-wing individualism. Her two most important novels were *The Fountainhead* (1943), the tale of an objectivist architect, and *Atlas Shrugged* (1957), the tale of an objectivist businessman. The latter concludes with a 60-page speech in which the hero, John Galt, sings the praises of selfishness. Although Rand is derided by most literary critics, she has become a kind of patron saint of unabashed capitalism. Her funeral included a six-foot floral arrangement in the shape of a dollar sign.

More on 'Box Sets' overleaf

William Shakespeare, playwright
and poet (1564–1616)

USAGE: The term 'Shakespearean' is usually used, approvingly, to describe a play or film in which the characters are larger than life, flawed, and, often, meet deservedly violent ends.

The actor Kevin Spacey has said that the TV show *House of Cards* – about an unscrupulous, corrupt American politician named Frank Underwood – is 'based on Shakespeare'. How so? Well, in its use of 'asides', for one thing, where Underwood speaks his mind to the camera, just as Shakespeare's villains sometimes address the audience directly. But there's more to it than that. Underwood and his wife, in their ruthless mutual ambition, are like the two protagonists of Shakespeare's *Macbeth*: a deranged power couple, mesmerising in the sheer focus of their schemes.

Underwood also has more than a little of the psychotic Richard III about him, or of Iago, the smiling villain in *Othello*. How did William Shakespeare, the son of a glover from the provincial town of Stratford-upon-Avon in England, create these unforgettable characters? Some have said he can't have done. It must have been someone else who wrote his plays, someone more educated, the Earl of Oxford perhaps, or Francis Bacon*. But don't waste time on that nonsense – and equally, don't waste time on the bad plays and boring bits of Shakespeare. Just because the man was a cast-iron genius, doesn't mean we shouldn't admit he could be bad. All those clever-clever plays-on-words? Yawn. All those supposedly funny scenes involving working-class characters being stupid? Oof.

Stick to the good ones, though, and the great lines just keep coming. (Did we mention that he was a phrase-maker?) 'My fate cries out!' 'Frailty, thy name is woman!' 'Give me that man that is not passion's slave, and I will wear him in my heart's core.' Almost any line from *Hamlet* makes the point. It's no exaggeration to say that Shakespeare's influence can't be exaggerated. As well as *House of Cards*, there are the musicals (if that's your thing): *West Side Story*, which is an adaptation of *Romeo and Juliet*, or Cole Porter's *Kiss Me Kate*, which is inspired by *The Taming of the Shrew*. On which note, here's a quiz question on a similar theme: which novelist produced the book behind the musical *Cabaret*?

Musicals!

*Musicals often get sneered at by intellectuals
as frothy and lightweight. But many of them
have an impeccable literary pedigree.*

Christopher Isherwood, writer (1904–86)

USAGE: Taking a photograph of a friend, first murmur, 'I am
a camera.' If challenged, you can explain that this is the first
sentence of Isherwood's *Goodbye to Berlin*.

When Christopher Isherwood went to Berlin to visit his boy-friend, the poet W.H. Auden, he intended to stay only a few weeks. But although Auden didn't hang around, Isherwood did, finding the anything-goes atmosphere of the Berlin nightlife up his street. He gave English lessons to pay the bills, and meanwhile jotted down his thoughts and experiences in a series of short stories that focused on those who were most vulnerable to the rising threat of Nazism. The result was the collection *Goodbye to Berlin* (1939), which would form the basis for the hit musical *Cabaret*.

Everyone remembers the flamboyant nightclub singer Sally Bowles, particularly as played by Lisa Minnelli in the wonderful 1972 film adaptation. But the book is worth read-ing for its qualities as pure prose, its quiet precision summed up in its famous opening sentence, 'I am a camera', meaning that the author intended to record faithfully what he saw without prejudicial comment.

If Isherwood's time in Berlin had been overcast by shadows, he found a contrasting sunlit paradise in California after he and Auden moved there in the late 1930s. Their relationship had always been on-off, and Isherwood, who found work as an English professor at an LA university, eventually hooked up with an eighteen-year-old named Don whom he met on a beach. The author was then 48, so the age gap raised a few eyebrows. But the pair stayed together until his death three decades later. The relationship also inspired what some say is his best novel, *A Single Man* (1964), about an erudite Englishman in LA who has an affair with – you guessed it – a much younger, but dazzlingly beautiful man. Colin Firth played the Isherwood figure in a 2009 film adaptation.

Jean Cocteau, poet, novelist, playwright, artist and film-maker (1889–1963)

USAGE: If someone seems to be eternally playing games and faking their emotions, describe them as an 'an enfant terrible, in the Cocteauesque sense'.

If you're ever in Villefranche on the French Riviera, pay a visit to the little Chapelle St-Pierre by the sea front, which houses murals by Jean Cocteau. The images, which depict events in the life of St Peter, give a sense of the man who created them: languid, effortless, light – but are they brilliant, or an effeminate imposture? This question hangs over the whole of his remarkably varied *oeuvre*.

When Cocteau was nineteen, the impresario Sergei Diaghilev instructed him: 'Astonish me!' The young man duly did so, writing *Parade*, a one-act ballet, with music by Erik Satie and sets by Pablo Picasso. It is to this day regarded as a pivotal work of modern dance. Cocteau went on to publish volumes of poetry, novels and memoirs, produce endless paintings and drawings, and direct films that are hailed as classics of world cinema. His entrancing gothic fable *La Belle et la bête* (1946), which starred his strong-jawed lover Jean Marais as the Beast, would inspire Disney's animated musical *Beauty and the Beast* a half-century later.

As a writer, Cocteau is best remembered for his 1929 novel, *Les Enfants terribles*, about two wilful siblings who play a relentless game that ultimately leads to their deaths. This theme – leaving the reader to wonder when the characters are experiencing real emotions and when they are merely playing – casually pre-empted similar postmodernist concerns by decades.

T.S. Eliot, poet, playwright
and literary critic (1888–1965)

USAGE: A prose-like style of poetry, which involves precisely described images, pervaded by a sense of existential despair, may be said to owe something to T.S. Eliot.

There are some reactionaries who believe modern poetry isn't proper poetry, because it doesn't rhyme or scan. In their eyes, T.S. Eliot has a lot to answer for. For the American, who lived most of his life in London, was one of the first to introduce the rhythms of prose into poetry. After works such as *The Waste Land* and *Ash Wednesday*, poems that rhymed and scanned seemed old hat.

Thin-lipped and conservative in dress, Eliot looked more like a schoolmaster or an accountant than a poet. He looked repressed, and that was how he felt, to judge from *The Love Song of J. Alfred Prufrock* (1915), in which a middle-aged man laments his sterile existence. The poet's real breakthrough was *The Waste Land* (1922), which expressed the sense of existential despair that pervaded Europe after the First World War. Influenced by Eliot's study of Eastern philosophy, the long, disjointed poem seemed incomprehensible to many. Yet whether or not it coheres into a satisfying whole, the poem is rich in lines of haunting if somewhat chilly beauty.

The Waste Land is undoubtedly depressing. A response to the slaughter at the Somme, it was also, the author confessed, influenced by the horrific state of his private life (especially his excruciating first marriage to a mentally unstable Englishwoman named Vivien). But Eliot wasn't all doom and gloom. He had a secret passion for the comedy of Groucho Marx. He published a volume of poetry about cats (complete with rhyme and metre), which was adapted into the musical *Cats* by Andrew Lloyd Webber. And notwithstanding his conventional appearance, he was the first author to use the word 'bullshit' in print. That was considered racy stuff in those days – although when it came to profanities, Eliot was a boy scout by comparison with one of his foul-mouthed contemporaries …

F*** You

We're now accustomed to characters in movies saying f*** every third word, but there was a time when it was considered controversial.

D.H. Lawrence, novelist and poet (1885–1930)

USAGE: If anyone says that something you've written is a bit sloppy, you can claim you were aiming for a kind of Lawrentian spontaneity of style.

In London in 1960, there was a court case to decide whether the publishing house Penguin should be allowed to print for the first time in the UK the final novel of D.H. Lawrence. *Lady Chatterley's Lover* told the graphic tale of the love affair between a salt-of-the-earth gamekeeper and the aristocrat of the title. Some regarded it as pornographic for its liberal use of four-letter words (particularly f*** and c***), but the jury decided it was an interesting, not a dangerous book. The publication went ahead, some 30 years after the book had been written.

It's generally agreed it wasn't Lawrence's best work. That would be *Sons and Lovers* (1913) or *Women in Love* (1920). The books' titles give away the author's obsession with love, which in his eyes meant a spontaneous, deep and generally rather carnal passion between men and women. Lawrence thought the West over-emphasised the mind, neglecting our animal reality. Spontaneity was his watchword, as is clear if you read his novels and poems, some of which are sloppily written. But this was in keeping with his crazy, sometimes crazed belief system: the well-lived life was one of enthusiasms, passions – even hatreds.

Some of Lawrence's political beliefs were extremely dodgy: hate-filled and hateful. He fantasised in a letter to a friend about building gas chambers for exterminating 'the weak'. Nevertheless, his cultural impact was huge, as a successful working-class author (he was born into a coal-mining community in Nottinghamshire) at a time when that was rare, as an exemplar of the writer as visionary, and as a thinker impatient with the politenesses of the English tradition.

Kenneth Tynan, theatre critic (1927–80)

USAGE: To heap praise on a play or film, conjure the spirit of Kenneth Tynan by declaring, 'I doubt if I could love anyone who did not wish to see ...' (Add name of latest play.)

Some have argued that the Irish playwright Brendan Behan* was the first to utter the word f*** on British TV. But it's more generally accepted that it was the theatre critic Kenneth Tynan. On a live show in 1965, he was asked if he would put on a play that showed people having sex on stage. He replied that he didn't imagine it should shock people any more than it would if they heard the word f***. Moral crusader Mary Whitehouse declared that in her opinion Tynan should have 'his bottom spanked'. Little did she know, but he would have loved that, since he was into S&M.

Apart from the fact that he wasn't gay, Tynan had a lot in common with Oscar Wilde. He was a brilliantly witty writer with a flair for flashy phrases. While Wilde wrote plays and poetry, Tynan poured his talent into a higher form of journalism, serving as drama critic for the *Evening Standard* and then *The Observer*. He championed the so-called Angry Young Men and lambasted what he called 'the Loamshire play', the conventional kind of drama that was often set in a large house in the English countryside. He hailed Samuel Beckett's* *Waiting for Godot* as a masterpiece and was equally excited by John Osborne's *Look Back in Anger*, famously declaring, rather preciously, in 1956: 'I doubt if I could love anyone who did not wish to see *Look Back in Anger*.'

Tynan's motto as an author was: 'Write heresy, pure heresy.' Pretty good advice for any young gun starting out in journalism. But it also points to a weakness in his makeup (something else he shared with Wilde), which was his irresistible need to show off. It's why he's more likely to be remembered for saying f*** than for his wonderful prose style. This may have stemmed from insecurity rooted in the discovery, when he was 21, that his father was actually called Sir Peter Peacock, wasn't married to his mother, and had a second, secret family with his real wife. It was a traumatic discovery on a par with that of the next author, who didn't discover until early adulthood that the woman he'd been told was his sister was actually his mother ...

Bastards

Thankfully, the stigma of being born out of wedlock isn't as much of a big deal now as it once was. Back in the day, it was a tough burden to carry – but in the cases of some 'bastards', as they used to be known, it seems to have spurred them on to greater endeavour.

Louis Aragon, writer (1897–1982)

USAGE: When talking about Surrealism, name-check Salvador Dalí, André Breton and Louis Aragon. It's your mention of the relatively obscure Aragon that will really impress.

The French author Louis Aragon had an unconventional childhood. He was born out of wedlock, the result of an affair his mother had with a much older married man, who refused to acknowledge him. To conceal the scandal, the boy was brought up believing his mother was his older sister and his grandmother (whose husband had abandoned her) was his foster mother. The secret was revealed only as young Louis was leaving to fight in the First World War. It was decided that, since there was a good chance he wouldn't return, it was time he learnt the truth.

This wayward upbringing left Aragon with an instinctive sympathy for women, and a deep need to belong to groups. He duly joined the Dadaists, who successfully strove to create art and poetry that were total gibberish. Later, along with André Breton*, he founded the Surrealist movement, which was similar to Dadaism, but not as silly. Nevertheless, Aragon would look back on his fifteen years of Surrealism, writing automatic poetry (i.e. whatever came into his head), etc., as 'an error of youth'. Like other Surrealists, he found himself increasingly drawn to communism and in due course he joined the party: another group for him to belong to, and one with a powerful father figure in the form of Josef Stalin to replace the one missing from his childhood.

A war hero, a founding Surrealist, an author of communist poetry and novels, Aragon is much loved in France. Several of his poems were set to music by crooners such as Leo Ferre, which boosted his popularity. In person, he was the embodiment of the elegant man of letters (or *homme de lettres*). He also had a glamorous wife, the Russian author Elsa Triolet.

Jean Anouilh, playwright (1910–87)

USAGE: If someone is raving about the latest trendy play, you could mention that, according to Jean Anouilh, the bourgeoisie go to the theatre primarily to demonstrate how cultured they are.

The French playwright Jean Anouilh (pronounced: an-WEE) was born out of wedlock, the result of his mother's affair with a fellow actor. In due course, history would repeat itself when Anouilh married an actress who proceeded to carry on a series of affairs behind his back. If this all sounds like something out of a Greek tragedy, that's fitting, for it was for his modern-day adaptations of ancient plays that Anouilh would become best-known. He started out in advertising, and later said that inventing punchy advertising jingles had taught him brevity as a playwright. Then he followed his heart and got a job as a director's assistant in a theatre. This didn't pay, and, to help him out, at the end of each play's run, the crew used to donate the furniture to Anouilh.

His first efforts as a playwright were set in his own time, but they were mainly flops. Then, just as the Second World War kicked off, Anouilh turned to times past and began writing plays that were reinterpretations of ancient myths. Like *Antigone*, his biggest hit, which pitted moral integrity (as represented by Antigone, intent on giving her warrior brother an honourable burial) against political expediency (in the form of King Creon, enemy of the dead man, who wants to leave the corpse to be eaten by vultures). In the end, in defiance of the king, Antigone does succeed in giving her brother a proper send-off. The French theatre-going public interpreted this as a call to act like Antigone and courageously oppose the Nazi-supporting French Vichy government.

Later, the young turks Eugene Ionesco* and Samuel Beckett* appeared on the scene. Their crazy experimentalism wowed audiences, making Anouilh's stuff look dated, and the older man found himself shunned. But he probably didn't care much. He had a pretty dim view of the theatre-going public, believing they went to plays not to see them, but in order to be seen.

François Truffaut, film director (1932–84)

USAGE: To anyone claiming that critics can rarely do the thing they criticise, you can mention François Truffaut as a counter-example.

So ashamed was the mother of François Truffaut (pronounced: troo-FOE) at having a child out of wedlock, she sent him to live with his grandmother. As a result, Truffaut always felt unwanted. He went off the rails for a bit in his teens, doing a stint in a reformatory after he was caught stealing metal doorknobs to sell them. Cinema saved him. He began spending as much time as he could watching movies, particularly adoring the American films that flooded into Paris after the end of the Second World War. Then he was befriended by the critic André Bazin, who employed the young man to review films for his magazine *Cahiers du cinéma*.

Truffaut's journalism was so brutal he became known as 'the gravedigger of French cinema'. He became so hated that in 1958 the organisers of the Cannes film festival refused to let him attend. Yet as it turned out, he was a rare example of a critic who could actually practise what he preached. The following year, his debut feature *The 400 Blows* won the director prize at Cannes. It was an autobiographical story of a delinquent youth, but what most impressed was its innovative style (including jump-cuts and a disconcerting voice-over). It was the start of a distinguished career as a film-maker, whose other highlights included *Jules et Jim* (1961): the charming tale of a woman (Jeanne Moreau) who can't choose between two men, so hangs out with both of them.

Along with the likes of Jean-Luc Godard* and Claude

Chabrol, Truffaut played a key role in the *Nouvelle Vague* (New Wave) in French movies, which meant he made films that were cool and edgy. It's probable that – as much as for any of his movies – he'll be remembered for developing what became known as the 'auteur theory'. Essentially, this is the idea that, though it may take many people to make a film, it's basically the creation of the director. This notion of the film as the product of a single unifying mind resulted in cinema being taken more seriously as an art form.

Desiderius Erasmus, scholar and theologian
(1466–1536)

USAGE: A humanitarian thinker, who displays bewilderingly broad learning, might be praised as 'a modern-day Erasmus'.

Desiderius Erasmus was *the* Renaissance scholar. Even the theologian Martin Luther* admitted he was a man of vast scholarship, whose intellect was superior to his own. The pair later fell out, because Luther believed that Erasmus' quizzical examinations of Church doctrine didn't go far enough. Enraged, Luther slagged him off as a 'viper', a 'liar', and, startlingly, 'the very mouth and organ of Satan'. It's surprising that Luther should have had such harsh words for Erasmus, as the latter is now widely accredited as the man who 'laid the egg that hatched the Reformation'. Which is to say, Erasmus' learned and non-partisan questioning of Catholic dogma helped create an intellectual climate in which Protestantism could arise.

Erasmus, who was born out of wedlock in Rotterdam,

enjoyed many friendships with other intelligent, highly educated men. In his youth, he took this too far and fell in love
with a young chap named Servatius Rogerus. He wrote him
some passionate letters, but later got a hold of himself and
denounced homosexuality as a vile aberration. He kept up his
letter-writing though, corresponding with everyone from the
painter Albrecht Dürer to the English statesman Thomas More.

At one point, Erasmus spent time in England, staying at
Queens' College, Cambridge. He developed a violent distaste
for the weather (understandably) and English ale (oddly). In
the meantime, he weighed into the theological debates of the
day, some of which seem pretty musty today: for instance,
whether Jesus' mother Mary remained a virgin all her life
(Erasmus believed she did). Other questions to which he
wrote hefty, reasoned answers included some that are still fairly
crucial, such as the matter of whether we have free will. In
accordance with Church teaching, Erasmus argued that we do.

Thomas Paine, writer (1737–1809)

USAGE: When naming Thomas Paine as one of the founders of
liberal thought, it's customary to refer to him as 'Tom Paine', or
even 'old Tom Paine', as if he were a personal friend.

Born out of wedlock into a working-class family in Norfolk,
Thomas Paine devoted his life to promoting the rights of ordinary people against their presumptuous overlords. He sailed
to America in time to witness the War of Independence, and,
by writing the 50-page pamphlet *Common Sense*, inspired

its army to push for total freedom from the English king. It's believed almost every American soldier either read or heard a reading of the work, whose very title was revolutionary in its implication that you didn't have to be an aristocrat to understand the difference between right and wrong. Sense was common to all. Even common people had it.

Paine returned to Europe when revolution was brewing in France. He was so appalled by the conservatism of Edmund Burke's* *Reflections on the French Revolution* that he penned a response, *Rights of Man* (1791), in which he argued that when a government fails to defend its people's interests, they are entitled to rise up against it. The book's huge success led to further switchbacks in his turbulent life. He was tried and convicted for libel against Burke, but escaped punishment. He became a hero in revolutionary France, but fell foul of Robespierre's supporters and escaped the guillotine only by the skin of his teeth. He met Napoleon, who told him he slept with a copy of *Rights of Man* under his pillow. After observing Napoleon's increasing usurpation of power, Paine responded by calling him 'the completest charlatan who ever existed'.

Paine lived his last years in America, ostracised for declaring himself a deist: i.e. a man who thought god existed, just not the God of the Christian Bible. He wasn't a man who believed in hiding his feelings. In fact, practically his only pretence was in his name. He had been born Pain, but had added an E to make it look more distinguished. This, though, was a relatively mild stratagem of social pretension, by comparison with those of a certain painter …

Social Climbers

Creative types regard themselves as nature's aristocrats. A few have taken it further by actually inventing aristocratic backgrounds for themselves.

Balthus, artist (1908–2001)

USAGE: Balthus was certainly a bit louche. A high-brow way to imply that someone is extremely dodgy is to say, 'He's as impenetrable as Balthus, if you know what I mean.'

Born Balthasar Klossowski, Balthus (pronounced: bal-TOOS) was given his nickname by his mother's lover, the poet Rainer Maria Rilke*, who thought it sounded more distinguished. In later life, the painter went a step further and adopted the surname de Rola, which he claimed had belonged to the aristocratic ancestors of his father's family, though this has been disputed.

In his art, as in every area of his life, Balthus went his own way. He concentrated largely on painting naked, often pre-pubescent, girls. This may sound rather avant garde, yet he chose to do so in a conservative, figurative style. (This very conservatism was actually quite shocking at a time when most of his peers were pursuing the latest form of abstractionism.) In the best-known example of his work, *The Guitar Lesson*, a clothed older woman holds a semi-naked pre-pubescent girl across her lap as if she is a guitar. The implication of the composition is that the little girl is about to be 'played upon'. Balthus always insisted that such images were not erotic: he was just showing us an uncomfortable fact, namely that children have sexual organs too. Whether or not one is convinced by his denials, the painter was definitely not immune to the attractions of the young. He met his first wife when she was just twelve (though he waited fifteen years before marrying her). His second wife was 35 years his junior.

Balthus' fame grew over the years, helped by his friendships with other celebrated cultural figures such as Alberto Giacometti and André Malraux*. It also helped that he achieved such a distinguished age, so that in his latter years, he seemed a fascinating relic of a bygone era. Meanwhile, he encouraged people's curiosity using the technique that has served Kate Moss so well: by hardly ever agreeing to an interview. His funeral was attended by prime ministers and rock stars. U2's Bono sang a dirge and, in the pews, the model Elle Macpherson wept.

Gottfried von Leibniz, philosopher
and mathematician (1646–1716)

USAGE: After a couple of drinks, if you're feeling the love, you might observe that you 'can't help but feel there's a kind of benign Leibnizian order governing the universe'.

Gottfried von Leibniz was a bigwig, quite literally. He had a very big wig. Also metaphorically: he was a man of significance in an astonishing number of fields. He made refinements to Pascal's calculator, for example, and to the binary system now used in digital computers. He wrote essays and books about maths, logic, politics, law, ethics, theology and history, and that's just for starters. Indeed, it has been calculated that if you were to lay all of Leibniz's works end to end, and then set fire to them, you would save yourself a lot of reading.

To the non-specialist, he is remembered for having possibly plagiarised ideas from two contemporaries. Isaac Newton* accused Leibniz of stealing his theory of calculus (the mathematical measurement of change). At the time, Leibniz was judged guilty and the disgrace darkened his latter years. These days, however, it's generally agreed he came up with his calculus independently.

Leibniz has also been accused of ripping off ideas from a man with whom he is often contrasted, Baruch Spinoza*. While Spinoza stayed at home in Holland and was indifferent to worldly success, Leibniz was a globe-trotter, skipping his native Germany for England, France and elsewhere, and ever on the hunt for titles and accolades. (It's thought he had no

justification for the aristocratic 'von' he placed before his surname.) Spinoza envisaged a non-interventionist God. Leibniz
conceived a universe that was governed and guided by a
benign order; he thought we live in the best of all possible
worlds. This optimism was mocked by Voltaire*, who lam-
pooned Leibniz in his novel *Candide* as the eternally upbeat
Dr Pangloss. In Leonard Bernstein's musical version of that
book, Pangloss, about to be executed, declares rapturously,
'God in his wisdom made it possible to invent the rope, and
what is the rope for but to create a noose?' He is then hanged.

Honoré de Balzac, novelist (1799–1850)

USAGE: The name Balzac has become a byword for literary
productivity, for manic energy, for irrepressible verve. It also
refers to a kind of extremely detailed and wide-ranging realism.

After making love, Honoré de Balzac allegedly used to murmur, 'There goes another novel.' He always avoided having
an orgasm if he could, because he believed it depleted his
creative powers. He may have been right. Famously prolific,
Balzac poured forth a stream of words and works, his publications combining to form a masterpiece known as *La Comédie
humaine* (The Human Comedy).

When he first came up with the idea for this mam-
moth undertaking, which aimed to present the full pageant
of existence, he raced to his sister's apartment in Paris and
breathlessly declared, 'I am about to become a genius!'
Regarded as a sort of French equivalent of Charles Dickens*,

Balzac wrote novels remarkable for their detail and real-ism, their historical sweep, and for characters who, having appeared in one story, pop up in another. Those who are really pernickety say his writing style is a bit vulgar (the same has been said about Dickens), not so different from the trashy potboilers with which he began his career. Gustave Flaubert* remarked sniffily of Balzac, 'What a man he would have been had he known how to write.'

Having come from an ordinary background, through sheer energy Balzac had made himself a great man. To accompany the status, he added the particle 'de' to his name, to imply he had aristocratic forebears. By all accounts a jolly cove, Balzac was short and stout with a glorious mane of thick black hair. He used to go to bed at 5.00pm, then get up at midnight and write for fifteen hours straight, fuelled by (so we're told) as many as 50 cups of strong black coffee. There was only one other author, by all accounts, who has equalled this astounding level of caffeine consumption: a certain slippery French philosopher …

Coffee Addicts

Pro Plus became popular only in the 1980s.
Before that, anyone wanting to pull an all-nighter
had to rely on a series of double espressos.

Voltaire, writer and philosopher (1694–1778)

USAGE: 'Voltairean' means stingingly witty, with barbs aimed especially at organised religion or anyone in authority.

When Voltaire was on his death-bed, the priest asked him if he renounced the Devil. 'This is no time to be making enemies,' came the reply. The story sums up two key things you need to know about Voltaire. The first is he was witty. The second is that he was a sceptical thinker, who devoted his energies to annoying the clergy in particular and the authorities in general.

Voltaire wasn't an atheist. But he was vehemently opposed to the religious extremism of the Catholic Church in his native France, and inspired by the relative tolerance he had witnessed during a visit to England. 'Superstition engulfs the world in flames,' he once remarked; 'Philosophy quenches them' – a nice summary of the spirit of the 18th-century Enlightenment movement. No dry philosopher, Voltaire was a performer. Even his name was a mask (he was born François-Marie Arouet, the son of a lawyer). He wrote poetry, works of history (innovative in their emphasis on arts and customs rather than battles and kings), one of the first works of science fiction (1752's *Micromegas*), and most famously, the novel *Candide* in 1759.

That tale's hero is an optimistic young man who, after many sufferings, concludes: '*Il faut cultiver notre jardin*' (One must cultivate one's garden). What this means is open to interpretation. Don't engage in crazy schemes. Live quietly. Study. Be a free-thinker. Voltaire was certainly the latter. He had a long relationship with his niece, which caused general outrage. He annoyed so many people that he was banished from several countries. His intake of coffee was so vast (over 50 cups a day) it's a miracle he ever slept.

Søren Kierkegaard, philosopher (1813–55)

USAGE: If a film or novel involves a self-absorbed character who finds meaning in life through romantic commitment, you might observe that 'it follows the standard Kierkegaardian narrative arc'.

The Danish philosopher Søren Kierkegaard (pronounced: KEER-kuh-gard) had a strange way of drinking coffee. First he filled the little cup to the brim with sugar. Then he poured in coffee, so the sugar melted. Then he gulped it all down in one go. Is it possible he thought the procedure mirrored the three 'stages on life's way', as he saw them? Kierkegaard believed a man goes through an 'aesthetic' phase when he's young, which involves the selfish pursuit of sensual pleasures (the sugar). Then he enters the 'ethical' phase when he marries and has children and engages in civic duties such as being a magistrate (the bitter coffee). Finally, he suggested, he will enter the 'religious' phase, as he focuses on the most important things in life (the drink itself and how he feels afterwards).

Known as the father of existentialism, Kierkegaard was profoundly religious (unlike later existentialists such as Jean-Paul Sartre). He didn't use the phrase, but he argued that, since logical thinking couldn't get you to religious belief, you had to make a leap of faith. In what sense, then, did he pioneer existentialism? First, he believed that the most important questions, which you had to consider before all others, were who you were and how to live. This might provoke a degree of existential angst, which Kierkegaard called 'the dizziness of freedom'. He suffered from it himself. After falling madly in love with a girl named Régine and having his love returned, he broke off the engagement in 1841 for profound philosophical reasons he never divulged. He was miserable as a result. But, like all good creative writers, he turned his agony into art, and used it as inspiration for 1843's *Either/Or*, a kind of philosophical novel divided between a consideration of the aesthetic mode of living and the ethical mode. The transition from the former to the latter, found in many novels and films, is sometimes referred to as a 'Kierkegaardian narrative arc'. A passionate fellow, he had hair that stood up six inches above his head, and according to some accounts was a hunchback. If that report is true, it was a deformity he shared with one of the greatest German philosophers …

Misshapen

When the body is crippled, the mind can soar. The
following two characters provide a demonstration.

Immanuel Kant, philosopher (1724–1804)

USAGE: When discussing what qualifies as moral behaviour,
you can invoke Kant's 'categorical imperative': that we should
behave according to rules we'd be happy for everyone to follow.

The diminutive, hunchbacked German philosopher
Immanuel Kant lived an unbelievably boring life, on the face
of it. His daily habits at his home in the small seaport town
of Königsberg on the edge of the North Sea were so precise
and unvarying that his neighbours were reported to set their
clocks by his afternoon walks. Even when it came to giving
dinner parties, the little man was strangely methodical. He
divided the evening into set periods for exchanging news,
discussing serious matters, and making jokes. There was no
accompanying music. Amazingly, guests who attended these
occasions reported that they were a lot of fun.

But the professor's real adventures were reserved for the
library. He wrote long, complicated books with intimidating
titles such as *The Critique of Pure Reason*. Yet notwithstanding
these provisos, his philosophy was weird, ground-breaking
and – dare one say it – pretty exciting. He argued, for instance,

that it is impossible to understand the world as it actually is, which he called the 'noumenal world'. The idea we have of it relates only to the 'phenomenal world': what we perceive, conditioned by our brains, which are only able to understand things in terms of time and space, etc., when the universe's reality might be completely different.

Kant further tried to construct a basis for morality without reference to religion. This is harder than it sounds. He put forward the idea of 'the categorical imperative': you must choose rules for morality that you'd be happy for everyone in the world to follow. This is not so different from the injunction, 'Do as you would be done by', but it sounds more impressive if you refer to it as the Kantian categorical imperative.

Henri de Toulouse-Lautrec, artist (1864–1901)

USAGE: Caught visiting a brothel, you might claim to have been doing so 'in a spirit of creative fascination, like Toulouse-Lautrec'.

Henri de Toulouse-Lautrec is an easy artist to like, perhaps particularly for men. He produced portraits of prostitutes and specialised in brightly coloured posters of exuberant activity – e.g. women dancing the can-can, kicking their legs as high as possible, with the useful side-effect of revealing the thighs and maybe more.

There's a sad contrast between the physicality of these images and the artist's own physical limitations. He was preternaturally small, owing to a genetic disorder, which caused his legs to stop growing when he was thirteen. He spurned his aristocratic background, choosing instead to embrace the low life of the Paris red-light district. In part-payment for his posters, the Moulin Rouge nightclub reserved a seat for him. For a film about the artist, shun the 2001 film *Moulin Rouge* and seek out the 1952 movie of the same name: a conventional biopic, with an emphasis on its subject's unhappy love life.

It wasn't easy for the unbeautiful artist (who is said to have had unusually large genitals) to find tranquillity in romance. He became heavily dependent on alcohol, affecting an interest in inventing his own cocktails as an excuse for getting plastered. Shortly before his death at the age of 36, he took to supporting his 5ft frame with a walking stick that had a secret compartment for alcohol. Toulouse-Lautrec was proof personified that even small men can be big drinkers – although if you wanted another example, you might consider the author of *The Sound and the Fury* …

Midgets

'Little man syndrome' is a phrase sometimes used to describe the tendency of small men to overcompensate. Napoleon (5ft 6in) is often cited as a classic example. Picasso (5ft 4in) is another. The following two would also qualify.

William Faulkner, novelist (1897–1962)

USAGE: If anyone goes on for a bit too long, you can tell them – if you want to be cutting – that 'William Faulkner would have been proud of such a stream of consciousness.'

The American novelist William Faulkner was a big drinker, and a big deal as a writer. But he was a little man – just 5ft 5in, to be precise, which is why he was rejected by the American army. Nothing daunted, he duly enlisted in the British Royal Air Force, which had a base in Toronto. However, it seems his claims to have seen service with the RAF during the Second World War were invented.

His style as an author was often contrasted with that of Ernest Hemingway*. The latter was a big man who favoured short words, while Faulkner was the opposite, and as a result they each delighted in slagging the other off. Curiously, when it came to making a film adaptation of Hemingway's rather bad novel *To Have and Have Not*, it was Faulkner who got the job of writing the screenplay, and the result was rather a good movie. He also wrote the screenplay for the classic film of Raymond Chandler's novel *The Big Sleep*. But it's his novels for which Faulkner is remembered.

When his third novel was rejected by publishers, he was shocked. Yet counterintuitively, the experience gave him the courage to write for himself and become more experimental in his style. *The Sound and the Fury* (1929) was written in four parts, all told in stream-of-consciousness style from the viewpoint of a different character. The storyline, about the decline of a wealthy Missouri family called the Compsons, reflected the author's own experiences of a privileged upbringing in the American South. He always claimed to be uninterested in style per se: 'Let the writer take up surgery or bricklaying if he is interested in technique,' he once declared in an interview. Yet his own technical mastery earned him the Nobel Prize in Literature in 1949: an accolade about which he had profoundly mixed feelings. He was so suspicious of literary fame that his seventeen-year-old daughter learnt he had won the award only when she was told about it by her college principal.

More on 'Midgets' overleaf

Jean-Paul Sartre, philosopher, novelist, playwright (1905–80)

USAGE: If someone untruthfully pretends something is out of their hands, it may be described as an example of 'Sartrean bad faith' – or, better, '*mauvaise foi*'.

In 1964 Jean-Paul Sartre was offered the Nobel Prize in Literature. He declined it – the only author ever to do so – saying he did not wish to 'be turned into an institution'. By then, he already was one: the definitive French intellectual, smoking cigarettes in Parisian cafés, sporting berets and black roll-necks, banging on about socialism, and getting his leg over when he could. His success was contributed to by the fact that he expressed his ideas in novels and plays (key title: *Nausea*), as well as in more challenging philosophical works (key title: *Being and Nothingness*).

It also helped that Sartre's main concepts seemed complicated (because of the way he wrote about them), but were actually relatively simple. 'We are condemned to be free,' he said, meaning there's no such thing as god or fate, and we have to take responsibility for our actions. 'Existence precedes essence,' he also said. This was another way of saying we're free to do what we want with our life. First we realise we exist; then that we have no 'essence' (in the sense of 'set purpose or function') unless we choose one. In other words, we create our own meaning in life by an act of will. Sartre believed that people fear freedom, which makes them feel 'existential angst', and do all they can to deny it (e.g. by believing in God). He dubbed this denial 'bad faith': the pretence that you can't help the way you behave.

After nine months in a POW camp during the Second World War, Sartre decided it wasn't enough for an intellectual to write. He had to engage with the political issues of his day. During the student riots of 1968 he was arrested for civil disturbance but released by order of President De Gaulle. To lock up such a man, De Gaulle said, would be akin to imprisoning Voltaire*. Another quality Sartre shared with the great 18th-century gadfly was his diminutive stature. Voltaire was 5ft 3in; Sartre stood at barely 5ft. In the latter's case, this was in part the consequence of an illness he suffered as a child. As a result, he was confined to bed for long periods, which at least gave him time to read voraciously. This consolation of early illness was one that was also enjoyed by a certain German cultural critic ...

Sickly Children

If you scan the obituary pages of the newspapers, it's striking how many accomplished people suffered illnesses as children. Often, it seems to have given them time for reading while they convalesced, allowing their ideas to develop in tranquillity.

Walter Benjamin, cultural critic (1892–1940)

USAGE: In any conversation about movies, disconcert your interlocutor by remarking: 'Of course, cinema is a fundamentally post-auratic medium. Don't let's forget that.'

The German author Walter Benjamin (pronounced: VAL-tuh BEN-ya-meen) was a sickly child. Growing up in Berlin, confined to bed for long periods, he immersed himself in reading. And partly as a result, he emerged as one of the great public intellectuals of the 20th century. Like Simone Weil*, Benjamin produced no big book, yet his influence, through his erudite and varied essays, has been considerable.

In 1923's *The Task of the Translator* he argued that translation inevitably distorts, though it may also reveal virtues that were only latent in the original. In 1936's *The Work of Art in the Age of Mechanical Reproduction* he considered the negative impact of mass (particularly photographic) reproduction on culture. What is the difference between a poster of Van Gogh's *Sunflowers* and the original? The original has an 'aura', Benjamin said, an almost magical glow of authenticity. He believed that, in a sense, the 'auratic' work of art looks back at the viewer. This is what has been lost in the 'post-auratic' modern age. Moreover, the post-auratic medium of cinema lends itself to the communication of toxic political propaganda, as in the pro-Nazi films of Leni Riefenstahl.

Benjamin wrote in a style of fragmented brilliance. Here are some post-auratic snapshots to illustrate his life and personality. He avoided serving in the First World War by staying up all night with his friend, the Kabbalah scholar Gershom Scholem, drinking coffee to fake the symptoms of a weak heart. He had tiny handwriting, and often wrote with his pen upside-down, to make it even tinier. His life's theme was the perilous condition of Western culture, which seemed confirmed by the rise of the Nazis. The Jewish author fled, making it to the French–Spanish border, clutching a brief-case that he said contained a manuscript 'more important than I am'. He was turned back by the border officials and, in despair, committed suicide. The manuscript he referred to has never been found.

More on 'Sickly Children' overleaf

Marcel Proust, novelist (1871–1922)

USAGE: Proustian effect: when a sensual experience (sipping a certain drink, say, or hearing a certain song) releases a flood of memories.

Who was the greatest novelist of the 20th century? Two names that often get mentioned are those of James Joyce* and the French author Marcel Proust. As it happens, they did once meet at a party in Paris. The rendezvous was deliberately engineered by a couple of friends, but it wasn't a success. Although accounts vary as to what they actually said to each other, it seems that each confessed to not having read the other's work, before going on to complain about his physical ailments – which in Joyce's case were eye-related, while Proust had been sickly since childhood, a martyr to stomach cramps.

In fact, Proust was such an invalid he spent much of the last few years of his life in his bedroom, whose walls were covered in cork to deaden distracting outside noise. It was here that he applied the finishing touches to his masterpiece, the vast, seven-volume *À la recherche du temps perdu* (In Search of Lost Time). The story begins when the narrator dunks a cake known as a madeleine into a cup of herbal tea. The taste reminds him of his childhood and sparks the 3,000 pages of pin-sharp memories and exquisitely phrased reflections that follow. This reaction, where a sensual experience triggers memory, has henceforth been known as 'the madeleine effect' or sometimes 'the Proust effect'.

Preternaturally pale, with dark, heavy-lidded eyes and a quizzical moustache, Proust was a homosexual attracted to men who resembled himself. Although he is seen as something of a literary saint by his fans, some have accused him of anti-Semitism (though his attitude was mild by the standards of the time), while others regret that he wasn't more open about his sexuality (again, this was hardly unusual). When a journalist hinted in an article that Proust was having an affair with one of his male friends, the author challenged him to a duel. Both fired their pistols and, thankfully, missed. Otherwise the absurd ritual could have put an end to a mighty literary career – as it had a century earlier, in the case of one Russian author …

Pistols at Dawn

They say the pen is mightier than the sword. But the pen is not much use if you're taking part in a formal bout of single combat over a matter of honour: a fact that could be attested by such duelling authors as Cervantes, Ben Jonson and others …

Alexander Pushkin, poet, dramatist, novelist (1799–1837)

USAGE: When referring to Pushkin's most famous work, *Eugene Onegin*, use the Russian pronunciation of its title, *yev-GAYN-ee on-YAY-gin*.

It sometimes seems as if the lives of Russian novelists tend to be as extreme as the plots of their books. In *Eugene Onegin*, for example, a verse novel by Alexander Pushkin, the main character kills one of his close friends in a duel over a woman. And in reality, its author would also die in a duel: the woman in his case was his beautiful, wilful wife Natalya, whom his rival, he believed, had tried to seduce. Pushkin had already survived 28 duels, but on this occasion his luck ran out. He received a bullet in the stomach, and expired at the age of 38.

By then, it is said, he had invented Russian literature. The meaning of this extravagant claim is that Pushkin was the first real giant of Russian writing. As Chaucer did with the

English language, he brought together from different dialects the Russian vocabulary that would come to be accepted as suitable for literary works. And he made his mark on all the major genres. As well as his poetry, and his plays (the most famous of which is the historical drama *Boris Godunov*), he excelled at writing short stories. In *The Queen of Spades*, a man accidentally kills an old woman while attempting to persuade her to reveal a secret to winning at cards. The old woman then haunts him and he goes mad. It's all in the telling, of course, and because Pushkin mainly wrote in verse – whose qualities are inevitably diluted in translation – he doesn't enjoy the same standing abroad as he does in his native land. For this reason, he's a good one to admire.

A final piece of Pushkin-related trivia: on his mother's side he was descended from an African, a slave of Peter the Great who had risen to be a distinguished general. The author took great pride in this fact, and reminded himself of it by using an ink-well that had as its centrepiece the figure of a small African boy.

Tristan Tzara, artist (1896–1963)

USAGE: Accused of being silly, you could claim you're actually making a Dadaist statement about the meaninglessness of existence.

Did Tristan Tzara fight in a duel? He told the newspapers he did, engaging in single combat with fellow artist Hans Arp in Zurich in 1919. Several shots were fired, but when Arp's thigh was grazed, the duel was abandoned. Later Arp and

Tzara declared they'd actually made up the whole story. Either way, it was another wacky incident in the history of that most wacky of art movements: Dadaism.

Dadaist art, of which Tzara is the best-known pioneer (and the author of several of its manifestos), usually took the form of theatrical performances that were designed to shock. The aim was meaninglessness, as was suggested by the name Dada (chosen to resemble the inarticulate noise a baby makes). For instance, Tzara might dress as a clown and encourage the audience to pelt him with fruit. To attract the crowds, he once claimed that the movie star Charlie Chaplin was going to appear on stage. Needless to say, he didn't. If this all sounds like self-conscious student antics, it was: Tzara was in his teens when he launched the movement, and within a few years it was over. But put the Dadaists' silliness in context. It was, at least in part, a reaction to the horrors of the First World War.

And it must be said, Tzara has proved remarkably influential, inspiring the absurdism of Samuel Beckett* and Eugene Ionesco*, the situationism of Guy Debord*, and rock stars such as David Bowie and Thom Yorke. Among other things, they were impressed by Tzara's exoticism as a Romanian who migrated to Paris via Switzerland, and by his inventive personal style. Even his name was made up. He'd been born Samuel Rosenstock, but changed it to Tristan Tzara, partly because the first word sounded like '*triste âne*', the French for 'sad donkey': an image that amused him. If you bear that in mind, the pseudonym gives a sense of the character of the man – as too did the pen-name of one of the great English short-story writers …

Names that Mean Something

'What's in a name?' Shakespeare asked. The
answer, sometimes, is more than meets the eye.

Saki, short-story writer (1870–1916)

USAGE: If a story has a coldly macabre twist to it, particularly if
the whole thing is done with a dispassionate elegance, you can
describe it as Saki-esque.

There's some dispute about why the author Hector Hugh
Munro chose to write under the pen name Saki (pronounced:
SAH-kee). According to one theory, he borrowed it from a
character in the Persian poem *The Rubaiyat of Omar Khayyam*.
But the word also refers to a type of South American monkey,
which may have been why he picked it. In many of his crafted,
witty, often disturbingly dark short stories, Saki shows a curious empathy with animals, contrasting the naturalness of
their lives with the artificial propriety of humans. In others,
he tends to side with children against adults.

In *The Open Window*, a fifteen-year-old girl tells a neu-
rotic male visitor named Framton Nuttel that his hostess's
husband and brothers were killed in a tragic accident, which
she describes in some detail. When the three men turn up,
Nuttel thinks they must be ghosts and rushes away, terrified.
Needless to say, it was a prank. Or, to give an example of one

of the animal stories, in *Tobermory* an animal trainer has taught a cat – the Tobermory of the title – how to talk. The other characters are thrilled, until the cat starts revealing all their most embarrassing secrets. In a characteristic comedic flourish, Saki mentions casually at the end of the tale that the trainer later dies, squashed by an irritable elephant in Dresden Zoo while attempting to teach the animal to speak German.

Some of the details of Saki's life sound like vignettes from one of his own stories. When he was two years old, his mother was frightened by a bull, which caused her to miscarry, leading to complications that killed her. He worked as a foreign correspondent for *The Morning Post*, was gay (a fact he felt forced to conceal), and was killed in the trenches during the First World War. His last words, it's said, were, 'Put that bloody cigarette out!' spoken to a fellow soldier who was unwisely smoking. A German sniper, spotting the glow of the man's cigarette end, aimed at it and shot Saki dead.

Plato, philosopher (428–348 BC)

USAGE: The most common references to Plato are in the phrases 'Platonic relationship', 'Platonic ideas' and 'the Platonic philosopher-king'.

Plato's name means 'broad', and it's thought this may have been a nickname given him by his Athenian contemporaries, in reference to his unusually broad shoulders, or else because he had a massive forehead. In any case, the name is suitable when one considers the broad range of his philosophy. It has been said that all Western philosophy has been little more than 'footnotes to Plato'.

A failed poet, he was practically a playwright. That is, he expressed his ideas in the form of written 'dialogues': staged conversations in which two main speakers, one of whom is usually Socrates, discuss a question, progressing towards a conclusion. Often, they try to define a concept, asking, 'What is courage?' or 'What is justice?' etc. In Plato's *Symposium*, several men meet for a dinner party, then in turn answer the question, 'What is love?' One theory is that true love is usually found in a relationship between an older and a younger man, in which the older offers wisdom in return for the younger's beauty. Hence the expression 'a Platonic relationship' has come to mean one that doesn't involve sex (though this wasn't quite what Plato had in mind).

In Plato's *Republic*, as well as arguing that the ideal state would be ruled by philosophers (or Platonic philosopher-kings), he also suggests that most people are, so to speak, stuck in a cave, able to see only shadows thrown on a wall. Most people, that is, are thickies. So far, so good. Where Plato loses the plot is where he says that if they could only free themselves from the cave, they'd be able to see the world as it really is: a place of eternal 'forms' such as the perfect chair and the perfect essence of beauty, which are sometimes referred to as Platonic ideas. If this is hard to understand, that's because it's basically a bit potty.

Louise Bourgeois, artist (1911–2010)

USAGE: If you ever hear someone dismiss something as 'bourgeois', you can ironically ask if they intend a reference to the work of the French artist, Louise Bourgeois. In the process, you will demonstrate, via this superior reference, that you yourself are definitely not bourgeois.

As a noun, the word 'bourgeois' is often used pejoratively to refer to someone who is boringly conventional – an amusingly unsuitable surname for Louise Bourgeois, given the markedly unconventional nature of her art. Most of her *oeuvre* seemed to be devoted to exacting a furious revenge on her father, who had tyrannised her and her mother. Possessed of an explosive temper, he had used to put down the young Louise, mocking her in front of others. Then, when her kindly, supportive mother fell ill, he seized the chance to cheat on her with Louise's governess.

With such memories to work with, it's little wonder that Bourgeois' art was all about her parents. One of the first practitioners of what's referred to as 'confessional art' (meaning it's relentlessly autobiographical), she is noted most especially for the work she called *Maman* (lest anyone should be in any doubt as to what it was about). It's a huge bronze sculpture of a spider, which, at a height of 30 feet, towers over the viewer. Menacingly? Actually not, according to Bourgeois. 'Spiders are friendly presences that eat mosquitoes,' she explained. 'So spiders are helpful and protective, just like my mother.' Papa got a rougher ride. The work she called *Destruction of the Father* (again, the clue's in the title) consisted of the corpse of a man surrounded by the vague forms of children. The implication is that they have just murdered and eaten their father: a case of wishful thinking for Bourgeois, perhaps.

It was all rather dark and disturbing, yet Bourgeois was wildly successful. The year after she died, *Maman* sold for $11m, a record sum for a work by a female artist.

Marcel Mauss, sociologist and anthropologist
(1872–1950)

USAGE: After presenting someone with a gift, disconcert them by saying, 'I hope you realise you've just agreed to a Maussian gift-debt.'

In spite of his surname, Marcel Mauss (pronounced: MOUSE) was French, not German, and no rodent but a veritable lion in his field of socio-anthropology. He is now best remembered for his analysis of the complicated business of gift-giving. This was what Mauss referred to as a '*fait social total*' or 'total social fact', which is a socio-anthropological way of saying that people give gifts in all societies, and there are certain rules attached, which you have to observe. To reduce Mauss's central insight to a rather trite observation, he basically argued that 'there's no such thing as a free lunch'.

When you accept a present, you're undertaking to return the favour at some point. More subtly, you're entering into a social relationship with the giver, which you can't easily back out of. In a sense, a gift is never given. It's just loaned. It has what is termed an 'inalienable' quality, meaning the ownership remains with the original giver. In the way anthropologists like to, Mauss supported his theories with examples from Polynesian tribal society. In those islands, apparently, if you failed to repay a gift, you lost '*mana*', which is the source of all authority and wealth.

Some have gently suggested that Mauss may have taken it all a bit too seriously – when he argued, for instance, that every gift possesses a magical power. But his keynote work, *Essai sur le don* (which was first published in 1925 and later appeared in English as *The Gift*), had a profound influence on the theories of Claude Lévi-Strauss*. Mauss himself had been inspired by the work of the founder of sociology and the world's foremost authority on suicides, who also happened to be his maternal uncle …

Actually, We're Related

It can't have done Jean-Paul Sartre any harm
that his mother was the first cousin of the Nobel
laureate Albert Schweitzer*. The following
few were also culturally well-connected …*

Émile Durkheim, sociologist,
philosopher (1858–1917)

USAGE: You can describe almost any aspect of society, from a
system of law to the existence of pets, as 'a social fact, in the
Durkheimian sense'.

The uncle of Marcel Mauss, Émile Durkheim wasn't just a
sociologist. He was one of the first great sociologists (and
France's first sociology professor) who established the subject
as a subject. While Freud* was delving into the individual
subconscious, Durkheim suggested it was more illuminating
to study the superstructures that govern the lives of all individuals. Also known as our societies.

The son of a rabbi, Durkheim devoted himself to science rather than scripture, and believed that religion could
be explained in terms of the need of a developing society
for social cohesion. That said, he lamented what he saw as
the shocks that had been delivered to societies by modern
developments such as the 'cult of the individual' (the phrase

was Durkheim's) and the worship of science. The result was what he called 'anomie': a state in which the old certainties had been taken away, and societies were destabilised. Anomie could occur in individuals too, as he pointed out in his seminal study *Suicide* (1897), which considered suicide as a 'social fact' (another of his terms) as stark and inevitable as infant mortality, say, or the number of citizens with blue eyes.

He was the first to note many now-accepted facts about suicide, such as its higher incidence among men than women. As well as the anomic suicide (who finds himself at sea in a society that no longer tells him how to behave), he classified the egoistic suicide (the gloomy loner), the altruistic suicide (the crazed soldier) and the fatalistic suicide (the depressed prisoner). For all his insights, critics have argued that Durkheim doesn't take into account individual complexity – or sufficiently acknowledge the part played by mental illness.

François Mauriac, writer (1885–1970)

USAGE: Asked to comment on the latest novel by some whippersnapper, you might refer to François Mauriac's view that no one can write really good fiction until they're middle-aged.

In France, François Mauriac is revered as one of the great novelists of the past hundred years. Internationally, he's best known for his masterpiece *Thérèse Desqueyroux* (1927), the tale of a bored housewife in rural France who is rightly accused of trying to poison her husband. What was striking about the book – apart from the way Mauriac incorporated cinematic techniques such as flashbacks, which he'd learnt from watching silent movies – was the way the author urged us to see things from Thérèse's point of view, to understand and even forgive her.

Reconciliation was a theme in Mauriac's life. He had a violent row with Albert Camus* after the Second World War when the hot-headed young philosopher was urging reprisals against all those who had collaborated with the Nazis. Bad idea, said Mauriac. What France needed was clemency. He often found himself in opposition to the younger generation, and sometimes even seemed to court their antipathy. In a famous interview with the *Paris Review*, for example, the distinguished novelist declared that years had to pass before you could write well about an experience in your life. As a consequence, no young man was capable of writing a good novel (unless perhaps it was about his childhood). Mauriac clearly knew what he was talking about: he was awarded the Nobel Prize in Literature in 1952.

A Catholic in an era of atheism, a pacifist in an age of extremism, Mauriac was generally speaking a square peg in a round hole. But he fitted in in one respect: he knew the right people, and so did his offspring. His son married the granddaughter of the brother of Marcel Proust, and his granddaughter, the actress Anne Wiazemsky, married a young film-maker by the name of Jean-Luc Godard.

Jean-Luc Godard, film director (b. 1930)

USAGE: To dissuade a friend from selling out artistically to make a fast buck, observe that that's how the screenwriter loses the love of Brigitte Bardot in Godard's *Le Mépris*.

For an artistic revolutionary, Jean-Luc Godard was extremely well-connected. His grandfather had founded Banque Paribas, and he himself later married François Mauriac's granddaughter (as observed above) – although the marriage didn't last. Troubled relationships were a bit of a theme for Godard. One of his most successful films was 1963's *Le Mépris* (Contempt), which opens brilliantly with an extended scene in which a young writer admires each part in turn of a naked Brigitte Bardot, sprawling on a bed. That certainly gets the viewer's attention. The film goes on to examine the break-up of the relationship, after the writer agrees to compromise his integrity by writing for a movie, and Bardot suddenly but irretrievably loses all respect for him.

Godard was one of the two best-known film-makers of the *Nouvelle Vague* (New Wave), a movement devoted to making ground-breaking movies that would shake up the fusty conservatism that was then the norm in French cinema. The other, François Truffaut*, helped Godard with his first movie, which remains his best-known. Based on a true story, 1960's *À Bout de souffle* (Breathless) follows a car thief (Jean-Paul Belmondo), who after murdering a policeman, returns to Paris to try to persuade his American girlfriend (a trendily short-haired Jean Seberg) to run away with him. The story, though, wasn't what caught the attention so much as the film-making style. Godard moved his cameraman around in a wheelchair, giving the film a shaky, home-made feel. And he didn't use a completed script. Every morning before arriving on set, he would dash off the dialogue for the day's filming. The result is a sense of spontaneity, casual and achingly cool.

Other things to know about Godard. He started out as a film critic and his films often seem to be commenting on the art of film-making. His great muse among actresses was Anna Karina, who appeared in such movies as *Vivre sa vie* (1962) and *Pierrot le fou* (1965). Sad to say, but it's generally agreed that Godard's films since the 1960s haven't been as good as his early work. Critics have complained of prolonged silences in some of his more recent movies. And the dialogue of his 1982 film *Passion* was almost impossible to follow, some said, on account of the main actress's stammer …

Stammerers

*Sometimes the fluency of the pen belies a stutter
in the speech. Kenneth Tynan and Adam Smith
were two examples of writers who suffered from
speech impediments. Here are three more.*

Charles Darwin, scientist (1809–82)

USAGE: Mentioning evolutionary arguments, refer to them as
'post-Darwinian', to indicate that you realise the theory has been
refined somewhat since the 19th century.

Evolution was a revolution. Before the 19th century, people
looked at nature's wondrous variety and concluded that God
must exist. Not necessarily, said the theory of evolution.
The cause could have been a process of 'natural selection'
or 'survival of the fittest'. In other words, the best-equipped
animals (fastest, best camouflaged, etc.) survive and pass on
those qualities to their offspring. This sometimes leads to the
extinction of entire species (such as the dinosaurs), sometimes to the creation of new ones, e.g. humans, who evolved
from chimpanzees.

Charles Darwin wasn't the only scientist developing a
theory of evolution in the 19th century, but he's the one who
took most of the credit. This is partly because of his exhaus-
tive research, partly because of the verve and clarity with

which he set out his conclusions in *On the Origin of Species* (1859), and partly because he grew an enormous beard. As a result, he was a gift to cartoonists who wanted to mock the idea that humans are related to chimps. One sketched a hairy-bodied, ape-like Darwin and the image became fixed in the public imagination.

An agnostic, Darwin himself had no desire to shake people's belief in God and delayed publishing his theories for years for fear of upsetting his devout wife Emma (who was also his first cousin). Explaining evolution to people, he once remarked, felt like 'confessing a murder'. It ran the risk not only of 'killing' God, but also of wounding the high opinion humans like to have of themselves as superior, god-like creatures. Darwin himself certainly had feet of clay. He was racked by doubts. He spoke with a hesitant stutter. And he was assailed throughout his adult life by crippling health problems, which he treated with an interminable series of cold showers.

John Updike, novelist (1932–2009)

USAGE: If someone criticises you for failing in something you never attempted, you could remind them of John Updike's first rule of book reviewing.

It was curious that John Updike should have had a stammer when he spoke. For when he wrote, the American novelist was incredibly fluent, not only in terms of how much he wrote (lots), but in the elegant and apparently effortless rhythm of his sentences. Some critics have even seemed to feel that he wrote 'too' well, as if the beauty of his prose suggested that he wasn't deeply engaged with the subjects he was writing about. Others – such as the literary critic Harold Bloom, who called Updike 'a minor novelist with a major style' – said that he focused on rather light, trivial themes.

For example, sex and adultery, marriage and divorce. These were among the themes of Updike's two great novel sequences. (He had so much to say, he couldn't say it in one book at a time, but had to spread it out over 'sequences'.) The 'Rabbit' books are his best known, charting the adventures of an ordinary American guy called Harry 'Rabbit' Angstrom who was far from perfect, but not villainous: a guy readers could relate to. The hero of the other series, Henry Bech, was a kind of anti-Updike, a reclusive, Jewish, Nobel Prize-winning novelist who rarely put pen to paper.

The gregarious, Protestant Updike never won the Nobel but he did walk away with two Pulitzers (one of only three novelists ever to manage that trick). Clearly he had succeeded in his stated aim, which was 'to give the mundane its beautiful due' (by 'the mundane', he was referring to ordinary, everyday life). As well as his fiction, he was a distinguished man of letters, *The New Yorker* providing a conduit for his poetry, short stories and literary criticism. When it came to reviewing books, he laid out the rules he stuck to, which included not attacking a work for failing at something it never attempted, and always trying to include lengthy quotations from the work itself, so readers could make up their own minds.

Aristotle, philosopher, scientist
(384–322 BC)

USAGE: If you hear anyone refer to 'strict Aristotelian logic', stay calm. All they really mean is 'logic'.

It may be harsh to describe Aristotle's prose style as dry, since his more entertaining works were lost through the ages. What we have are probably his lecture notes, and they extend to thousands of pages on subjects ranging from poetics and politics to geology, theology and meteorology. Even in performance, it must be said, his lectures may have been hard work, since he's thought to have stammered.

For centuries, Aristotle's theories went uncontested in almost every area of human thought. He may not have set the pulse racing, but about most things he had got it more or less right. These days, he casts the longest shadow in two fields. The first is logic. He essentially invented inductive and deductive reasoning (forming a general rule based on examples, or proceeding by pure reason, respectively). The second is morality. In his *Nicomachean Ethics*, Aristotle argues that virtue consists in fulfilling your primary function. In a horse, this might be speed. In a man, it's reason. The man who reasons best is the best man. (Which makes it sound as if Aristotle must have regarded himself as a fine fellow.) He goes on to argue that in many cases, this will lead men to follow a middle course, halfway between excess and restraint. You should also serve the state, performing civic duties. Ho hum.

More attractive is the emphasis he places on friendship as an essential component of the well-lived life. It's possible that Aristotle may have particularly valued the kindness of friends, as one who had lost both his parents at an early age and subsequently been adopted …

Adopted

Psychologists have observed that adopted children often feel unloved, not necessarily because of a lack of affection on the part of their adoptive parents, but as a result of feeling 'dumped' by their natural parents. To compensate, they are often exceedingly ambitious – as in the case of the next two characters …

Edward Albee, playwright (b. 1928)

USAGE: Any couple who argue in public, but love each other really, may be said to be a bit like George and Martha in Albee's play *Who's Afraid of Virginia Woolf?*

Edward Albee has written 28 plays during his career, but his name instantly conjures the title of just one of them. It's not that his other works aren't any good (1975's *Seascape*, and two others, have earned him Pulitzer Prizes). It's just that *Who's Afraid of Virginia Woolf?*, which premiered in New York in 1962, is so brilliant that, once seen, it's almost impossible to forget.

In the 1966 film version Richard Burton and Liz Taylor play George, a sardonic college professor, and Martha, his ball-busting wife, who tear strips off one another – wielding words like knives – before the horrified gaze of a younger couple. During a late-night drinking session, they play verbal and non-verbal games that include George pretending to shoot Martha, and finally revealing that the child they've been referring to throughout the evening doesn't actually exist. The fascination of the film, which is often very funny, was added to by the possibility that it offered an insight into the real-life marriage of its stars, though in fact it was inspired by the combative relationship between the playwright and his boyfriend, a composer named William Flanagan.

The play, its author remarked, has 'hung around my neck like a shining medal of some sort – really nice but a trifle onerous'. This is what's known as a five-star problem. The play is revived regularly, guaranteeing attention to Albee's later works – such as 2002's *The Goat*, about an architect who falls in love with the four-footed beast of the title. Forever opposed to authority, Albee had come into conflict with it from an early age. He tells a story of how, as a child, he had been chastised for taking down a book, because the hole it left on the shelf was unsightly. Albee said this was when he first began to suspect he had been adopted – which, as it turned out, he had.

Muhammad, spiritual leader (c. 570–632)

USAGE: The Arabic pronunciation of 'Muhammad' roughens the 'h' and lingers on the 'mm': 'Mookh-AMMM-ad'.

Most Christians (population: 2.4bn) know little about the life of Muhammad, who founded the Islamic faith of Muslims across the world (population: 1.6bn). Here's the lowdown. An illiterate orphan who was brought up by his uncle, he started out as a camel driver – or rather an organiser of trading trips, which were taken by camel, across the Arabian desert. Aged 40 he had a revelation while meditating in a cave. The angel Gabriel embraced him, telling him to spread the word of God. Muhammad thought he was going mad, but his wife Khadijah assured him that such experiences came from God.

That was the same angel Gabriel, incidentally, who crops up in the Christian and Jewish traditions. Muhammad didn't exactly found a new religion: what he did was urge his people to drop the polytheistic ways they had fallen into, worshipping many gods, and instead return to the faith of their ancestors, who had worshipped the God of Abraham. Where he diverged from tradition was in setting down a new set of divinely inspired rules and observances, which he recited in verse over the course of many years, and which make up the book called the Quran.

Unlike Jesus, Muhammad – or The Prophet, as he became known – never claimed divine descent. He did, however, report that he had flown to Jerusalem on a winged creature named Buraq, and there spoken to Jesus, Moses and Abraham.

A couple of common misconceptions about Muhammad. He didn't propose the universal use of the veil for women to preserve their modesty; this was a later innovation. Although a successful military leader, he taught that forgiveness was better than vengeance. 'Whoever kills a human being,' the Quran states, 'it shall be as if he killed all mankind.' As a sentiment, it bespeaks the wisdom of a man who didn't come to his vocation until his fifth decade …

Late Bloomers

*There are advantages to hitting the big time at a more
mature age. One is that you're less likely to waste it.*

Kurt Vonnegut, novelist (1922–2007)

USAGE: If an author is described as 'Vonnegutesque' it usually
means they combine a dark sense of humour with a zany prose
style, while mixing up their literary genres (e.g. history and sci-fi).

The novelist Kurt Vonnegut had the hangdog features of a
man who had known failure. Before becoming a novelist he
had run a nappy-cleaning business and managed America's
first Saab dealership, which folded after a year. He used to say
that he'd been a failure until he was 47 – which was when he
published *Slaughterhouse-Five* (1969): his satirical, mordant
novel that dealt with the horrors of the Allied bombing of
Dresden during the Second World War (while throwing in
some sci-fi elements). This Vonnegut had experienced first-
hand, after being captured at the Battle of the Bulge and taken
to Dresden as a prisoner of war.

The anti-war sentiments of the book chimed with the
mood of the time, and its author became a celebrity. At one
point he was the most studied novelist at US universities.
Since then, his reputation has declined, not helped by the
discovery that in *Slaughterhouse-Five* he got some of his facts

wrong. For instance, the Dresden bombing had killed around 30,000 people, not 135,000 as he had stated. (He had taken his figures from a book by Nazi apologist David Irving.)

Vonnegut's is a terrific name to drop, because he sounds German, while actually being American. This makes him an easier read, as does the fact that he wrote in a trendy, relaxed, wry style. He was nothing if not natural. He's as likely to indulge in a comic riff about the smell of farts as he is to present some reasoned argument about historical method.

William S. Burroughs, writer (1914–97)

USAGE: To invoke the spirt of William S. Burroughs is to refer to life choices that involve Class A drugs and transgressive sex.

William Burroughs didn't really hit his stride until he killed his second wife, Joan, when he was 37. It was an accident. Both were drunk, and she agreed to balance a gin bottle on her head, which he tried to shoot off with a handgun, a bit like William Tell. He missed and shot her dead. Burroughs managed to evade a prison sentence by telling the police in Mexico, where the tragedy occurred, that the gun had gone off accidentally. He later claimed the guilt had some-how 'made' him a writer, but this is a little dubious, since by then he'd already all but finished his first classic work, *Junkie* (1953), which describes in detail his experience of being a heroin addict.

Burroughs lived life to extremes. As well as taking a lot of drugs, he was, despite his two marriages, a homosexual who wrote graphically about gay sex. How much you admire him may depend on how interested you are in things of this nature. His hallucinatory novel *The Naked Lunch* (written in Tangiers, where he took drugs and slept with boys) has its fans, including the director David Cronenberg, who adapted it into an acclaimed film. The author took his literary experiments further, writing several novels by a 'cut-up' technique, which involved putting together randomly chosen words and phrases.

In the spirit of cut-ups, here are some randomly chosen facts about Burroughs. He invented the phrases 'soft machine', 'heavy metal' and 'blade runner'. He created art works by putting cans of spray paint near canvases and shooting them with a shotgun. And on one occasion, he cut off the last joint of the little finger of his left hand in an attempt to impress a man he was in love with. Clearly Burroughs was a bit deranged – although in the madness stakes, he can't compete with the French author who believed his urine was made of diamonds …

Insane in the Membrane

*There's a fine line between artistic genius and
sheer lunacy. Here are three who crossed it.*

Guy de Maupassant, writer (1850–93)

USAGE: An even better name-drop (because less obvious) than
Hemingway, if you wish to indicate a certain kind of laconic
prose style.

Like many a 19th-century *littérateur*, Guy de Maupassant
(pronounced: GHEE duh MOE-pass-on, though the n is
almost silent) contracted syphilis and went mad. He became
convinced that his brain was dribbling out of his nose and
mouth, and that his urine was made of diamonds. Not that
he needed unconventional sources of revenue. Maupassant
made a fortune by writing an enormous number of short stories at a furious pace (too furious, some said) and publishing
them in newspapers, which paid rather better in those days
than they do now.

One risk with reading the work of foreign authors is that
the translations mislay the poetry of their carefully chosen
words, which is what literature is ultimately all about. The risk
is less in the case of those such as Maupassant who wrote in
a stripped-down style. He is sometimes referred to as one of
the fathers of the modern short story. What this means is that

he favoured an economical way of writing, never using two words where one would do, and holding back from offering overt value judgements on the behaviour of his characters. The approach had a huge influence on many 20th-century writers of short stories, such as Ernest Hemingway*.

There was also something avant garde about Maupassant's apparently bleak outlook on life. And indeed in himself the author seems to have been something of a curmudgeon, even before he lost his mind. He so loathed the sight of the Eiffel Tower that he habitually ate in a restaurant at the foot of the monument, which he said was the only place in Paris where he wasn't forced to look at it.

Augustus Pugin, architect (1812–52)

USAGE: Pugin should always be referred to as 'poor Augustus Pugin', which indicates that you know something about the sad end to his life.

The clock tower of Big Ben in London's Parliament Square is one of the symbols of Britain. Its sturdy silhouette seems to proclaim solidity, apt for a democratic system that prides itself on tradition and common sense. Yet the tower's architect was a troubled figure who finally lost his mind completely.

The son of a French father and an English mother, Augustus Pugin (pronounced: PYOO-jin) was a man with a religious sense of mission. He deplored the flat pragmatism of the Industrial Revolution, with its factories and smokestacks, as much as he despised the effete foibles of the Regency architecture among which he grew up. What he thought was needed was a return to the austere beauty of Medieval Gothic.

It was a vertical style, its church steeples and window shapes pointed, like signposts directed at heaven. 'There is no likelihood of my ever having any initials after my name unless VP (Very Pointed),' he once endearingly confessed. Yet after the Palace of Westminster burned down in 1834 and Sir Charles Barry was chosen to rebuild it, Pugin was commissioned to design the lavish interiors, the vanes and spires of the exterior, and, of course, Big Ben. He threw himself into the work with such fervour that it brought on a nervous breakdown, which overwhelmed him on a train. By the time he reached his destination, he couldn't string a sentence together or recognise his wife or children.

Pugin was confined in the Royal Bethlem Hospital (whose name is the origin of the term 'bedlam' for a lunatic asylum). Over the road was St George's Cathedral, Southwark, which he had designed himself. He never fully recovered and expired at the age of 40, possibly of syphilis contracted in his teens. His posthumous reputation suffered from the fact that the great arbiter in these matters, John Ruskin, thought he was second-rate.

More on 'Insane in the Membrane' overleaf

Leopold von Sacher-Masoch, writer (1836–95)

USAGE: When you use the word 'masochist' to refer to someone who gets a kick out of pain, be sure to pronounce the S as a Z, to emphasise that you're aware of the derivation.

In 1869 the young Austrian novelist Leopold von Sacher-Masoch signed a business contract with his mistress, who revelled in the name of Fanny Pistor. The deal stated that for the next six months, he would be her slave. In return, she had to wear fur as often as possible, especially when she was in a cruel mood.

The pair set off by train for Venice, where they knew they wouldn't be recognised. On the journey, Fanny sat in first class, while Leopold debased himself by travelling in third. These details and the events that transpired (including enthusiastic whipping sessions) found their way into the novella *Venus in Furs*, which is the only book by Sacher-Masoch that is now available in English. His surname, though, was immortalised by Richard von Krafft-Ebing's *Psychopathia Sexualis* (1886), which used it as the basis for the term 'masochist', to describe anyone who gets a sexual kick out of receiving pain – as opposed to a sadist (named after the Marquis de Sade), who gets a kick out of inflicting pain.

When he wasn't being whipped, Sacher-Masoch campaigned for women's rights and tolerance for Jews. He came to a sticky end, but not quite as sticky as that of his favourite cat, whom he strangled. When his wife Hulda found him with the mangled animal, he raved on about the joy it brings to murder the thing one loves. Understandably, she had him confined in an asylum, where he is reported to have died in 1895 (though some say he may actually have survived for another decade).

Sacher-Masoch became an unlikely hero during the mid-20th century counterculture. His descriptions of perverse love appealed to The Velvet Underground's Lou Reed, who wrote a song named 'Venus in Furs' for the rock group's first LP. The title must also have been intended, at least in part, as a display of erudition – the same motivation as, presumably, impelled the rock group Steppenwolf to name themselves after a novel by a trendy German author …

Inspired Rock Singers

Serious rock singers have always been keen to show off about their reading habits. The song 'Killing an Arab' by The Cure was inspired by Albert Camus'* novel L'Étranger. *'Calypso' by Suzanne Vega is based on a scene in* The Odyssey *by Homer*. Here are a couple of other examples.*

Hermann Hesse, novelist (1877–1962)

USAGE: If you wanted to seem incredibly in touch with your spiritual side, you might claim to have been smoking dope and reading Hermann Hesse's *Siddhartha* by the light of a full moon.

When Dennis Hopper and Peter Fonda roar along the freeway on their Harley Davidsons in 1969's *Easy Rider*, they do so to the song 'Born to be Wild' by the American rock group Steppenwolf. The latter had named themselves after the 1927 novel *Steppenwolf* by the German author Herman Hesse, who was particularly popular with the followers of the hippy counterculture in the 1960s. Why? Because Hesse said that the most important thing a man could do was be a free spirit and try to 'fulfil himself' with 'the gifts bestowed on him by nature'. He was so convinced of this that he used it as an excuse when he walked out on his wife, who suffered from mental illness. All that mattered, apparently, was Hesse's duty to be a great writer.

The quest for self-fulfilment was the theme of his novels, as well as his life. This was clearest in his novella *Siddhartha* (1922) in which a young Indian man embarks on a quest for spiritual enlightenment in the time of the Buddha*. This was the Hesse novel most likely to be seen in the hands of 1960s hippies, since it was short and relatively straightforward. Hesse went on to express his ideas in more complicated forms in *Steppenwolf*, in which a man tormented by the split in his character between the civilised and the wild finally escapes his suicidal impulses, and in *The Glass Bead Game* (1943). Set in the distant future, the latter features a man groomed to be a member of an intellectual elite, who turns his back on it to seek his own meaning in life.

By the time that novel appeared, Hesse's books had been banned by the Nazis for their 'degenerate' content. In response to anyone who criticises his *oeuvre* as pretentious and self-indulgent, you might observe that at least he had political integrity: the author persistently denounced nationalism, even as many of his peers embraced it.

More on 'Inspired Rock Singers' overleaf

Mikhail Bulgakov, novelist
and playwright (1891–1940)

USAGE: Be sure that, whenever you refer to Bulgakov, you emphasise the second syllable of his name.

According to Mick Jagger, the Rolling Stones song 'Sympathy for the Devil' was inspired by the novel *The Master and Margarita* by Mikhail Bulgakov. It was yet another accolade that came too late for the author, who hadn't lived to see his book in print. For he had been writing it in Russia at a time when anything deemed remotely 'subversive' was banned.

In fact, Bulgakov had had a rather complicated relationship with the Communist state. Josef Stalin was a big fan of some of his plays. Reportedly, he had so adored his *Day of the Turbins*, for instance, he had been to see it fifteen times. However, several of Bulgakov's other plays were deemed so off-message they were banned before they reached the stage. It drove the author to despair and eventually he wrote a personal letter to Stalin, asking permission to leave the USSR, since the country seemed to have no use for him as a writer. Shortly afterwards, the phone rang and it was Stalin. Did Bulgakov really wish to leave Russia, he inquired icily. The author tactfully replied that a Russian writer could not exist outside of Russia, and lived to write another day.

Latterly he devoted his energies to *The Master and Margarita*, an extraordinary, visionary novel that soared across centuries – from 1st-century Jerusalem to contemporary Russia – and included the Devil among its cast of characters. Bulgakov slaved at it for twelve years, only for it to be rejected by publishers. Little wonder, since it provided a severe critique of the Soviet regime. When it eventually saw the light of day, the book was instantly hailed as a masterpiece. Sadly for Bulgakov, this wasn't until 26 years after his death – an interval almost, but not quite, as long as that between the death and due recognition of one of the most gifted pop artists of the 1960s …

Very Late Bloomers

*There's a downside to being ahead of one's
time. One is only appreciated posthumously,
and by then it's rather difficult to enjoy it.*

Pauline Boty, artist (1938–66)

USAGE: If you want to talk about Pop Art, it's fine to drop the
obvious names of Roy Lichtenstein and Andy Warhol. But you
might want to throw in the comparatively little-known name
of Boty, too, as a sure proof of your connoisseur status. Oh,
and make sure you pronounce her 'BOAT-ee', to avoid any
confusion.

After her death, the work of Pauline Boty lay forgotten for 30
years, languishing in a barn on her brother's farm in Kent.
Then an art historian discovered it and hailed it as touched
by genius. A retrospective exhibition followed. Suddenly Boty
was big news again, her place in the pantheon of Pop Art
practitioners confirmed.

She and her fellow pop artists had caused a stir back in
the day by introducing elements from supposedly trashy
popular culture into the high-brow world of contemporary
art. They produced artworks that had a disposable, bubble-
gum feel, like the latest song by The Beatles. Boty herself often
included more sophisticated references, just to show that

she could. For instance, she created two collages, which she pointedly exhibited side-by-side. One was entitled *Is it a bird? Is it a plane?*, quoting the popular Superman comic books, while the other was titled *A rose is a rose is a rose*, which is a quote from that high priestess of poetic pretentiousness, Gertrude Stein*. The artist was admired by feminists, not only for being a successful woman artist in an era when that was a rarity, but also for using her work to draw attention to the objectification and oppression of women. Her work *It's a Man's World II*, for example, was a collage comprising cut-outs she had taken from pornographic magazines.

The embodiment of cool, Boty was a very hip chick in the Swinging Sixties, friends with everyone from Bob Dylan to David Hockney. She died of cancer at the tragically young age of 28.

El Greco, artist (1541–1614)

USAGE: Always refer to him as Domenikos Theotokopoulos first. Then, if anyone looks confused, explain that you mean El Greco.

The great thing about stand-alone geniuses is that you don't need to know much about the artistic traditions in which they worked. All you need do is gawp and agree that something pretty extraordinary is going on here. That's how it is with the paintings of El Greco, which look like hallucinogenic visions. Indeed, some have suggested that the reason for the weird colours and oddly elongated limbs of the figures in his paintings is that he had smoked an enormous amount of marijuana. Others believe, more prosaically, he may have had defective eyesight, possibly astigmatism.

'El Greco' – meaning The Greek – was only his nickname. It's hardly surprising he was given it, since his real name was Domenikos Theotokopoulos, which is a bit of a mouthful. (N.B. He signed his paintings with his real name, using Greek lettering.) Born in Crete, which was then controlled by the Venetian Empire, as a young man he moved to Venice and trained as a painter under Titian. Later he settled in Toledo in Spain, where King Philip II was looking for painters to decorate his new monastery-palace, El Escorial. Unfortunately, El Greco's arrogance (he dismissed Michelangelo, on the grounds that he 'didn't know how to paint'), combined with his eccentric style of painting, irritated Philip, and so he was forced to proceed without the support of royal patronage.

A classic example of an artist who was under-appreciated in his own lifetime, El Greco wasn't hailed as a genius until the Romantic era of the 19th century. Those he has inspired since then include Pablo Picasso* and Paul Cézanne (with both of whom, it has been said, he has more in common than with any of his contemporaries), as well as the Greek film composer Vangelis, known for his soundtrack to the film *Chariots of Fire*. The latter composed an entire album in tribute to the greatness of El Greco.

Henry David Thoreau, writer (1817–62)

USAGE: When citing Thoreau as an inspiration for living a more simple, rural existence, don't make the mistake of pronouncing his surname as if he were French. Say it to rhyme with 'borrow'.

The American author Henry David Thoreau didn't enjoy much success in his lifetime. Yet his influence has been huge in two quite separate spheres. Firstly, he has become the patron saint of an idea beloved of eco-warriors the world over, of going back to basics and living at one with nature. For that was what Thoreau did. Admittedly not all his ventures into the wild were a success. On one occasion, he and a friend accidentally let a fire get out of control, leading to the destruction of 300 acres of woodland. But he had a happier time between 1845 and 1847 when he lived entirely alone in the Walden woods in Massachusetts, in a hut he had built himself: an experience he described in his eloquent, stirring, albeit often rather preachy book, entitled *Walden*.

Another key work is *Civil Disobedience*, which promoted the idea that if the government was immoral, you had a right to defy it. Thoreau – always one to practise what he preached – personally did this, refusing to pay his taxes on the grounds that the state of Massachusetts at the time allowed slavery. For this he spent the night in prison before being released when one of his aunts, against his will, paid his tax bill for him. Among those influenced by Thoreau's example were Leo Tolstoy, Mahatma Gandhi and Martin Luther King. Above all, he is an American hero, embodying the virtues of hardiness and self-reliance that his friend Ralph Waldo Emerson* praised, and the philosophy of oneness with nature known as Transcendentalism.

It was somehow fitting that this earnest, awkward-looking man – another of his friends, Nathaniel Hawthorne*, said he was 'as ugly as sin' – should have perished as a result of his relentless spirit of enquiry. He went out in the midst of a thunderstorm to count the rings around tree stumps, and contracted bronchitis, which eventually killed him. Talk about devotion to duty. In retrospect, his death seems symbolic – the man of science oblivious of mortality – and, perhaps, reminiscent of that of the Greek mathematician, who was so engrossed in his studies he didn't bother defending himself against an assailant …

Just Let Me Find Out If ...

Greater love of learning hath no man than that he
should perish while engaged in scientific work.

Archimedes, mathematician and inventor
(c. 287–c. 212 BC)

USAGE: Archimedes is most often referred to by implication
in the phrase 'to have a eureka moment', meaning to realise
something suddenly.

In his *Dictionary of Received Ideas*, Gustave Flaubert* wrote
satirically: 'ARCHIMEDES. On hearing his name, shout
"Eureka!" Or else: "Give me a fulcrum and I will move the
world." There is also Archimedes' screw, but you are not
expected to know what it is.' What a cynic Flaubert was. After
reading this entry, you will be expected to know something
about Archimedes' screw.

'*Eureka!*' is Greek for 'I have found it!' and it's what
Archimedes shouted after he climbed into the bath at his
home in Sicily, and noticed that the water level rose. What
he realised was that, to find out the volume of an irregu-
larly shaped object, all you had to do was fill a container to
the brim with water, drop the object in it, and then catch
and measure the volume of water displaced. Simple. His
remark about a fulcrum made the point that, if you had a

long enough lever and a pivot on which to rest it, you could shift even something as enormous as a planet.

Some of the maths you learnt at school (and may have since forgotten) was discovered by Archimedes: e.g., how to calculate the area of a circle. Yet in his lifetime, he was better known for his inventions, which included the afore-mentioned screw. This was not a sexual technique but a type of pump for removing bilge water from a boat.

When his home town of Syracuse was sacked by the Romans, a soldier burst in on the mathematician. 'Do not disturb my circles,' Archimedes is said to have murmured, meaning he would prefer not to be bothered until he'd solved the geometric problem he was considering. This so enraged the soldier that he killed him.

Francis Bacon, philosopher, scientist, statesman (1561–1626)

USAGE: Never, on any account, make any bacon-related puns. That would be hammy. Instead, limit your references to strict 'Baconian' scientific method.

Did Francis Bacon write Shakespeare's plays? No. But the fact that some think he did, secretly, using Shakespeare as a front, is a sign of just how brilliant the man was. It's also an example of the kind of flawed logical thinking that Bacon would have deplored. Bacon was brilliant – Shakespeare's plays are brilliant – therefore Bacon wrote Shakespeare's plays. What rot!

Bacon's life, though, could provide material for a whole host of plays. He trained as a lawyer; married a fourteen-year-old (when he was 45); rose to be attorney general; was prosecuted for taking bribes (which he did) and imprisoned in the Tower of London; released, he retired to his study to devote himself to philosophising. His major work, never completed, was *The Great Instauration*, in which he planned to set out a method for advancing all human knowledge. First, he explained various ways in which men's view of the world is distorted. There are errors of the 'tribe' (those we make because we are human), of the 'cave' (our personal prejudices), of the 'marketplace' (linguistic confusions), and of the 'theatre' (the mistakes of past philosophers).

He went on to detail a strict method for scientific enquiry, based on experimentation and the consolidation of results. This is why he's sometimes known as 'the father of scientific method', and sometimes as 'the father of empiricism' (enquiry based on experimentation). In the end, his theories killed him. He went out, one cold winter's day, to discover if stuffing a chicken with snow would help preserve it, caught a chill and died. An absurd end to an intellectual titan, who must never be confused with his 20th-century namesake ...

Not to Be Confused With

The blush of shame is rarely hotter than when one confuses one important cultural figure with another. So note well the distinctive features of the following.

Francis Bacon, artist (1909–92)

USAGE: Score extra points by referring to him as 'Fran' Bacon, which was what his friends called him.

The painter Francis Bacon may occasionally have been confused with his 17th-century namesake (see previous entry) but there's little chance of his paintings ever being mistaken for anyone else's. They are, it must be said, not the sort of thing most people would want to hang in the home. His works are bleak, distorted, his human figures hunched or twisted like trapped animals. Yet to admirers, these glimpses of emotional pain say something profoundly, if depressingly, accurate about what it meant to be alive in the midst of the gratuitous 20th century. To make the point, a figure in one painting wears a swastika armband. (Bacon claimed, not very convincingly, he had included it only because he liked the symbol's shape.)

Sad to say, but if you really want to capture the public imagination, it helps if your private life is as colourful as the work you produce. And it was in the case of Bacon, a pudgy homosexual with a face like a boxing glove, who haunted the dives of Soho in London. As well as fellow artists such as Lucian Freud, he enjoyed the company of ruffians such as his long-term boyfriend George Dyer, whom he met when Dyer tried to burgle his flat. Dyer bungled it and Bacon bundled him into bed. The relationship was tempestuous, eroded by alcohol and the fact that Dyer couldn't understand Bacon's art. 'I fink they're reely 'orrible,' he once observed of some intense but tender portraits the artist had done of him. Yet when the affair ended in 1971 with Dyer's suicide, Bacon was devastated.

After that, death became more than ever a theme in his work, along with pain and decay (he was particularly inspired by a book of photographs illustrating diseases of the mouth). A rare example of an important British painter, Bacon today routinely commands prices in the tens of millions.

Irving Berlin, composer (1888–1989)

USAGE: Many of Berlin's lyrics have become well-known sayings, which makes his an easy name to drop. For instance: 'In the words of Irving Berlin, there's no business like showbusiness.'

You should never on any account mix up the American composer of popular songs Irving Berlin with the philosopher Isaiah Berlin – although if you did, you'd be in good company, since it was a mistake once made by no less a personage than Winston Churchill.

'White Christmas'. 'What'll I Do?' 'There's No Business Like Showbusiness'. Irving Berlin racked up so many hit songs that when he died, the *New York Times* credited him with having written 'the tunes America played and sang and danced to for much of the 20th century'. One of the keys to his success was that he wrote simple lyrics that sounded like ordinary spoken dialogue. There was also an energy and verve to his brand of 'ragtime' music (a precursor of jazz) that meant, for the first time, young people could really cut loose and go crazy when they danced to his tunes.

Berlin's biography was a rags-to-riches story. Born to Jewish parents, he was brought up in abject poverty in rural Russia, along with his seven siblings. When he was five, the family migrated to New York to escape the growing climate of anti-Semitism in Russia. A few years later, he was working selling newspapers, when he noticed that more people would stop to buy one if he sang the latest songs. His musical talents recognised, he was recruited to write songs for a musical publisher and went on to become one of the most accomplished American songwriters in history.

Somehow, his fame failed to impinge on the consciousness of the British PM. When Churchill was introduced to Irving at a lunch in London during the Second World War, he mistook him for the philosopher Isaiah Berlin (up next) and asked how he thought the war was going. To his surprise Irving replied, in a pronounced American accent, that he was honoured to be asked such a question and that he would boast about it to his grandchildren when he returned to his own country. Assuming he had been the victim of an obscure practical joke, Churchill made his excuses and left.

Isaiah Berlin, philosopher (1909–97)

USAGE: If one of your friends is wrestling with a major life dilemma, it may be that their difficulty stems from what Isaiah Berlin called 'value pluralism'.

The philosopher Isaiah Berlin once suggested that thinkers, writers, artists and the rest could be divided into two categories: hedgehogs and foxes. Hedgehogs, by his definition, were those who had one big idea, which influenced everything they did. He categorised Plato and Nietzsche as hedgehogs. Foxes were those who darted about, being interested in and good at a number of things. Examples of foxes were Shakespeare, Balzac – and, it seems fair to say, Berlin himself.

His obituaries described him in hyperbolic terms. For instance, he was said to have been the best talker of his generation and the pre-eminent scholar of the 20th century: both rather dubious claims. But he does seem to have been a pretty interesting guy. Born in Russia, he witnessed the revolutions of 1917 before fleeing to Britain. There, having learnt the language in a few months, he established a reputation for intellectual brilliance. He also found time to marry a golf champion and work for the British as a spy, the latter service earning him a knighthood in 1957.

These days, Berlin is best remembered for his scintillating essays. It was in one of these, for instance, that he set out the difference between 'foxes' and 'hedgehogs' (though the old fox claimed he hadn't meant the essay seriously). In another essay, he defined his notion of 'value pluralism'. In essence this is the idea that humans create their own values and these sometimes come into conflict with each other. For example, it's good to keep a promise, and it's good to tell the truth. But sometimes, to keep a promise you have to tell a lie. Or take the example of a man wondering if he should leave his wife for his mistress. The value of 'family life' says he should stay with his wife. The value of 'true love' tells him to run off with his mistress. A great deal of individual suffering, Berlin suggested, boiled down to cases of value pluralism.

Lao-Tsu, spiritual leader (6th century BC)

USAGE: If anyone ever accuses you of being lazy, you could claim you have merely been striving to live in accordance with the philosophy of the Tao.

In the 6th century BC, a Chinese scribe named Lao-Tsu (pronounced: LAO-tsuh), who had grown tired of imperial corruption, travelled west on a water buffalo until he reached the country's border. There the border official, whose name was Yinxi, didn't mistake him for the military strategist Sun Tzu (up next), as others have done since. He knew exactly who Lao-Tsu was, and he asked him to write down his wisdom so it wouldn't be lost. The resulting book was called the *Tao Te Ching* (pronounced: DOW DEY JING) and to this day hundreds of millions of people worldwide subscribe to its gentle philosophy of stillness, living in the moment, and enjoying the things that are already around you, instead of yearning after impossible dreams.

The story goes that Yinxi was so impressed, he quit his job and followed Lao-Tsu to the end of his days. However, very little can be known about Lao-Tsu for certain. Some scholars even believe there never was such a person and that the *Tao Te Ching* was compiled by many authors over the centuries (cf. Homer*). His followers have claimed that Lao-Tsu later taught the Buddha* – or even that he was the Buddha. However, they also claim that he was born fully formed from his mother's womb at the age of 63 with a grey beard and long earlobes (a sign of wisdom).

Let's say no more, for as Lao-Tsu put it, 'Those who know do not say. Those who say do not know.' Yet before falling silent for ever, we might make one last point. The tenets of the *Tao Te Ching* and its quest for the Tao (meaning a calm spirit that pervades the universe, and a way of living in accordance with it) have been co-opted in all sorts of different disciplines. Some Method actors try to channel the Tao in their performances. And there are those who see in Lao-Tsu's teachings a paradigm for free-market economics.

More on 'Not to Be Confused With' overleaf

Sun Tzu, general and military strategist (6th century BC)

USAGE: Take your copy of Sun Tzu's *The Art of War* into a business meeting, and lay it down on the table in front of you. This will set your opponents worrying: a very Sun Tzu-ian stratagem.

In the 6th century BC, the story goes, the Chinese potentate King Helu of Wu set his general Sun Tzu (pronounced: sun ZOO) a whimsical challenge. Could he transform the king's concubines – palace women who knew only a life of pleasure – into an effective fighting force? Of course, Sun Tzu replied. He told the women what to do, but when the time came to carry out an exercise, they just giggled. Sun Tzu promptly cut off the heads of the two he had put in charge. After that, all the women did as they were told, no questions asked, and it was agreed that Sun Tzu had accomplished his task.

This anecdote gives a flavour of the occasionally psychotic wisdom contained in Sun Tzu's slim military manual, *The Art of War* (which could barely be more different from the approach to life advocated by his contemporary Lao-Tsu). The book consists of epigrams about how to defeat an enemy, but is couched in such simple language it has more recently been applied to many areas of human endeavour: politics, human relationships, or the world of business, as in the 1987 film *Wall Street*, in which the unscrupulous Gordon Gekko quotes Sun Tzu. 'Every battle is won before it is fought,' he declares. Most battles, that is, are about preparation, rather than actual skill at fighting.

The enduring popularity of *The Art of War* owes something to its small size: it runs to a mere 6,000 words, i.e. not much more than 20 or 30 pages, although most copies today will be padded out with a long introduction. Its simplicity and its ruthless tone give a thrill to the armchair dictator in all of us. Who could fail to smile as they read Sun Tzu's advice to 'Let your plans be dark and impenetrable as night, and when you move, fall like a thunderbolt'? Mao Zedong, it is said, was rarely without his copy of Sun Tzu, using it to extend his control over all of China, and in the process, murdering more people than anyone in history. It was also reported to have been among the final reading of a troubled French author ...

Murderous Types

The more extreme the talent, the more likely,
it sometimes seems, that the artist in question
will lose all control and try to kill someone.

Guy Debord, writer (1931–94)

USAGE: Justify any extreme action – from emigrating to Australia
to letting out a shriek during a church service – with the claim
that you're trying to free yourself from the tyranny of 'what Guy
Debord liked to call *le spectacle*'.

When the publisher and film producer Gerard Lebovici was
found dead in a Paris car park in 1984, shot in the back of the
head, a chief suspect in the investigation that followed was
the French writer and film-maker Guy Debord (pronounced:
GHEE duh-BOR). At least, that's the way it was presented in
news reports. Some have claimed there was nothing to link
Debord with the unsolved murder, apart from the fact that he
had known Lebovici, and had always been a bit of a nutter. In
a sense, the perception of his involvement only goes to prove
that Debord was right all along. For his pet theory, articulated
in his best-known book, 1967's *The Society of the Spectacle*,
was that reality had been replaced by '*le spectacle*': capitalist
imagery designed to soothe us into a state of contented idiocy.

Debord had been developing these ideas since his late

teens, when he had fallen in with a group of post-Surrealist pranksters known as the Lettrists, whose serious aim was to shock people out of their apathy. There was the time in 1950 when one of Debord's associates ascended the pulpit in Notre Dame Cathedral, disguised as a priest, and announced the death of God to the bewildered congregation. Or there was the film Debord himself released a couple of years later, *Howls for Sade*, which consisted of a totally white screen when you could hear people talking, and a totally black screen when there was silence. Not everyone was impressed. With time, however, Debord's anti-capitalism found increasing favour, and when Paris was rocked by student riots in the summer of 1968, many of the protestors chanted slogans they borrowed from *The Society of the Spectacle* or from the Debord-led group that called itself Situationist International. According to one fellow Situationist, the growing power of *le spectacle* forced a stark choice: revolution or suicide. Having tried one, Debord eventually resorted to the other, shooting himself in the heart at the age of 63.

Werner Herzog, film-maker (b. 1942)

USAGE: To declare, 'This isn't a Werner Herzog movie,' would be an innovative explanation for your reluctance to go for a long walk.

'Ask for forgiveness, not permission.' 'Never wallow in your troubles; despair must be kept private and brief.' 'I believe the common character of the universe is not harmony, but chaos, hostility and murder.' These quotes, eagerly exchanged on the internet by his fans, give an idea of the gloomily – sometimes gleefully – Teutonic personality of the German film-maker Werner Herzog (pronounced: VUR-na HURT-sog).

Since he came to prominence back in the 1970s, Herzog has been drawn to stories about eccentrics, obsessives, men driven to wrestle with the pitiless forces of nature. One of his leading men, the demonic Klaus Kinski, brought the requisite intensity to early films – for instance in *Fitzcarraldo* (1982), in which he played a man determined to transport a steam ship over a mountain in Peru. In fact, he brought a little too much intensity to the set, constantly falling out with Herzog and everyone else. However, Herzog gave as good as he got, once threatening to shoot Kinski if he caused any more trouble (and anyone who knows Herzog confirms that he was quite capable of carrying out that threat). He had the last word after Kinski's death when he released a documentary about his friendship with the tempestuous actor, including footage of Kinski being generally beastly.

Having long been a cult figure, Herzog has recently become better known through the success of his documentary *Grizzly Man* (2005) about the naturalist Timothy Treadwell, who was eaten by a grizzly bear. The director has begun playing up to his image in cameo roles in other people's films. In the Tom Cruise action movie *Jack Reacher* (2012), for example, he is disturbingly convincing as the sociopathic villain. In acting, as in directing, commitment has always been his watchword. 'There is nothing wrong with spending a night in a jail cell,' he once observed, 'if it means getting the shot you need.'

Vaslav Nijinsky, dancer (1889–1950)

USAGE: Commenting on a rugby match, you might say that 'the side-step of the fly-half exhibited a Nijinskian grace'.

When Vaslav Nijinsky danced, it was as if his feet never touched the ground. He is widely regarded as the greatest male dancer of the 20th century, and it's unlikely that this judgement will ever be revised, since we have no film footage of him in action. His mentor, the manipulative impresario Sergei Diaghilev – who was also, incidentally, his lover – forbade anybody to film his star, fearing it would fail to do him justice. It was a canny move, since all we're left with are the ecstatic accounts of those who saw Nijinsky dance. Our imagination is left to do the rest.

The ballet equivalent of a rock star, Nijinsky outraged the conventional with his spontaneity and innovation, by daring to disregard the traditions of dance, which ordained above all that performances should be decorous and beautiful. In *L'Après-midi d'un faune* (1912), which was inspired by the poem of the same name by Stéphane Mallarmé*, Nijinsky mimed masturbating with a piece of cloth. His fans thought they were in the presence of divinity, and Nijinsky appears to have agreed. Always a little unhinged, he later lost it entirely and developed murderous inclinations, attempting to push his Hungarian wife Romola and their child downstairs, before announcing that he was going to marry God.

Romola had a heavy cross to bear. First she had to wean Nijinsky from his homosexual proclivities. Then, after he was diagnosed as a schizophrenic, she had to look after him for the last 30 years of his life. To be fair, it can't have been all that much fun for Nijinsky either.

Luis Buñuel, film director (1900–83)

USAGE: A fine way to allude to Buñuel is to thread the titles of his films into conversation. You might, for instance, describe someone you fancy as 'the obscure object of my desire'.

The Spanish film director Luis Buñuel believed in acting on impulse, even if the impulse was a violent one. There was the occasion when, during dinner, he tried to strangle Salvador Dalí's girlfriend. Dalí later got his own back by naming Buñuel as a communist, at a time when, in America, that was considered poor form. Buñuel raced round to Dalí's hotel room in New York with the aim of shooting him in the knee. But for once he managed to control himself.

A rare example of a film director whose work bears comparison with that of the great modernist painters and sculptors, Buñuel was an artist who hung out with other artists. He was officially invited to join the Surrealist movement by André Breton*, and his first film, the twelve-minute short *Un Chien andalou* (1929), was a collaboration with Dalí. Like many of Buñuel's films, it caused a scandal when it was released, which was ever his intention. For a taster, the opening scene shows a woman's eyeball being sliced in two by a razor blade.

Highlights of the remarkably long and distinguished career that followed included *Belle de jour* (1967) and *The*

Discreet Charm of the Bourgeoisie (1972). The first of these featured a conventional-seeming housewife pursuing a secret life as a prostitute; in the second, a group of middle-class people are repeatedly prevented from sitting down to dinner. In Buñuel's final film, *That Obscure Object of Desire* (1977), an elderly man is romantically obsessed by a woman who is inexplicably portrayed by two different actresses. As ever, the director succeeded in dividing opinion between those who thought him a genius, and others who found him whimsical at best. Although he was always a consummate provocateur, he achieved his greatest scandal, arguably, back in the early days of his career with *L'Age d'or* (1930). Perceived as an anti-Catholic diatribe, this movie prompted riots in Paris and was eventually banned by the authorities 'in the name of public order'. Buñuel, it seems, was undaunted by the response – unlike a certain Russian playwright, who when one of his plays was booed by the audience, decided to abandon the stage entirely ...

Succès de Scandale

*It's the duty of the artist to outrage the
bourgeoisie. The following all managed it.*

Anton Chekhov, playwright
and short-story writer (1860–1904)

USAGE: The adjective 'Chekhovian' refers to a mood or attitude
that is wistful or whimsical or both.

Let us consider, in a spirit of Chekhovian whimsy, the part
played by birds in the life of the Russian playwright. When he
was young, he caught and sold goldfinches for pocket money.
He later kept pet cranes. In his first theatrical masterpiece,
The Seagull, a tortured young man shoots a seagull and presents it as a love offering to the object of his desire. The girl
isn't impressed.

Nor was the audience of *The Seagull* when it premiered
in 1896. Confused by the originality of the work, and unsure
whether they were supposed to laugh or cry, they booed,
prompting the author Anton Chekhov to declare that he
would never write another play. Fortunately, his mind was
changed by the director Constantin Stanislavski*, who found
in his writings the avant garde naturalism he was looking for.
Chekhov avoided the 'event plots' of the past, more interested
in mood and character. Nor did he cater to genre. His plays,

which also include *The Cherry Orchard* and *Uncle Vanya*, are somewhere between comedies and tragedies. There's a vagueness to them, just as there's a vagueness to life. But don't be fooled: every component serves its purpose. Commenting on the art of writing stories (at which some say the author excelled even more than he did at writing plays), Chekhov declared that if you mention early on that there's an ornamental gun hanging on the wall of a room, by the end of the tale 'it absolutely must go off'.

Chekhov was in Germany when he died of tuberculosis. His body was transported home in a railway carriage also used for refrigerating oysters. At his funeral, some of the mourners mistakenly followed the coffin of an army general, who happened to be being buried on the same day.

Michelangelo Antonioni,
film-maker (1912–2007)

USAGE: If you wanted to express a feeling of deep despair, you might say, 'I've just been sitting around at home, endlessly rewatching my favourite Antonioni movies.'

An Italian film director of staggering pretentiousness, Michelangelo Antonioni epitomises everything arty, intellectual and profoundly suspect to the sensible Anglo-Saxon mindset. One of his films, the baffling *L'Avventura*, scandalised critics at the Cannes film festival when it premiered in 1960, and was greeted with a resounding chorus of booing. Another of his works, *L'Eclisse* (1962), ends with a seven-minute sequence in which nothing happens. Literally. Two characters arrange to meet on a street corner, but neither shows up. Antonioni films the pavement, and we all sit, waiting for a punchline that never comes. He's best known to British viewers for the film *Blow-up* (1966, filmed in English), about a randy photographer in the Swinging Sixties, which boasts a scene in which Vanessa Redgrave reveals her breasts. Despite this promising subject matter, the film is as peculiarly dull as the rest of Antonioni's output.

Lest we seem prejudiced, let's try to understand why the Italian is held in high esteem. When abstract art was invented in the first half of the 20th century, it raised the question of whether something similar could be pulled off in cinema: films more interested in mood and composition than dialogue or plot. This is tricky. With a painting, viewers can turn away whenever they want. In the cinema, you're trapped for the full two hours, and it's hard not to grow a little resentful as one prolonged scene follows another. We should, perhaps, salute Antonioni's ambition, and admire the way, in his abstractions, he cut the egos of actors down to size. On the set of *The Passenger* (1975), he told Jack Nicholson that for him, actors were no more important than the scenery.

Henrik Ibsen, playwright (1828–1906)

USAGE: If you're up for a heavy but potentially interesting conversation, you could ask someone to reveal their Ibsenite 'life lie'.

The life lie. That was what Henrik Ibsen called the delusion – it differs for each of us – that helps us get up in the morning. For bourgeois society as a whole, the 'life lie' is that husbands and wives stay together. No one has affairs. Everyone is basically a good person. Nonsense, Ibsen declared, and he wrote a series of plays to prove his point. *The Doll's House*, for example, ends with the main character Nora leaving her children and boring husband, saying she owes it to herself to live a fuller life. Audiences were outraged, but the critics hailed him as a genius.

The playwright – who is said to be the most performed in the world after Shakespeare – had experienced his fair share of domestic upheaval. Aged eighteen he got a serving girl pregnant, and though he wasn't allowed to see his son, he had to support him for the next fifteen years. He eventually left his native Norway and thereafter lived in Italy and Germany. His provocative plays made him famous as an author, helped by his knack for creating unforgettable characters: the dreamy hero of *Peer Gynt*, for example, or the doomed, self-destructive heroine of *Hedda Gabler*.

Then there are Gregers and Hjalmar in *The Wild Duck*, which some consider Ibsen's masterpiece. Gregers insists on telling Hjalmar that his wife once had an affair with Gregers' father. His belief that Hjalmar will be happier for knowing the truth turns out to be misplaced. The play is on some level a self-criticism by Ibsen, questioning his obsession with revealing painful truths. What was his own life lie? It's hard to say, but he seems to have been deluded about his hairstyle, which was ridiculous. He cultivated crazy mutton chops that looked as if they'd been stuck on with glue.

Igor Stravinsky, composer (1882–1971)

USAGE: Stravinsky's *The Rite of Spring* created the ultimate *succès de scandale* and can be referred to accordingly.

They howled. They cheered. They jeered. Insults and blows were exchanged. The opening night of *The Rite of Spring* at Paris's Théâtre des Champs Élysées in May 1913 was one of the great scandals in the history of the arts. The ballet's dancing, choreographed by Vaslav Nijinsky*, appalled some as much as it enthralled others – as too did the jerky, pounding, deliberately unbeautiful music by the Russian composer Igor Stravinsky. Although there were those who loathed it, claiming it threatened to destroy music itself (whatever that might mean), one listener was so excited he began to beat the rhythm with his hands on the head of the man in front of him. The man in question, the story goes, was so mesmerised that he didn't notice.

Over the course of his long career, Stravinsky's output was extraordinarily varied. He first caused a stir in his native St Petersburg by his interest in Russian folk music (at a time when that was deeply unfashionable). He later experimented with atonal music. Later still, he wrote for Hollywood (for instance, for the 1943 film of *Jane Eyre*, which starred Orson Welles).

A witty, mischievous man, he had many extramarital affairs, including one with the couturier Coco Chanel (or at least, that's what she claimed). Relishing his status not only as a composer but also as a celebrity, he spent his latter years in LA, hanging out with the rich and famous, and the poor and talented. It's possible his friendships with British authors such as Dylan Thomas and Christopher Isherwood owed something to their mutual appetite for heavy drinking. In his spare time, he loved to watch James Bond movies. A thematically related quiz question: which Scottish psychologist was friends with the James Bond actor Sean Connery, and is said to have engaged in a friendly grapple with him at a party?

Shaken Not Stirred

It's all very well being a high intellectual, but everyone knows that James Bond is as important a cultural phenomenon as anything written by T.S. Eliot or D.H. Lawrence. The next three names are all linked in surprising ways to the suave super-spy.

R.D. Laing, psychiatrist and writer (1927–89)

USAGE: In any discussion of madness, you might remark, 'I think there's a lot to be said for R.D. Laing's critique of rigid psychiatric categories.'

As psychiatrists go, R.D. Laing (pronounced: LANG) was a little out of the ordinary. In his later career, the Glaswegian shrink practised 'rebirthing' techniques, in which a patient tries to break out of a ring of people, thereby experiencing again the trauma of being born – and hopefully, feeling better as a result. Another time, treating a naked mute schizophrenic woman, Laing took off all his clothes and sat beside her, rocking back and forth to the same rhythm. Comforted, the woman spoke for the first time in months.

Although he always denied the association, Laing was viewed as part of an 'anti-psychiatry movement'. In other words, he criticised certain inhumane treatments applied to those regarded as mentally ill: for instance, electroconvulsive therapy. Further, he argued that much of what is called madness is actually a sane reaction to the crazy demands of life. In particular, in his influential work *The Divided Self* (1960), Laing set out his theory that what is termed schizophrenia is less a medical condition than a response to the pressures imposed on an individual by a dysfunctional family. 'Schizophrenia,' he famously declared, 'is a theory, not a fact.'

Laing blamed his own depression (which he medicated with heavy drinking) on his parents. (He had never got over the discovery, he said, that they had lied to him about Santa Claus.) He went on to be an erratic father to his own children, and the psychological problems they suffered in their turn seemed to bear out his theories. He died aged 61 of a heart attack while playing tennis in St Tropez. Though he was later seen as a crank, in his heyday Laing's idiosyncratic philosophy made him a celebrity. He counted among his friends (and patients) the James Bond actor Sean Connery, with whom he once wrestled at a party.

Bertolt Brecht, playwright (1898–1956)

USAGE: After witnessing a terrible play, to avoid hurting anyone's feelings, you might remark that you admired the Brechtian *Verfremdungseffekt*.

Who could forget the terrifying Spectre agent Rosa Klebb – the one with the knife concealed in her shoe – in the James Bond film *From Russia with Love*? She was played by Lotte Lenya, a wonderful if rather intimidating-looking actress who in Berlin in 1928 had appeared in the first-ever production of the musical *The Threepenny Opera* by Bertolt Brecht.

This classic work was definitively Brechtian in two respects. The first was that it was political, offering a socialist critique of the capitalist system (the playwright was a lifelong Marxist). The second was that it was an example of what became known as 'epic theatre'. This slightly misleading term meant that, a bit like Ancient Greek drama, Brecht's plays made no attempt to convince audiences that what they were seeing was real. On the contrary, he kept reminding them that it wasn't, by for instance flooding the stage with harsh lighting, or having actors hold up placards commenting on the action. Brecht called this a *Verfremdungseffekt* or 'distancing effect' (which is sometimes badly translated as 'alienation effect').

The idea was that, instead of getting emotionally involved, as you might while attending a realistic drama, at one of Brecht's plays you were left free to engage your brain. You might feel less, but you learnt more. (And it should be noted that Brecht was capable of writing movingly when he wanted to. In the 2006 film *The Lives of Others* the Stasi agent is so moved as a result of reading a poem by Brecht that he starts to question the whole communist system.) If this all sounds rather serious, those were serious times. Brecht wrote plays such as *Life of Galileo* and *Mother Courage and Her Children* that implicitly criticised the ruling Nazi party. In the process, they earned him a reputation as probably the pre-eminent modern German playwright.

Werner Heisenberg, physicist (1901–76)

USAGE: In any situation where it's possible to determine either one, but not both, of a pair of quantities, it may be called an equivalent of Werner Heisenberg's Uncertainty Principle.

The physicist Werner Heisenberg was once played in a TV movie by future James Bond actor Daniel Craig. Got that? Good, because it's unlikely you'll understand much about Heisenberg's best-known contribution to physics. In one of the great leaps forward of quantum mechanics – the study of how the universe behaves at the nanoscopic level (for instance, what happens inside atoms) – he delineated the limits of how far science can go, positing that certain pairs of quantities relating to particles cannot be accurately measured simultaneously. One example is position and momentum. You can measure the position of a particle, but the more accurately you measure it, the less accurately you are able to measure its momentum. And vice versa. Unless you have a special interest in and knowledge of quantum physics, you may struggle to fathom why this should be the case.

There is also, so to speak, a degree of uncertainty regarding the moral principles of the creator of the Uncertainty Principle. After the outbreak of the Second World War, this bright young man of German physics (he had received the Nobel Prize when he was just 30) became one of the scientific leaders of the Nazi effort to harness nuclear energy, and if possible, develop a nuclear weapon. In 1941, he visited his former mentor and colleague, the Danish physicist Niels Bohr, at his home in Copenhagen. The question of what was said, and why it resulted in an argument, provides the focus of Michael Frayn's acclaimed 1998 play *Copenhagen* (which was adapted into a film starring Craig and Stephen Rea). Was Bohr simply offended by Heisenberg's jingoistic conviction that Germany would win the war? Did Heisenberg intend, but fail, to reveal that he was secretly sabotaging the Nazi quest for an atomic bomb? Frayn's nanoscopically detailed examination of these questions provides a good introduction to quantum mechanics for the non-specialist. But it leaves the viewer in a state of uncertainty as to whether or not the scientist was a supporter of Hitler.

Adolf

The following three names are said, in their different ways, to have had an influence on Adolf Hitler's deranged worldview.

Richard Wagner, composer (1813—83)

USAGE: The adjective 'Wagnerian' tends to mean bombastic in sound or behaviour, though it may also refer to a woman's buxom figure.

In 1855, Richard Wagner conducted his *Tannhäuser* overture in London for Queen Victoria, who seems to have thoroughly enjoyed it. She later met the composer, noting in her diary that he was 'short, very quiet, wears spectacles & has a very finely-developed forehead, a hooked nose & projecting chin'. He may have been quiet but his music wasn't. Oscar Wilde* remarked that he loved Wagner's operas because they were so loud. This meant he could talk to his neighbour throughout without annoying anyone. Mark Twain simply observed that Wagner's music was 'better than it sounds'.

A musical revolutionary, the German composer practically invented modern music. He was obsessed by the philosophy of Arthur Schopenhauer*, who argued that the human condition is one of endless striving 'will', doomed never to be satisfied. Wagner boldly tried to represent this idea in his music, favouring cacophonous complicated chords, which seem to cry out for the resolution of a return to a simple chord: a comfort the composer rarely extends. His music wasn't meant to be comfortable but stirring, his aim to give expression to the rising tide of nationalist feeling in Germany. This, and the fact that Hitler was a huge fan of Wagner's *oeuvre*, has led to a widespread, if somewhat bizarre, perception that the composer was a kind of proto-Nazi.

Wagner's finest *Gesamtkunstwerk* (his own phrase for a huge multi-faceted work of art) was his *Ring* cycle, a saga of dwarfs, stolen treasure and buxom women. Its first production in 1876 at the composer's own opera house at Bayreuth had been made possible by the financial support of his patron, mad King Ludwig of Bavaria. The homosexual young monarch was romantically obsessed with the older man and Wagner pretended to reciprocate the feeling, so Ludwig would keep the cash flowing.

Ludwig Wittgenstein, philosopher, logician, mathematician (1889–1951)

USAGE: If two people are attempting to discuss something that can't be usefully tackled in words, you might observe that they are experiencing a Wittgensteinian difficulty with language.

Bertrand Russell* once described Ludwig Wittgenstein as 'the most perfect example I have ever known of genius as traditionally conceived: passionate, profound, intense and dominating'. He was also odd, occasionally very funny, and

– most often – exceedingly arrogant. When Russell, one of the pre-eminent philosophers of his day, attempted to adjudicate Wittgenstein's PhD at Cambridge, the younger man clapped him on the back and exclaimed cheerfully, 'Don't worry, I know you'll never understand it!' Naturally, he passed.

Yet if Russell couldn't fathom Wittgenstein's arguments, what chance do the rest of us have? Not much, but here are one or two ideas even dummies can grapple with. Wittgenstein believed that some things can't be meaningfully discussed in words (e.g. the existence of God). Indeed, it's only because of the flawed way people speak of them that they seem worth discussing at all. Thus, his *Tractatus Logico-Philosophicus* (1921) concluded with the line: 'Whereof one cannot speak, thereof one must be silent' – i.e. don't try to speak about things that can't be spoken about in any meaningful way. In his *Philosophical Investigations*, he went on to examine the ways in which some language – particularly that used by philosophers – is meaningless because it's removed from any grounded context.

Quite apart from being regarded as one of the greatest philosophers of the 20th century, Wittgenstein led an extraordinary life. He was a homosexual who was decorated for bravery in the First World War. He dabbled in sculpture and built his own house. Despite being born into one of the wealthiest families in Austria, he gave away his inheritance and lived frugally. At one stage he worked as a schoolteacher (getting into trouble for boxing the ears of his less gifted pupils). During his own schooldays, by a bizarre twist of fate, he had attended the same school as one Adolf Hitler: the Realschule in Linz, Austria. One historian has alleged that the two children hated each other, and that the friction between them inspired the violent anti-Semitism (Wittgenstein's ancestry was part-Jewish) that characterised Hitler's worldview ...

Friedrich Nietzsche, philosopher (1844–1900)

USAGE: An egotist who justifies their behaviour on the grounds that they are a superior human being may be described as having a kind of Nietzschean superman complex.

'Become who you are,' Friedrich Nietzsche (pronounced: NEECH-uh) liked to say. In the end, he became a gibbering wreck. Witnessing a horse being flogged in Turin, he threw his arms around the animal's neck and suffered a complete nervous breakdown. It was once thought his madness had been caused by syphilis contracted from a visit to a brothel, but that is now disputed. It may have been brain cancer.

The German philosopher, who suffered all his life from terrible indigestion, believed in the idea of the superman (*Übermensch*): the superior being who would bend the world to his will. He didn't have in mind a political dictator, more a man of superior intellect who could refashion the world through creativity. Yet it's hardly surprising that Nietzsche's name has been hijacked by right-wing fanatics. His cause wasn't helped by the fact that his sister Elisabeth was a Nazi sympathiser who after Friedrich's death presented his walking stick as a gift to Adolf Hitler. Hitler was later photographed staring intensely at a bust of the great philosopher, though it's thought he hadn't actually read any of his books.

A brilliant classics scholar who wrote of the eternal struggle between Apollonian (rational, controlling) and Dionysian (mad, creative) impulses, Nietzsche was more poet or prophet than political thinker. The sensational titles of his works, such as *Thus Spake Zarathustra* and *Human, All Too Human*, give the game away. Among his beliefs, which were often expressed in epigrams, were that 'God is dead' and 'Morality is the herd instinct of the masses'. He also had a magnificent walrus-like moustache, and suffered from appalling eyesight. But blindness, of course, doesn't preclude literary greatness …

As Blind as a Bard

*In Greek mythology, the blind prophet Teiresias
could 'see' more than those with keener visual sight.
The following are, so to speak, his descendants.*

Homer, poet (12th–8th century BC)

USAGE: As an adjective, 'Homeric' is often used loosely to
mean 'epic', particularly when describing a grand confrontation
involving a clash of heroic warriors or personalities.

Was Homer blind? So it used to be said, but the truth is, we
don't know anything about him. Or her. He may have been
a she. Or even a they. Few now accept the old tradition that
Homer was a blind wandering poet. It's widely accepted that
'his' two great epics, *The Iliad* and *The Odyssey*, were actually
by different authors. In fact, since they are both oral poems,
meaning they were memorised and passed on from one
generation to the next, with improvements being made over
time, you could reasonably say that each poem was actually
by many different authors.

So when anyone refers to 'Homer', they're referring not to
a person but to two long narrative poems (they don't rhyme
but they follow a metre) composed in Greek between the
12th and 8th centuries BC. *The Iliad* recounts episodes in the
Trojan War, culminating in the death of the Trojan Hector at

the hands of the Greek Achilles. Simply written, alternating passages of poetic beauty with graphic violence, it achieves an overwhelming accumulative force. *The Odyssey* is a different kettle of fish. It describes the return of the Greek Odysseus from Troy, his adventures (fighting witches and monsters), and how he defeats the thugs who have been courting his wife Penelope in his absence. It's a jollier tale, enlivened by humour, homely details and occasional gory horror.

Because so little is known about Homer, there have been some crazy theories as to his identity. When the Emperor Hadrian asked the Delphic oracle, he was told that Homer was Odysseus' grandson. The 19th-century novelist Samuel Butler argued that the poet of *The Odyssey* was a young Sicilian woman. There's even a wild theory, which has its attractions, that he may have been Odysseus himself.

John Dos Passos, novelist (1896–1970)

USAGE: Dos Passos is a good name to mention as a demonstration of the vicissitudes of literary fame.

Ernest Hemingway*. William Faulkner*. F. Scott Fitzgerald. And John Roderigo Dos Passos. He's not so famous now, but there was a time when the last of these was as big a name to conjure with as any of the other three. Specifically, Dos Passos is credited with having written a classic example of The Great American Novel in the 1930s – though it was a bit of a cheat in his case, since the *USA Trilogy*, as his masterpiece is known, actually consists of three novels (*The 42nd Parallel*;

1919; *The Big Money*). Yet it still appears on lists of the great novels of the 20th century.

Like Hemingway, he's counted as a member of the so-called Lost Generation: a phrase coined by Gertrude Stein* to refer to authors who were psychologically scarred by the horrors of the First World War. (They were 'lost' in the sense that they were left not knowing what to believe in.) In the case of Dos Passos (whose surname was testament to paternal Portuguese ancestors), he served as an ambulance driver in France and Italy, an experience that would inspire his anti-war novel *Three Soldiers* (1921). Later he broadened his remit in order to write his great trilogy, which amounts to a chronicle of American life from 1900 to 1930, told from the point of view of twelve diverse characters, ranging from a haughty social climber to a good-natured mechanic.

As well as being generally hefty, the work was innovative in its use of 'collage technique', meaning the text was interspersed with cut-outs from fictitious newspaper articles. It so impressed Jean-Paul Sartre* that he proclaimed Dos Passos the greatest living author. With time, the latter, who had once been a committed socialist, became less popular with the literary establishment owing to his increasingly right-wing views. In his fifties, Dos Passos was struck by tragedy when he was involved in a horrific car accident that killed his wife and left him blind in one eye.

Jorge Luis Borges,
short-story writer (1899–1986)

USAGE: Any high-brow science-fiction story, especially if it raises profound existential questions (and even more so if it involves a library or a labyrinth), may be said to be 'essentially Borgesian in tone' (pronounced: 'Bor-HAY-sian').

The great Argentine author Jorge Luis Borges wrote short stories not only out of a love for that genre, but also because his eyesight was so bad, he could write only for short periods of time. His is an excellent name to drop, because whenever you do, you demonstrate that you're aware of its surprising pronunciation, as well as being familiar with his *oeuvre*. As time went by, he increasingly favoured writing poems, because that meant he could hold the whole work in his head, instead of examining it with difficulty on the page. In any case, his longest work was a fourteen-page short story. Of the practice of novel-writing, he once remarked: 'It is a laborious madness, setting out in 500 pages an idea that can be perfectly related in five minutes.'

Was he entirely serious? It's often hard to tell with Borges. A literary prankster, he wrote reviews of books that had never existed except in his head. Occasionally, he would produce a 'translation' of an obscure short story supposedly by some famous author such as Emanuel Swedenborg, but which he'd actually invented himself. He is credited with having single-handedly created the genre known as magical realism (as practised by Gabriel García Márquez, Salman Rushdie et al.), but this is misleading. Borgesian stories don't tend to have the fairy-tale once-upon-a-time mood that is characteristic of that type of writing. They do, however, involve weird and magical things taking place, usually of a rather cerebral and obscure kind. In his story *The Aleph*, for instance, a man stumbles on a time machine that allows him simultaneously to witness everything that's happening in the world. Recurring motifs in Borges' work are mirrors, libraries and labyrinths.

Eventually Borges went completely blind. He was devotedly cared for by his mother, with whom he lived until her death at the age of 99 – a domestic arrangement similar to that of a certain Parisian intellectual, who also lived with his mum until she died …

Where's Your Laundry?

A lot of authors and artists seem to have had
appalling relationships with their parents (cf.
Louise Bourgeois*). So it's nice to see there
were a few who lived with their mothers.

Roland Barthes, philosopher (1915–80)

USAGE: Next time you want to get out of a shopping trip, you
could plead that you have 'a Barthesian aversion to rampant
consumerism'.

The consummate Parisian intellectual, Roland Barthes (pronounced: BART) was a writer who loved to criticise the
bourgeoisie for being boringly conventional. But he wasn't
exactly daring himself, at least when it came to his living
arrangements. He shared a flat with his mother for 60 years
until her death at the age of 85. Admittedly, he would often
flee the nest in order to engage in decidedly un-bourgeois
activities, such as cavorting with young boys in Morocco.

The main problem with the bourgeoisie, according to
Barthes, wasn't that they were boring. It was that they ignored
the real meaning of things, being duped instead by the 'myths'
that had been concocted about them, usually by advertising
companies. In his seminal book *Mythologies* (1957), Barthes
used the word 'myths' to refer not to ancient stories about

heroes and monsters, but to false beliefs regarding every-day objects. One example was wine. Barthes claimed that the French bourgeois had completely accepted the 'myths' about wine that had been dreamed up by wine-sellers: e.g. that it is the French national drink, so that to drink it was practically a patriotic act.

Or consider books. Barthes argued that the bourgeois reader no longer saw a book for what it was – a self-contained story that conveyed experience – but instead regarded it as a mystery to be unravelled by examination of the author's life. This was because the publishing houses were always arranging interviews with their authors, implying that authors' opinions were somehow essential to appreciating their works. The reader mistakenly believed that the aim was to understand the motivation behind the book. The book would then be rendered a 'knowable text' (to use Barthes' term) and they could discard it and buy a new book. Thus the cycle began again.

Gertrude Jekyll, garden designer and author
(1843–1932)

USAGE: There aren't many universally famous garden designers. Jekyll's is a decent name to toss into the mix, perhaps mentioning that her colour schemes were inspired by the Impressionists.

The first thing you need to know about Gertrude Jekyll is that she pronounced her name JEEK-le, to rhyme with treacle, as opposed to JECK-le, to rhyme with shekel – not, in other words, the way the name tends to be pronounced in Robert

Louis Stevenson's horror novella *Strange Case of Dr Jekyll and Mr Hyde*, although Stevenson, who happened to be friends with Gertrude's brother, did borrow the family's name for the story. The second thing you need to know about her is that she's probably the most influential gardener, and writer about gardening, who ever lived.

Jekyll was brought up in the English county of Surrey, the daughter of a soldier. Her childhood was one in which artistic interests were encouraged (there was a life-size copy of the Venus de Milo in the dining room) and in due course she enrolled at the South Kensington School of Art. She didn't embark on a career as a garden designer until middle age, possibly because it was then that her eyesight began to fail her, making painting difficult. But she brought an artist's sensibility to her bold choices of colour in her borders and confessed to being inspired by J.M.W. Turner and the Impressionists.

Jekyll, who never married, lived in later life with her mother. As time went by, she increasingly resembled Queen Victoria. There was something imperial in her dominance of her craft, as she created some 400 gardens in her distinctive style, mixing audacity with formal order (as too, it might be said, did her friend and frequent collaborator, the architect Edwin Lutyens). The resemblance was also physical, for, like Queen Victoria, Jekyll was decidedly plain, and on the large side. (Her nieces nicknamed her 'Aunt Bumps'.) Yet obesity has never been a bar to creative achievement – nor, as a Greek philosopher proved, to being found irresistibly attractive ...

Fatties

If you have a beautiful mind, you don't need to worry so much about piling on the pounds.

Socrates, philosopher (470–399 BC)

USAGE: 'Socratic irony': to pretend to know nothing, while actually knowing more than anyone. 'Socratic method': to conduct or teach philosophy by a conversation, not a lecture.

Socrates could drink anyone under the table. He was extremely fat and ugly, with a snub nose, but everyone found him strangely attractive, because he was so incredibly clever.

As if that wasn't enough, he was also a war hero. He fought for Athens against Sparta, and when all around him fled, he stood his ground. No weedy scholar, he could endure harsher conditions on campaign (sleepless nights in the bitter cold) than the ordinary soldier. Basically the man was a legend – although his pupil and number one fan, Plato*, may have exaggerated when describing him. So why did the Athenian state execute Socrates? Because he made it his business to wander (invariably barefoot) around the city, making important people feel like idiots. His normal form was to engage someone in a chat about a particular topic – say, the nature of virtue – and by question and answer, force them to admit they didn't know the first thing about it.

Socrates always claimed that he himself knew nothing. But this, paradoxically, made him the cleverest man in town, because no one else even knew that they knew nothing. His message was basically that people should re-examine their assumptions about everything. 'The unexamined life,' he famously declared, 'is not worth living.' His life was one long examination, but an intoxicating one. Be brave, was the theme, and think hard, and live well.

It's worth bearing in mind that when we talk about Socrates, we're basing our knowledge largely on the descriptions in Plato's works such as *The Symposium* and many others. Socrates himself was far too busy wandering around annoying everyone to bother to put pen to paper. As far as we know, he never wrote a word.

Buddha, spiritual leader (6th century BC?)

USAGE: Always refer to him as 'the Buddha' rather than merely 'Buddha', as it sounds more impressive.

The Chinese are responsible for the Buddha's reputation as a fattie. During a key stage in the spread of Buddhist teachings across China, there was a general perception that being fat was a desirable sign that you were not only rich, but also happy, lucky and wise. The result was that when artisans came to create their gold statues of the Buddha, they invariably depicted him as exceedingly rotund. (In reality, this is highly unlikely to have been the case, since the Buddha preached self-control in all things, including food.)

Born the son of a wealthy Indian landowner, Siddhartha Gautama – who came to be known as the Buddha, meaning 'enlightened one' – rejected his luxurious background and set off on a spiritual journey that would change history. For wherever he went, he so impressed people with the profundity of his insights that he accumulated a horde of followers. This enraged his envious cousin, who tried to kill him. Fortunately for the Buddha, his relative proved an incompetent murderer. He got an elephant drunk and directed it towards his intended victim, hoping it would trample him to death. No such luck. The sozzled animal merely wandered off in another direction. Sounds like the cousin should have heeded the Buddha's advice. Riches don't make you happy, he argued, but that didn't mean you should give away your possessions. The path to enlightenment (or 'nirvana') was through regular meditation. Only then would you free yourself from negative emotions.

Some of the Buddha's followers tried to claim he was divine, superimposing the standard deistic narrative onto his life. The rumour arose, for instance, that his mother had given birth to him without the preamble of intercourse. But he himself always denied being a god. So be quick to correct anyone who refers to Buddhism as a religion. It's a self-professedly human self-help course.

Thomas Aquinas, philosopher (1225–74)

USAGE: For an argument in favour of vegetarianism, look no further than Aquinas', formulated eight centuries ago.

Thomas Aquinas (pronounced: uh-KWEYE-nuhs) was a compulsive over-eater who was by all accounts morbidly obese. He apparently had to have a semi-circle cut into the table for his meals. Otherwise, his massive stomach would have made it impossible for him to reach his food. Born into an Italian family that was wealthy enough to keep him in pies, Aquinas decided one day that he was going to give up his luxurious lifestyle and become a priest. But on his way to Rome, he was stopping off for a drink from a spring, when his brothers kidnapped him. They incarcerated him in the family castle and even sent a prostitute to his room to remind him of the pleasures of the flesh. Instead of extending a Christian welcome, Aquinas chased her out with a red-hot poker.

Why is he so revered? He applied his fine academic mind to considering the more difficult points of Christian theology, and giving them a convincing intellectual underpinning. Or to put it another way, he successfully fused Christian thought with the teachings of the Ancient Greek philosophers. One way he achieved this was by giving primacy to the Greek concept of 'logos' or reason. If your reason tells you that a course of action is morally right, Aquinas argued, you could go ahead, without first needing to find some kind of confirmation in the Bible. In another well-known argument, Aquinas claimed to prove the existence of the soul. His reasoning went as follows. We can all understand statements that are universally true, such as 'All dogs bark'. And since it 'takes one to know one', there must be something universal within us that is capable of comprehending these universal statements. This universal thing, said Aquinas, is our soul.

What was he on about? That's a good question. But if you think you can come up with a better proof of the existence of the soul, you're welcome to try. And for the record, Aquinas did have a few other theories, which were a bit more grounded. For example, he argued that we shouldn't eat animals, if we could survive on fruit and vegetables. For plants, he said, were inferior life forms to animals, and so should be killed and eaten first.

Oscar Wilde, playwright, poet, wit (1854–1900)

USAGE: To describe someone's wit as 'Wildean' suggests that they have a knack for coming out with facetious but amusing one-liners.

'We are all in the gutter, but some of us are looking at the stars.' 'All women become like their mothers. That is their tragedy. No man does. That's his.' 'To love oneself is the beginning of a lifelong romance.' 'I can resist everything except temptation.' 'The truth is rarely pure and never simple.' Oh, Oscar! It was as if the man just couldn't help expressing himself in epigrams.

An Irish upstart, he conquered London society by his wit, by his pose of taking nothing seriously except frivolity, and by having, whatever else you might say about him, a certain style. All these qualities are evident in his masterpiece, the (ironically titled) play *The Importance of Being Earnest*, which manages the trick of being completely charming from beginning to end: as perfect, in its way, as a Mozart symphony. Some of his short stories are pretty good too (for instance, *The Selfish Giant*), but on the whole Wilde is best remembered for his one-liners and his personality.

And for his downfall. For it turned out that Wilde, who was a married man with two children, had been spending his spare time consorting with male prostitutes. He was imprisoned in Reading Gaol, and by the time he'd served his sentence, was a broken man. High society turned its back on him – which for Wilde, was as painful a punishment as could be imagined. He mustered his energies for one last great work, the long and lyrical poem *The Ballad of Reading Gaol* (with its pertinent refrain, 'Each man kills the thing he loves'). Then he retired to Paris to die at the age of 46 in a down-at-heel hotel with questionable decor: fat, ugly and unloved, but still displaying flashes of the old style. His reported last words showed characteristic concern for the important things in life: 'Either those curtains go or I do.' Moments after he gave up the ghost, his body is said to have poured (forgive the disgustingness) fluids from every orifice. He died a foreigner in France – as would a certain American dancer a few decades later, although the way she went was far more gruesome …

Gruesome Deaths

The lives of the following three figures were rather beautiful and inspiring. Their deaths, not so much.

Isadora Duncan, dancer (1877–1927)

USAGE: A stylish way to say goodbye is to exclaim, 'Adieu, mes amis. Je vais à la gloire!' If possible, fling a scarf over your shoulder as you say it.

The sculptor Auguste Rodin called her perhaps 'the greatest woman the world has ever known'. The choreographer George Balanchine remembered 'a drunk fat woman … rolling around like a pig'. The American free spirit Isadora Duncan is often referred to as the creator of modern dance. What you think of modern dance will probably dictate what you think of her.

By the end of the 19th century, ballet had developed certain accepted gestures. Duncan, the daughter of a Californian banker, favoured more natural movements such as skipping and waving her arms around, inspired by ideas of how the Ancient Greeks may have done it (she used to loiter in the British Museum, gazing at the vase paintings). She danced barefoot, clad in a white Greek-style tunic. Spontaneity was her watchword. On stage in Boston, she expressed her pro-Soviet sympathies by waving a red scarf and baring her breasts, shouting, 'This is red and so am I!'

She later founded a dance school in Moscow, and married the alcoholic Russian poet Sergei Yesenin. As unconventional in her private life as in her art, she drank a lot, and slept with women as well as men. Her children, both born out of wedlock, were killed in an accident. Isadora herself died one night after setting off from a hotel in Nice, ill-advisedly wearing a long, flowing scarf. '*Adieu, mes amis,*' she exclaimed. '*Je vais à la gloire!*' (Goodbye, my friends. I go to glory!) The scarf caught in the car's wheels and Duncan was flung into the road, her neck broken. Some, such as Jean Cocteau*, felt her death was a work of art. Others were more cynical. 'Affectations can be dangerous,' Gertrude Stein* wryly observed.

Federico García Lorca, poet and playwright
(1898–1936)

USAGE: When considering whether a work of literature qualifies as truly great, you might question if it fulfils the three criteria set by Lorca.

The Spanish author Federico García Lorca once wrote that great art invariably displayed the following characteristics: an awareness of the inevitability of death, an engagement with the 'soil' of the land in which it was created, and an acknowledgement of the limitations of reason. Needless to say, this sounds a little like a description of much of his own work.

Lorca – who strictly speaking should be referred to as García Lorca, though the shorter form is fine in conversation

– started out as a poet. His *Gypsy Ballads* (1928) made him a star but also triggered a personal crisis. He became convinced he was going to be pigeonholed as an author of naive, rural verse. At the same time, he was distraught when his close friend, the artist Salvador Dalí, rejected his sexual advances. Did Dalí and Luis Buñuel* intend their film *Un Chien andalou* as a mocking satire aimed at their friend Lorca? Probably not, but Lorca thought they did.

'To burn with desire and keep quiet about it is the greatest punishment we can bring on ourselves,' he once remarked. In the conservative atmosphere of 1930s Spain, the homosexual author was forced to keep quiet about his deepest desires. He channelled his feelings into tortuous, passionate plays such as *Blood Wedding*, in which a bride runs off with her former lover directly after getting married, and *The House of Bernarda Alba*, in which a matriarch's desire to keep her daughters cloistered at home has disastrous consequences. Lorca became one of the first victims of the Spanish Civil War when he was executed by forces loyal to General Franco. One of the soldiers reportedly shot him twice in the backside, as an expression of disgust at his sexual orientation.

Che Guevara, revolutionary (1928–67)

USAGE: To describe someone with rather hazy left-wing views, you could say, 'I doubt his politics extend much further than the poster of Che Guevara on his bedroom wall.'

You could be forgiven for thinking Che Guevara was as much a rock star as a revolutionary. One particular photograph of his intense, simian features, the long hair splayed out beneath the dashing beret, adorns student bedrooms across the West, alongside posters of the likes of Jim Morrison and Kurt Cobain. He was young. He was handsome. Women found him irresistible.

Although he's known for the role he played in the revolution that brought Fidel Castro to power in Cuba in 1959, Guevara wasn't Cuban. He was from Argentina (he earned the name Che from his Argentine habit of addressing everyone as 'che', which is a bit like 'mate' or 'dude'). A trained doctor, he was incensed by the economic injustices he witnessed across South America during a road trip he took with a friend (as depicted in the 2004 film *The Motorcycle Diaries*). He promptly became a communist, convinced that the US was 'the enemy of humanity', and determined to spread revolution throughout the globe.

He started in Cuba, taking to the hills with Castro, and earning a reputation as a fearless soldier (braver, it was said, than Castro) as well as a ruthless killer. His unemotional diary descriptions of the executions he carried out make chilling reading. After the triumph in Cuba, he tried to take the revolution to the African Congo, without much success. Then he did the same in Bolivia, where his luck finally ran out. He was captured by Bolivian forces in 1967, shot in cold blood, and then had his hands cut off so his fingerprints could be used to prove it was he who had been killed. An attractive, intriguing and intimidating figure, Guevara was more literate than your average revolutionary, being particularly fond of poetry (he could recite Rudyard Kipling's poem 'If' by heart). Another curious fact about him is that, as a young man, he was so careless about his hygiene that his friends nicknamed him The Pig. It seems, though, that he wasn't the smelliest communist in history …

Stinkers

Real men are too busy and important to wash properly. At least, that's what the next two figures seem to have thought.

Mao Zedong, revolutionary (1893–1976)

USAGE: The phrase 'Maoist communist' usually refers to guerrilla revolutionaries from peasant backgrounds (by contrast with Lenin's vision of an uprising led by an urban intellectual elite).

You can bet your bottom renminbi no one ever told Mao Zedong that he stank. But stink he did, for the Chinese communist leader never bothered to wash properly. The most he stooped to was a daily rub-down with a hot towel by an attendant. His teeth remained resolutely unbrushed, and rather green, since he habitually drank green tea. A slovenly fellow, he rarely dressed up, conducting most of his business either in bed or else lounging beside a swimming pool. Meanwhile, out in the towns and countryside, his people perished in their tens of millions.

Some of these deaths were executions. The majority, though, were caused by the famine resulting from Mao's catastrophically misguided agricultural reforms of the 1950s, which were known, in what now seems like a sick joke, as The Great Leap Forward. In an attempt to drive industrial progress, Mao forced farm workers to abandon their farms and instead build power plants. But, as a result, grain production collapsed, and there was mass starvation. As many as 30 million died. Those who complained were deemed 'counter-revolutionaries' and murdered in the 1960s in a purge known as (sick joke number two) The Cultural Revolution. So many committed suicide that in Shanghai, people avoided walking near buildings for fear of being struck by falling bodies.

Mao is notorious for having probably caused more deaths than anyone else in history. What can be said in his favour? Some have argued that he didn't know about the executions, suicides and starvations. (Some chilling remarks attributed to Mao suggest otherwise. For instance, he's said to have declared: 'It is better to let half of the people die so that the other half can eat their fill.') Others point out that the revolutionary – who had grown up in the countryside, the son of a farmer – was a masterly tactician when it came to guerrilla warfare. Also that he promoted women's rights. And that his modernisations dragged China, kicking and squealing, into the 20th century. If you think that justifies a total of between 40 and 70 million deaths, feel free to admire the guy.

Ernest Hemingway, writer (1899–1961)

USAGE: It's fashionable, these days, to sneer at Hemingway as a boastful fool and hypocrite. But you're on relatively safe ground if you praise his early short stories.

There's a problem with Ernest Hemingway, which is that the caricatured idea of him – a bearded American braggart swaggering around the world getting drunk, shooting animals, and banging on about bravery – has obscured his early achievements as a writer. Of course the blame for this is largely his. He did get drunk. He did shoot animals. He did bang on. And according to his third wife, the journalist Martha Gellhorn, he was also filthy and stank of onions.

But first consider his achievements. Hemingway realised that using long words and a flowery style draws attention to the author. If you use short words and simple direct sentences, the emotion of the situation described comes through more strongly – especially if you don't say what that emotion is, but leave it to the reader to work it out. In his writing, he committed to these principles, and produced some of the best short stories ever written (try *The Killers*). His novels are more hit-and-miss (*A Farewell to Arms* is good; *Across the River and into the Trees* is terrible). But his influence is enormous. Every tough guy who writes quietly about tough things, such as war or deep-sea fishing, is operating in the shadow of Hemingway.

He got the Nobel Prize in Literature in 1954 after he published *The Old Man and the Sea*: a novella about a tough guy doing some deep-sea fishing. By then, he was already losing it. Drinking too much, forgetting the writing rules he'd invented himself, resorting to an embarrassing comb-over to hide his baldness. He killed himself in 1961. By then, it was a mercy. He was miserable and had suffered acute physical pain for years, exacerbated by his involvement in two separate plane crashes.

Plane Crashes

Icarus flew too close to the Sun and fell to Earth.
These two suffered more prosaic in-flight hitches.

Walter Gropius, architect (1883–1969)

USAGE: To justify embarking on a diet, you could claim to be
inspired by Walter Gropius' dictum that form should follow
function.

While serving his country in the First World War, Walter
Gropius earned two Iron Crosses for bravery. On one occasion, he survived being shot out of the sky. On another, he
was buried under rubble. But he arose from that ordeal and
went on to put those bricks to better use when he became one
of Germany's greatest architects.

After the war, the new Weimar Republic permitted a
greater level of experimentation in architecture than had previously been welcome in Germany, and Gropius seized his
opportunity. He set up what became known as the Bauhaus
school of architecture. The term meant, literally, building
(*bau*) house (*haus*). An unpretentious title for an unpretentious idea: to design buildings, above all, to serve a purpose,
without wasting space, materials and money on attempting
to make them beautiful as well. This was a revolutionary programme at the time, which annoyed conservatives. When the

Nazis rose to power in the 1930s, they drove out the Bauhaus architects (who also included Le Corbusier) along with other avant garde artists they regarded as 'degenerate'.

Gropius fled to America, where he set up a new and thriving practice as an architect, pursuing his key principles. Among these were the idea that 'ornamentation is crime' (which speaks for itself) and 'form follows function' (i.e. a building is designed solely and sufficiently to serve a particular purpose). Gropius encapsulated the latter when he was asked to build a factory whose main purpose, he was instructed, was that it should attract the attention of people passing in a train. Accordingly, he slanted the facade of the building so it would reflect the sunlight into their eyes.

Joseph Beuys, artist (1921–86)

USAGE: If you wanted to slag off 'performance art' as pretentious and self-indulgent, you might remark that 'Joseph Beuys has a lot to answer for.'

While serving as a Nazi pilot during the Second World War, Joseph Beuys (pronounced: BOYS) crashed in the Ukraine. He was discovered, he claimed, by a strange Tatar tribe which nursed him back to life. It was a nice story, but unfortunately it wasn't true. He had crashed but, less glamorously, been rescued by a fellow Nazi, who later revealed that Beuys had made up the bit about the tribesmen.

After recovering from his injuries, Beuys put his penchant for inventing stuff to better use and went on to become one of the world's most famous artists. His goal, he said, was to bridge the gap between reality and spirituality. For instance, one of his works comprised 600 pictures full of curious symbols, which Beuys claimed held the key to connecting the real world and the spirit world.

He was one of the first and best-known exponents of performance art. (The term refers to any artwork that involves someone, usually the artist, doing something in person in front of an audience.) The most notorious example in his *oeuvre* was a piece entitled *Explaining Art to a Dead Hare*, which involved Beuys wandering around cradling a dead hare, and occasionally whispering into its ear, in front of a bemused audience. What was his point? Perhaps that animals – even dead ones – are more instinctively perceptive than some humans. We need to get in touch with our animal nature if we're to have any hope of crossing the divide that separates us from the spiritual life. To some, this was exciting, vibrant, even witty. Others said the man was clearly a lunatic. To support their argument, they pointed to his eccentric style of dress. In Beuys' invented narrative about being rescued from the burning plane, he had claimed the Tatars had swaddled him in a layer of fat and felt – and in honour of this, the artist not only made as much use as possible of these two materials in his artworks; he also wore a felt hat at all times. Of course, in so doing he was also proclaiming himself as an artist who didn't abide by the normal rules of society: a stratagem that would also be adopted by an eccentric English poet ...

Sartorially Strange

'The apparel oft proclaims the man',
Shakespeare noted. If that's true, the next
three must have been very peculiar people.

Edith Sitwell, poet (1887–1964)

USAGE: Witnessing any self-consciously zany performance
– especially if the performer is posh – you might remark,
'Channelling the spirit of Edith Sitwell, I see.'

Dame Edith Sitwell once wrote a rather entertaining book
called *English Eccentrics*, and though she devoted most of
her energy to writing poetry, she is best remembered for her
eccentricities. Six feet tall, thin, angular, with an exceedingly
pointy nose, she decided to make a virtue out of her appearance, and habitually wore turbans and exotic outfits made
of brocade and velvet. Her most famous performance was
Façade, with music by William Walton, during which Sitwell
concealed herself behind a curtain and boomed nonsense at
the audience through a megaphone.

Sitwell herself was no slouch as a poet. She's little read
now, though, certainly by comparison with her protégés
Wilfred Owen and Dylan Thomas, whose verse she championed tirelessly. In her own work, she tried to recreate the pure
sound effects of music, and the rhythms of the new musical

form of jazz. Some thought her a poseur, a flashy amateur. F.R. Leavis* was particularly dismissive.

Sister of the extravagantly named Osbert and Sacheverell Sitwell, friend of Marilyn Monroe (whom she met while writing scripts in Hollywood) and enemy of Noël Coward, she didn't have an easy life. Her only love affair, with the homosexual Russian artist Pavel Tchelitchew, was probably never consummated. The extremities of her adult life were likely part of a long journey of escape from her miserable childhood. Her mother was an alcoholic, her father, Sir George Sitwell, a half-mad aristocrat who strapped a contraption to his daughter's face in the hope of making her nose shorter.

Rainer Maria Rilke, poet (1875–1926)

USAGE: In a mood of inner torment, exclaim, 'Who, if I cried out, might hear me, among the ranked angels?' Then mention that this is a quotation from Rilke.

The Austrian poet Rainer Maria Rilke could hardly have helped ending up a rather delicate sort of fellow. That's not just because he had the middle name Maria – which is more normally associated with girls – but also because his sister died a week before he was born. Accordingly, his grief-stricken mother dressed her son in girl's clothes for a time, and even used to address him as Sophie.

He went on to become a sensitive, angst-ridden poet. 'Who, if I cried out, might hear me, among the ranked angels?' he demanded in the first line of his masterpiece, *Duino Elegies*. He heard these words, he said, uttered by a voice in the wind as he was out walking on the cliffs, and scribbled them down in his notebooks. One answer to his question about who would hear him if he cried out, was generations of readers to come, since Rilke has enjoyed remarkable longevity as a poet. Today, despite the problems of translating his ecstatic verse, he rivals Rumi* and Khalil Gibran for popularity in the US.

As a young man, Rilke had enjoyed the mentorship of the sculptor Auguste Rodin, who had encouraged him to temper the wilder excesses of his style, and introduce a little objectivity. In due course, the poet also found himself buttonholed by younger men in search of guidance. He replied to one of them, a certain Franz Xaver Kappus, in a famous series of ten long letters that were later published as *Letters to a Young Poet*. In these, he advised him how a poet should feel. Love, he noted, was 'the hardest thing it is laid on us to do, the utmost, the ultimate trial and test, the work for which all other work is just preparation'.

Epicurus, philosopher (341–270 BC)

USAGE: The word 'Epicurean' means not 'pleasure-seeking', as many mistakenly believe, but 'tranquil and meditative'. To be on the safe side, you should spell this out whenever you use it.

Epicurus only owned two cloaks. In other words, his reputation as a self-indulgent hedonist couldn't have been further from the truth. Even during his lifetime, gossips claimed that the commune where he lived with his friends was a place of debauchery. There was a story that he once spent the night with several virgins and enjoyed eighteen orgasms. And if that's true, all one can say is: nice going, Epicurus! But it wasn't his style. In reality, he lived a simple, sober life, abstaining from sex and drugs, and restricting his diet to bread and olives with the occasional hunk of cheese as a treat.

Consider the moments in your life when you've actually felt happy. Now consider what it was that made those moments happy. What if you altered the way you live in order to maximise the likelihood of enjoying more of these moments? Epicurus said that if we were honest about it, we'd have to agree that, by these lights, the way most of us live is profoundly misguided. He believed the aim of existence is not pleasure exactly, but freedom from pain, which he called *ataraxia* (literally, lack of disturbance). So he didn't pursue the wild life. He lived with his friends precisely because he thought that pursuits such as love and sex didn't bring as much happiness as friendship.

Love was fool's gold. So too was money (what makes us happier is satisfying work). So too was luxury: Epicurus said what we really want is the inner peace we think (quite wrongly) that luxury will bring. He set up The Garden, a kind of commune where he lived quietly with his friends, dividing tasks of cooking, cleaning, etc., and discussing philosophy. The idea caught on and Epicurean 'gardens' sprang up all around the Mediterranean. They were later adapted by Christians into monasteries, which operate along similar principles.

Constantin Stanislavski, actor, theatre director, author (1863–1938)

USAGE: To deflate the ego of any actor you know, ask if the reason they're behaving so arrogantly is because they're using The Method to prepare for their next role as a dunderhead.

The Russian actor Constantin Stanislavski took his holidays at Yalta by the Black Sea. For an hour every morning, he used to wander the streets in the character of whatever role he was preparing for at the time. If he was going to play a tramp, he would step out looking and acting like a tramp, in filthy clothes and a battered hat. Or if he was playing a dandy, he'd be impeccably dressed.

This may sound pretty self-conscious, but Stanislavski was actually trying to rid himself of self-consciousness. The more he practised, he believed, the more naturally the performance would come. It was a key part of a method he worked out, which is deemed so important by actors today that it is known simply as The Method. Before Stanislavski, it had been thought that acting came largely by inspiration. His key work was *An Actor Prepares* (1936), and the title says it all, really. It's partly due to him that certain actors these days take themselves so seriously (and, perhaps, that the public accords them so much respect). On the other hand, The Method has produced some extraordinary results. Marlon Brando was famously a fan. Robert De Niro piled on the pounds to play Jake La Motta in *Raging Bull* and Daniel Day-Lewis insisted on staying in his wheelchair during the filming of *My Left Foot*. Both earned Best Actor Oscars for their efforts.

If Stanislavski had just been an actor, it's a safe bet no one would have heard of him. For by all accounts, he wasn't much good – a bit over the top, and with a tendency to deliver his lines in a hammy, declamatory style (which he'd picked up after hiring an opera singer as his voice coach). Then one day it occurred to him that, whatever the quality of his own performances, he should share the thoughts about acting that he'd been jotting down in notebooks ever since his teens. This 'eureka moment' sent him off on a new path, which would secure his place in history.

Eureka!

*For convenience's sake, it's helpful to think of
talented individuals having sudden moments of
realisation, which alter the courses of their lives.
In some cases, it may actually have been true.*

Jean-Jacques Rousseau, philosopher (1712–78)

USAGE: Any reference to the French Revolution is bolstered by
a mention of Rousseau. For bonus points, add that you mean
'Jean-Jacques, of course, not Henri' (who was a 19th-century
painter).

Edmund Burke* believed the excesses of the French Revolution
could be laid at the door of one Jean-Jacques Rousseau. The
self-taught son of a Swiss watchmaker, Rousseau wrote the
bestselling novel of the 18th century (*Julie*), pioneered the
autobiography with his *Confessions*, and even found time to
compose the odd (not very good) opera. Yet he's best remembered for a sudden realisation he had one day while walking
from Paris to Vincennes. People are unhappy. The reason
they're unhappy is because of the laws of society, which have
been corrupted by the powerful to suit their own ends. What
is needed therefore is a new society devoted to equality and
'the will of the people'. Enter Robespierre.

'Man is born free, but everywhere he is in chains,'

Rousseau observed in *The Social Contract* (1762). Because he believed people in primitive societies were happier than those in 18th-century Paris, he's often credited with inventing the concept of the 'noble savage'. But he wasn't suggesting we should all strip off and don loin cloths (more's the pity).

He did, though, think the best education for a child was to be brought up in the country rather than the city, as he detailed in one of his tracts on education. His critics point out that it's hard to be lectured on such matters by a man who deposited his five children in a foundling hospital because he was afraid they would interfere with his work. In person, Rousseau was a nightmare: paranoid and vain, liable to fall out with anyone who helped him. In 1766, after Rousseau's provocative publications had stirred his detractors to throw stones at his house, he fled to Britain. There he took shelter with the enlightenment thinker David Hume*, before inevitably turning against him.

Ralph Waldo Emerson, philosopher (1803–82)

USAGE: The next time someone tells you, 'I don't really believe. But I do think God's all around us, in the trees and the oceans', you can respond: 'So you're an Emersonian Transcendentalist!'

It was while he was wandering through the Jardin des Plantes in Paris that the American philosopher Ralph Waldo Emerson had his sudden moment of realisation. It wasn't only the astonishing beauty of the place that inspired him. It was also the methodical way everything had been arranged, which helped clarify his vision of the great connectedness of things. From that moment on, it's said, Emerson ceased to be a Christian and became what would later be known as a Transcendentalist: a man who believed God was all around him, in nature, in everything.

Born and brought up in Boston, as a young man Emerson had been ordained as a minister. Then his wife and two of his brothers died, and, plunged in grief, he began questioning the Christian idea of a benign God who intervenes in human affairs. In due course, he embarked on a new career as a public lecturer. He consolidated the money he made from his talks by working them up into highly readable essays with titles such as *Self-Reliance*, which became bestsellers when collected and released in book form. As well as his spiritual Transcendentalism, Emerson advised that individuals strive for a kind of personal independence comparable to American political independence. His influence in giving expression to a species of hoary, eloquent, alternately plain-speaking and lyrical American 'individualism' (as his theme was known) was huge, influencing everyone from fellow Transcendentalist Henry David Thoreau* to the poet Walt Whitman*.

Emerson isn't a name that's much bandied about these days, though he has been called the most important American intellectual of the 19th century. According to the critic Harold Bloom, one unintended consequence of his theories was to inspire others to develop alternative belief systems to the Christian religion, paving the way for Mormonism and Christian Science.

Albert Schweitzer,
author and missionary (1875–1965)

USAGE: Confuse someone trying to mug you by inquiring, 'Where's your Schweitzerian reverence for life?'

'A man can only do what he can do. But if he does that each day, he can sleep at night and do it again the next day.' So said Albert Schweitzer, a rare example of someone who practised what he preached. When young, he resolved that from the age of 30, he would devote himself to helping others. Until then, he would do what he wanted. Being Schweitzer, he didn't chase girls or get loaded, but made a serious contribution to Biblical scholarship. Specifically, his book *The Quest of the Historical Jesus* (1906) argued that Jesus Christ had mistakenly believed the world was about to end.

True to his word, Schweitzer spent seven years studying medicine at Strasbourg University, before setting off for Africa. He founded the Albert Schweitzer Hospital in Gabon and stayed there for much of the rest of his life, caring for the sick. One day, while he was in a boat that was nosing its way through a herd of hippos, a phrase came to him for his entire philosophy: reverence for life (or in German, *Ehrfurcht vor dem leben*). It basically meant doing things for other people, but he expressed it so inspiringly in his subsequent books, he was awarded the Nobel Peace Prize in 1952.

Inevitably, there was a backlash. Schweitzer claimed he had been moved not only by Jesus' exhortation to his followers to be 'fishers of men' but also by guilt at his native Germany's colonial excesses. Yet some said his own attitude to the locals in Gabon smacked of colonial arrogance. In later life, he campaigned against the proliferation of nuclear weapons alongside the likes of Albert Einstein* and Bertrand Russell*. He was also, incidentally, a great expert on the music of Richard Wagner* and J.S. Bach, and a highly skilled organist.

Albert Einstein, physicist (1879–1955)

USAGE: Einstein's impact on his subject was so vast that, when referring to the state of physics today, you may safely use the phrase 'post-Einsteinian physics'.

In music, Mozart. In art, Picasso. But in science, the name most easily associated with the idea of pure unadulterated genius is that of Albert Einstein. In 1905, while working as a patent clerk in the Swiss capital of Bern, he was travelling home one day on the tram when he fell to wondering what the consequence would be if the tram were travelling at the speed of light. He realised that, for him, time would move more slowly. Thus was born his 'special theory of relativity', which he set out in a scientific paper that was published later that year: around the same time as he published another paper, which paved the way for quantum theory.

Einstein's theories about the universe eventually overturned the dominance that had been enjoyed by Sir Isaac Newton* for over 200 years. Most of us think of space and time as dependable constants. Yet Einstein proved it wasn't as simple as that. His 'general theory of relativity', which he published ten years after the special theory, showed that even Newton's idea of gravity is misleading. When a parachutist jumps out of a plane, he isn't sucked towards the Earth by an invisible force. The gravity of objects distorts space, pushing him towards the ground.

After winning the Nobel Prize in Physics in 1921, Einstein became a global celebrity. Since then, his very appearance – the broad face and unkempt hair – has become the public idea of what a genius looks like. Other trivia about the great man includes the fact that after he died, his brain was stolen by the pathologist on duty, who kept it for decades before subjecting it to tests to see if there was anything unusual about it. (Apparently, there wasn't.) It was an outrageous abuse of the great man's corpse, although not quite as outrageous as the treatment meted out to the body of one of the great originals of English literature ...

The Desecrated Dead

*The next three experienced macabre codas to
their lives – willingly, in Bentham's case – when
strange things were done to their corpses.*

Laurence Sterne, writer (1713–68)

USAGE: A propos any innovative technique used by a
contemporary writer, you can nod knowingly and say,
'I've a feeling Laurence Sterne did something similar in
Tristram Shandy.'

After the Anglo-Irish novelist Laurence Sterne died, his body
was illegally dug up from the London churchyard where it
lay, and sold to anatomists at Cambridge University. As it
happened, one of the surgeons there had known Sterne personally and recognised his corpse. He ordered that the great
man's remains should be returned to their original resting
place in Hanover Square.

It was a troubled afterlife to cap a troubled life. One of
the most extraordinary things about the playful, experimental, and often very funny novel *The Life and Opinions
of Tristram Shandy, Gentleman* (more easily referred to as
Tristram Shandy) was that it was largely written, as the author
himself confessed, 'under the greatest heaviness of heart'. His
father had died when he was eleven. He had become a priest,

but then decided he wanted to be a writer. So, aged 46, he delegated his parish duties to a curate, and sat down to write *Tristram Shandy* at around the time his mother was dying and his wife suffering a nervous breakdown and threatening to kill herself. The book, though, which appeared in instalments between 1759 and 1767, made him famous.

It's hard to summarise the plot, since it's one of those crazy early novels inspired by Rabelais*. It kicks off with Shandy describing his own conception. Then it digresses – and keeps digressing without ever getting anywhere, but all in a highly entertaining way. There are typographical peculiarities. One page is entirely blacked out. While writing it, Sterne suffered increasingly from tuberculosis, which eventually forced him to travel in the hope of alleviating the symptoms. His wanderings inspired another novel, *A Sentimental Journey Through France and Italy*, which appeared in 1768 shortly before his death. In his playfulness and experimentalism, Sterne is said to have pre-empted the modernist (and even the postmodernist) literature of the 20th century.

More on 'The Desecrated Dead' overleaf

Jeremy Bentham, philosopher (1748–1832)

USAGE: If you are attempting to construct a morality independent of religion, a 'Benthamite utilitarian approach' – asking what will create 'the greatest happiness of the greatest number' – is a good starting point.

If you're passing University College London, pop in and have a look at the mummified remains of Jeremy Bentham. They're there, in a cabinet, for all to see. In an exemplary display of independent thought, the oddball Englishman decreed in his will that it would please him if his corpse could be exhibited in this manner. In fact, the face you'll see is a wax replica, since the real one was thought to look too disturbing. After being removed, it was kept in the same cabinet for a while. But students kept stealing it and using it for pranks, so in the end it was moved elsewhere for safe keeping.

Curious that such a peculiar man should have invented one of the most straightforward and sensible systems of thought in history. He called it utilitarianism and it stated, quite simply, that what was morally good was whatever created 'the greatest happiness of the greatest number'. That may sound so obvious as to be unimpressive, but actually it isn't obvious at all. Most systems of morality are based on religious dogma, or else on far more complicated ideas cooked up by philosophers. Bentham's was plain and solid as a brick. And its implications were huge.

To start with, they prompted Bentham himself to argue in favour of women's rights (he never married); the rights of animals (the question, he said, is whether they can suffer);

the abolition of slavery, of the death penalty and of corporal punishment; and the decriminalisation of homosexuality (the latter wasn't unnatural, in his eyes, merely 'an irregularity of the venereal appetite'). No one can say that Bentham wasn't ahead of his time. A clumsy, impractical fellow in person, who some believe may have suffered from Asperger's syndrome, he arguably exaggerated the simplicity of things. Shouldn't a definition of moral rightness include not only happiness but also some concept of justice? Is it really okay, for instance, to torture someone (a man who knows the location of a bomb, for example), if it will probably save lives?

Ivan Turgenev, writer (1818–83)

USAGE: If someone seems too self-centred – or too generous – you might refer them to Turgenev's essay *Hamlet and Don Quixote*, warning of the dangers of being too much like either character.

Towards the end of the 19th century, scientists frequently cut out the brains from the skulls of intelligent people who had just died, to see if there was any link between their intelligence and the size of their brains. In the case of the brilliant novelist, Ivan Turgenev (pronounced: tur-GAY-nyev), it seemed that there was. For his brain was found to be the largest on record, weighing in at a hefty 2kg.

In addition to this huge organ, Turgenev was blessed with that other key resource of any writer: a miserable childhood. His father was a compulsive philanderer and his mother took it out on young Ivan, often beating him. Admittedly, life had consolations, since the family was rich and he could distract himself by going hunting in the 500 acres of forest surrounding his home. As he grew older, there was also the option of dallying with attractive serfs.

His first major publication, *Notes from a Hunter* (1852), was a collection of short stories inspired by these experiences. As well as being a milestone in the literary movement known as Russian Realism, it showed such empathy towards the plight of the serfs – who were the property of landowners – that it contributed to the abolition of serfdom in 1861. This, the author said, was his greatest achievement. His literary fans, though, might disagree, pointing to the novel *Fathers and Sons* (1862), which portrayed the conflict between the old, traditional Russia, and the new.

As a modern novelist, he seemed to represent this new Russia and was driven out of his native land by the stifling conservatism of life under Tsar Nicholas II. (He hung out in Paris and Baden-Baden and fell in love with an opera singer named Pauline.) Yet Turgenev was a moderate fellow. He once argued in an essay that men were habitually torn by the desire to be like Hamlet (a tortured intellectual) on the one hand, and Don Quixote (a generous child-like figure) on the other. A middle way, he said, was best. He was suspicious of novels that had too obvious a message or were imbued with too strong a religious feeling. Unsurprisingly, this caused him to fall out with Tolstoy, who challenged him to a duel (though he later apologised), and with another of his great contemporaries ...

Public Spats

Some writers are sensitive souls, liable to take offence at the smallest insult. Others are combative, ready to pronounce their views from the most public pulpits.

Fyodor Dostoyevsky, novelist (1821–81)

USAGE: If you've been having a tough week, with money worries, moral dilemmas, and the gradual feeling you're losing your grip on sanity, you might say you're in a Dostoyevskyan kind of mood.

Fyodor Dostoyevsky can't have been easy to live with. He was unfaithful to his wife and quarrelsome with his friends. (He fell out bitterly with Turgenev after lampooning him in *The Devils*.) Few have endured such a sharp decline in their fortunes. After one successful novel, his second one bombed, and shortly afterwards he was sentenced to death by firing squad for his membership of a subversive political group. At the last moment, he was spared by the Tsar, only to be subjected to eight years' imprisonment and hard labour in the wastes of Siberia. When he eventually re-entered society, he had to rebuild his literary reputation from scratch. This, after many setbacks, he managed with extraordinary success.

The extremity of his suffering fed his fiction. His characters wrestle with poverty, as did Dostoyevsky. *The Idiot*'s hero suffers from epilepsy, just like Dostoyevsky. *The Gambler*'s is addicted to gambling. So was Dostoyevsky. It isn't clear if he considered murdering his pawnbroker – as the tortured intellectual Raskolnikov does in *Crime and Punishment* – but it seems likely. His insight into marginal, flawed human beings, combined with the miseries of his plots, led to his being hailed as the poet of the Russian soul. Strangers doffed their caps to him in the streets of St Petersburg.

As regards his wider reputation, people sometimes ask who is greater, Tolstoy or Dostoyevsky. You should probably say Dostoyevsky: the less obvious and therefore more interesting answer. In defence, you might point out that he essentially invented the flawed and tortured anti-hero. Or quote Sigmund Freud*, who called Dostoyevsky's late masterpiece *The Brothers Karamazov* 'the most significant novel ever written'.

Theodor W. Adorno, philosopher (1903–69)

USAGE: The next time you see someone slope off from the dinner table to watch TV, you could shout out after them, 'This is exactly what Adorno warned us about!'

Theodor W. Adorno devoted his life to telling people unpalatable truths. Invariably the response was extreme. On one occasion, for instance, he was in the midst of giving a lecture when three women burst into the room, bared their breasts and scattered petals over his head. All to persuade him to stop talking, it seems.

Perhaps the best-known of the Adorno controversies centred on a series of debates between himself and his fellow-German Karl Popper (up next) on the thorny subject of how best to bring about political change. According to Adorno, the only way to effect real change was through revolution: one great event that would completely reconfigure people's mindsets. The problem with this, Popper countered, was that revolutions inevitably led to violence. He advocated a step-by-step approach, through gradual reform of the laws governing society. It might seem like a no-brainer that Popper was right about this, but the Adorno position certainly has its supporters: most recently the British clown-prince of philosophers, Russell Brand.

Some of Adorno's other arguments were rather more persuasive. For instance, in his book *The Dialectic of Enlightenment*, he pointed out that the popular assumption that we are all progressing towards a more enlightened state of being was disproved by the rise of Nazism. Far from achieving a state of affairs in which reason (and reasonableness) were king, in the 1930s Europe had been swamped by a wave of primitive superstition – most notoriously in the case of the persecution of Adorno's fellow Jews in his native Germany and elsewhere. Adorno went further, arguing that capitalism was partly to blame for these atrocities. In capitalist societies, so-called culture has become little more than a factory producing standardised goods designed to distract our attention from the real problems of society. One of Adorno's favourite examples was TV whodunits. They're all essentially the same: someone gets murdered, and the grizzled or eccentric detective has to work out who committed the crime. Yet we all watch them, mesmerised – which suits the politicians, who can meanwhile get on with doing whatever they want, unopposed.

Karl Popper, philosopher (1902–94)

USAGE: If anyone makes a claim that is impossible to disprove, you can observe, 'That's what Karl Popper would call an unfalsifiable assertion. In other words, it's meaningless.'

If we accept that scientists tell us what we know and philosophers what we don't know, then the Viennese thinker Karl Popper must be one of the greatest philosophers of all time. For he argued that most of what we think we know, we don't. 'Science,' he said, 'does not rest upon solid bedrock – the bold structure of its theories rises, as it were, above a swamp.' His justification for this enormous claim is that most of what we call science operates on a principle of induction, i.e. we observe several instances of a thing (we notice several green frogs) and draw from this a general principle (all frogs are green). Popper points out that this can only ever be conjecture, and may be exploded by a single exception (e.g. a Panamanian pink-sided tree frog).

This sounds a merely negative philosophy, but Popper claimed his 'falsificationist' approach, as it became known, was a kind of progress. For if we know a thing isn't true, we know more than we knew before. He also provided a handy dismissal of much of Sigmund Freud's teachings when he pointed out that if an argument can't be disproved, it's essentially meaningless. Freud's claim, for instance, that we all want to kill our fathers is arguably gibberish.

After escaping from Austria shortly after the Nazi invasion, Popper spent much of the rest of his life teaching in London. A difficult, arrogant man, by all accounts, forever spoiling for an academic scrap, he wrangled publicly with Adorno and privately with Ludwig Wittgenstein*. The latter was in the room in Cambridge in 1946 when Popper delivered a paper entitled *Are There Philosophical Problems?* His arguments so enraged Wittgenstein, he is said to have threatened Popper with a red-hot poker.

Jacques Derrida, philosopher (1930–2004)

USAGE: If someone urges you to bear in mind the context in which a novel was written, you might reply by quoting, or perhaps misquoting, Derrida: 'There's nothing outside the text.'

The slippery Continental philosopher Jacques Derrida was so annoying that he didn't just spark one row in particular. He sparked many. Noam Chomsky* called his scholarship 'appalling'. And he was being polite. When Cambridge University announced its intention to award the Frenchman an honorary doctorate in 1992, eighteen distinguished scholars from a range of countries wrote a letter complaining that Derrida's theories did not 'meet accepted standards of clarity and rigor' and were 'semi-intelligible attacks upon the values of reason, truth and scholarship'.

It's the last phrase that provides the key to the anger he provoked. For Derrida was known for 'deconstructionism': an approach to culture that he, with typical elusiveness, refused to define, but which seemed to be a reaction against 'structuralists' such as Claude Lévi-Strauss*. While the latter had been a positivist, generalising to make sense of human existence, Derrida was the opposite of a generaliser. He de-generalised. He de-constructed structuralism. Crucially, he argued that you couldn't say for certain what any work of literature meant. Every reader will bring his own prejudices to interpreting it. Derrida's often quoted as saying, 'There's nothing outside the text', though the old buzzard claimed he never actually said that. Or if he did, it wasn't what he meant.

Derrida's big idea was that language is incomprehensible and he demonstrated it with his own prose style, which is hard going, to say the least. Why, then, was he so popular and successful in certain quarters? He cut a dashing figure, with his thick crop of prematurely white hair and healthy tan. And he made literature professors feel an unfamiliar sensation: importance. For Derrida's arguments focused on a literary theory, and expatiated outwards from there towards an attitude that would encompass – and threaten to erode – the entire apparatus of Western thought.

John Maynard Keynes, economist (1883–1946)

USAGE: The phrase 'Keynesian economics' refers to a dominant mid-20th-century economic theory: that controlled government intervention is necessary to mitigate the boom and bust cycle.

Some critics, who loathed the economic theories of John Maynard Keynes (pronounced: KAINS), sniped that he didn't care what happened to the economy, because he didn't have any children to care about after he died. This was a way of referring to the fact that Keynes was a promiscuous homosexual; he had affairs with, among others, the artist Duncan Grant and the author Lytton Strachey. (The latter complained of Keynes' habit of jotting notes about his love life in his diary, as if recording economic statistics.) But in 1925 he took everyone by surprise and married a Russian ballerina named Lydia Lopokova. Grant was best man at the wedding.

So what was so controversial about Keynes' arguments? In short, they turned the world of economics on its head. Before Keynes came along, people believed that, if the economy ever got into trouble and unemployment soared, things would sort themselves out by a natural process. The unemployed would take whatever salary they were offered, since they were desperate for work. Keynes said this was all wrong. In reality, workers often refused to take a lower salary – because of pride, for example. No, the way to get the economy going again, said Keynes, was not to sit back and cross your fingers, but rather to persuade the government to spend money building roads and carrying out other public works, which would create more jobs – and, crucially, jobs that paid acceptable wages. He famously set out his arguments in *The General Theory of Employment, Interest and Money* (1936).

When governments put Keynes' methods to the test in the 1950s and 60s, they seemed to work. In fact, if it hadn't been for Keynes, some said, there might well have been a global revolution during those decades, as a result of a massive economic meltdown. This is why he has been called the man who saved capitalism. His theories remain hugely influential to this day – although the extent of that influence usually depends upon the state of the world economy. After the 2007/08 financial crisis, during the 'bust', everyone started talking about Keynesianism again. Back in the 'boom' years of the 1980s, by contrast, you were more likely to hear economists name-dropping a man with views that were diametrically opposed to Keynes' …

Friedrich Hayek, economist and social theorist (1899–1992)

USAGE: To claim to be a 'Hayekian' when it comes to the economy means you believe politicians tend to mess things up – so the less the state intervenes, the better.

In the 1930s, a series of debates were held in London in which J.M. Keynes* and the Austrian economist Friedrich Hayek (pronounced: HIGH-ek) argued about the best way to run an economy. Keynes advocated limited state intervention, while Hayek asserted that, because politicians were never sufficiently well informed, they invariably made things worse.

This in turn, Hayek believed, spurred a further, more extreme level of intervention, usually from the same politicians who had ballsed the economy up in the first place. And that damaging syndrome, as he warned in his 1944 book *The Road to Serfdom*, ran the risk of ultimately leading to dictatorship.

At the time, Hayek lost the argument. Keynes' ideas were generally adopted and the Austrian came to be regarded as something of a crackpot by his academic colleagues. He succumbed to depression, which plagued him until 1974 when, greatly to his surprise, he received the Nobel Prize in Economics. This marked the start of a major rehabilitation, not only of Hayek's emotional well-being, but also of his economic views – and his broader ideas regarding social freedoms. These too focused on non-interventionism and leaving breathing space for what he called 'spontaneous order'. The following year, the leader of the British Conservative Party, Margaret Thatcher, produced a copy of Hayek's *The Constitution of Liberty* from her handbag at a meeting, slapped it down on the table and declared, 'This is what we believe!' Her handbag must have been enormous, to judge from the number of weighty books she's reported to have carried around in it.

Adored by Maggie

The British Conservative prime minister Margaret Thatcher famously had a very large handbag. She had to, for she used it to carry around whatever weighty tome she happened to be reading at the time.

Adam Smith, economist (1723–90)

USAGE: If the name Adam Smith is conjured by a conservative, they may be claiming that if we all act like selfish bastards, everything will still work itself out all right in the end.

Adam Smith – sometimes known as the father of economics – never married, and little wonder. Everything in his face bulged: his eyes, his nose, his mouth. He stammered, and in company, would restrict himself to topics about which he knew nothing. If he revealed his theories, he reasoned, people might not bother to buy his books. As a result, he wasn't a scintillating conversationalist.

For all that, the Scotsman seems to have been a likeable sort of chap. (He once absent-mindedly stuffed a sandwich in his teapot, drank the ensuing brew, and declared it the worst cup of tea he'd ever had.) His economic theories seem attractive at a glance. In *The Theory of Moral Sentiments* (1759), he argued that most of us do most things not because they're morally right, but because it suits us. The book was a hit: readers were thrilled to be told they were all secret egotists, but shouldn't feel too bad about it. The latter conclusion was bolstered in Smith's masterwork. In *The Wealth of Nations* (1776), he set out his belief that if everyone pursues their own interest within an economy, they will be guided by what he called 'an invisible hand' to act in a way that will benefit society, since a stable society ultimately benefits our self-interest. This amounts to the idea that a free-market economy will produce the healthiest and most stable society.

Margaret Thatcher is said at one point to have carried around a copy of *The Wealth of Nations* in her handbag. No surprise that Smith is reviled by left-wingers. For his arguments sound pretty good in theory, but the question remains, was he right?

Edmund Burke, philosopher, politician (1729–97)

USAGE: In a conservative mood, you might remark, 'We shouldn't forget Edmund Burke's warnings about what happens when you abandon the system laid down by tradition.'

In the Enlightenment era of the 18th century, when brilliant men believed a new age was dawning, which would throw off the injustices of the past, there was at least one dissenting voice. The Irish author Edmund Burke was convinced that without the restraint of tradition, the lowest appetites would run riot, and the results would be chaos and bloodshed (cf. Thomas Hobbes*). This was the message of *Reflections on* *the French Revolution*, which he published in 1790 – and his predictions were to prove horribly accurate.

Burke didn't think much of humankind. Men, he once declared, are no more than the 'shrivelled, meagre, hopping, though loud and troublesome, insects of the hour'. Yet he wrote of them in such graceful prose that his works are still read to this day, and he displayed such a gracious temperament that he himself seems far more than an 'insect of the hour'. Dr Johnson once declared: 'No man of sense could meet Mr Burke by accident under a gateway to avoid a shower, without being convinced: "This is an extraordinary man."' His personality has proved so attractive that he has been embraced by readers of both political stripes, the left hailing his critique of the pitfalls of imperialism, and the right praising his measured cautiousness about half-cocked idealism.

Like anyone of serious intelligence, he can't easily be fitted into one political category, yet Burke has been regarded as 'the father of modern conservatism', particularly by conservatives such as Margaret Thatcher, who have been delighted to press-gang such a substantial figure into their service. Whatever else one might say of him, Burke had one claim to authority that isn't shared by most political commentators. He had first-hand experience of politics, serving for much of his adult life as a Member of Parliament. It was an index of his willingness to get his hands dirty, to do as well as to think: a trait he shared with one of the fathers of investigative journalism …

Wannabe Politicians

It's a lot easier to snipe from the sidelines than to achieve anything in politics. Here are a couple of authors who at least tried to get involved.

Upton Sinclair, writer (1878–1968)

USAGE: Any really extensive piece of investigative journalism, for which the writer has gone undercover, may be said to owe a debt to the example set by Upton Sinclair.

The American journalist and novelist Upton Sinclair ran for political office on more than one occasion, without success. His life was devoted to socialist causes, in particular the plight of those living in extreme poverty, as contrasted with the cushy existence of corrupt plutocrats. Sinclair knew what he was writing about. For one thing, he had experienced the wealth gap as exemplified by his parents. (His father was destitute, his mother was loaded.) Crucially, though, Sinclair knew his stuff because he did his research. He is regarded as one of the pioneers of investigative journalism.

The key work in this context was *The Jungle* (1906), a novel designed as an exposé of the dark heart of the American meat industry: the appalling conditions in which animals were kept, and the exploitation of wage slaves. The author worked undercover in the industry for seven years to write it. As a result of the book, in the year of its publication the Meat Inspection Act was passed to improve animal welfare. Even Winston Churchill admitted to being a fan, though he rejected 'Sinclair's conclusion that socialism was the answer to the problems he so convincingly describes'.

Among his countless other books were the non-fiction 1919 book *The Brass Check* (an exposé of corrupt practices in journalism) and the 1927 novel *Oil!*: a diatribe against greed in the oil industry, which was the inspiration for the 2007 film *There Will Be Blood*, starring Daniel Day-Lewis. As a moral conscience, and a tireless campaigner against corruption, the author was exemplary. 'It is difficult to get a man to understand something,' he once brilliantly noted, 'when his salary depends upon his not understanding it.' In person, he may have been harder to take, being keen on fasting for long periods at a stretch and believing that sex was best avoided except for the purpose of procreation. He also had a private interest in telepathy and the occult, which is always a bit suspicious.

Gore Vidal, writer and wit (1925–2012)

USAGE: If you think you're bisexual, consider whether you might actually be a 'pansexual' like Gore Vidal. In other words, do you simply not make a distinction between the sexes?

'You'll get more with Gore.' That was the slogan for Gore Vidal's campaign as a Democratic candidate for Congress in 1960. He did well but he didn't win. Perhaps voters feared they might actually get more: more than they bargained for. For the author, intelligent and articulate as he was, was a controversial figure. For instance, he believed himself a 'pansexual', by which he meant that gender was immaterial to him. And no one could deny he was a show-off. Summing up the two traits perfectly, he once confessed: 'I never miss a chance to have sex or appear on television.'

The flash and crackle of his wit rather distracted from his other achievements. He was, for example, an accomplished novelist, scoring a *succès de scandale* with 1948's *The City and the Pillar*, which shocked readers with its frank description of a homosexual affair. But his best novels, it's generally thought, were historical, most notably the seven-book series known as *Narratives of Empire*. For all his provocative views and lifestyle, the sleekly-groomed, smooth-cheeked author had a moneyed, patrician air, and seemed most at ease as a novelist when writing about the past.

Latterly, Vidal enjoyed a 53-year relationship with a man named Howard, which he insisted was not sexual. 'It's easy to sustain a relationship when sex plays no part,' he said, 'and impossible, I have observed, when it does.' Apart from his novels, he excelled as an essayist, but perhaps his greatest gift was for annoying the hell out of people. He and the author Truman Capote famously feuded. Then on TV he taunted the right-wing pundit William F. Buckley by calling him a 'crypto-Nazi'. To which Buckley retorted by calling him a 'queer' and threatening to 'sock' him 'in the goddamn face'. He didn't go through with it. However, there was one author who, faced with what he saw as Vidal's provocations, was unable to restrain himself.

Fisticuffs

Some writers slept together. Some got married.
Others preferred to punch one another.

Norman Mailer, novelist (1923–2007)

USAGE: Mailer's name can be used to refer to a certain kind of larger-than-life writer-celebrity, particularly of the male-author-as-action-man variety.

The American novelist Norman Mailer was one of the most pugnacious writers in history. So it was no surprise, given Gore Vidal's eminently punchable face, that when Mailer spotted him at a party, he angrily knocked him down. But on that occasion it was Vidal who had the last word. 'Once again,' he drawled from the floor, 'words fail Norman Mailer.'

'For the last 60 years of this man's life, he drank to excess every day. He was married six times. He smoked pot. He stabbed his second wife. I've never read one of his books, but I've gotta tell you, I'm a huge fan!' Thus did the stand-up comedian Ron White sum up the achievement of Mailer. And he made a good point. For truth told, Mailer is more likely to be remembered for who he was – the brawling, boozing, woman-abusing *enfant terrible* of American letters – than for what he actually wrote.

His major contribution to literature was to have had a hand (along with Truman Capote and others) in inventing the genre known as 'creative non-fiction'. This basically means writing a true-life story in an imaginative way, a bit like a novel – and if the truth has to be massaged a little, so be it (name-drop Mailer's 1968 book *The Armies of the Night*). His debut novel, *The Naked and the Dead* (1948), was inspired by his own experience in the Second World War. It was about a US platoon fighting the Japanese on a Pacific island. Published when he was 25, this raw, heart-wrenching book met with general acclaim – the only time, perhaps, that this could be said about anything in Mailer's *oeuvre*. Thereafter, the story was one of gradual decline, as he was increasingly forced to churn out potboilers to meet alimony payments. He did, after all, have eight children by six wives.

Mario Vargas Llosa, novelist (b. 1936)

USAGE: If talk turns to the Latin American literature boom, always cite Vargas Llosa as his name is less familiar than García Márquez's.

Apart from the brawl between Gore Vidal* and Norman Mailer*, the most famous punch-up between authors occurred at a film premiere in 1976. The Peruvian novelist Mario Vargas Llosa punched the Colombian novelist Gabriel García Márquez in the face. Why? The story goes that Gabriel had been advising Mario's wife Patricia on how to cope with her husband's frequent infidelities. 'You must pretend to have an affair with someone he's jealous of,' García Márquez had counselled, before adding: 'There's only one person in the world he's jealous of. Me.'

One-time friends, the pair were also literary rivals, both part of what became known as 'El Boom', when a group of authors from Latin American countries began to enjoy huge international success in the 1960s and 70s. These also included Pablo Neruda* and Jorge Luis Borges*. Apart from the continent of the authors' birth, there's not much to link their works except that (broadly speaking) they were all stylistically experimental, and engaged seriously with contemporary politics.

From the beginning, Vargas Llosa's work was politically inflammatory. The satire of his first novel, *The Time of the Hero* (1963), so enraged certain generals that they ordered it to be burnt. Having started as a socialist, the author was gradually convinced by the merits of capitalism. When he ran for president in 1990, his furious left-wing opponents read out graphic sexual passages from his novels, to persuade voters that he was unfit for government. In the event, Vargas Llosa lost badly. Returning to literature, he published perhaps his greatest work, *The Feast of the Goat*, about the dictatorship of Rafael Trujillo in the Dominican Republic. (One reviewer even declared it would overshadow García Márquez's *One Hundred Years of Solitude* as the great Latin American novel of the 20th century. This remains to be seen, but it's not looking good for *The Feast of the Goat*.) Vargas Llosa also succeeded in irritating the Catholic Church with his open and lifelong atheism, thereby contributing to the long and distinguished tradition of hostility between religion and the arts, which is being continued even now by a man known as 'the Elvis of cultural thought' …

Militant Atheists

Socrates was put to death for being an atheist – which
he probably wasn't. But these guys probably were.

Slavoj Žižek, philosopher (b. 1949)

USAGE: 'Slavoj' is pronounced 'Slavoy'. As for 'Žižek', each Z
is spoken as a soft 'j' sound, as in the word 'beige'. (In other
words, it's SLA-voy JHEE-jhek.) Remember: the trickier the
pronunciation, the more impressive the name-drop.

The Slovenian philosopher Slavoj Žižek doesn't have much
time for Christianity – but then, he's opposed to all ideologies.
He likes to argue that people with religious conviction are in a
sense just as bad as those responsible for the worst excesses of
Stalinism, since they are placing greater value on an ideology
than they are on simple human morality. Before you dismiss
this out of hand as bigoted atheist extremism, consider the
Catholic Church's policy, based on strict dogma, of forbidding
contraception to Africans in the midst of an HIV epidemic.

A man who has been described as 'the Elvis of cultural
thought', Žižek is the epitome of the celebrity academic.
With his dirty hair and black T-shirt, he looks like Russell
Brand's bad-tempered uncle. And like the British comedian,
he seems to have an opinion on every topic (although you're
less likely to have heard of the sources he cites), and it's

usually left-wing. He has argued that society's obsession with conspiracy theories is a sign that people miss the fairy tales (above all the fairy tale of Christianity) that sustained previous generations. Yet he also believes that all laws passed by politicians are designed not to benefit the people, as the politicos claim, but rather to line their own pockets. Communism, according to Žižek, may have failed, but that doesn't mean we shouldn't give it another chance.

Despite not being conventionally handsome, the scintillating, if often rather sweaty Žižek has been married three times, invariably to hotties much younger than he is. When he gets criticised it's usually for a lack of academic rigour and the fact that though he's a gifted critic of just about everything, he's not so convincing when it comes to suggesting alternatives. This may be deliberate. 'I despise the kind of book which tells you how to live, how to make yourself happy!' he has said. 'I believe the first duty of philosophy is making you understand what deep s*** you are in!'

Thomas Hobbes, philosopher (1588–1679)

USAGE: Adjective: 'Hobbesian'. You might encounter reference to the Hobbesian 'state of nature', or the Hobbesian 'social contract', both of which are explained below.

Why do we need a government? Wouldn't we all be happier if everyone was allowed to get on with their lives, without being told what to do? Not according to Thomas Hobbes. Without laws, he argued, humans would quickly return to 'a state of nature'. Our lives would be like those of animals, which Hobbes characterised as 'solitary, poor, nasty, brutish and short'.

The son of a vicar, he was born prematurely, it's said, after his mother heard news of the coming invasion of the Spanish Armada. Hobbes later witnessed the excesses of the English Civil War, which convinced him of the need for an absolute ruler. The title of his best-known book, *Leviathan* (1651), is derived from a Biblical sea-beast, but Hobbes uses it to refer to the 'monster' of the state – misleadingly, since he's arguing in its favour. His arguments, which reject religious justifications in favour of earthbound reasoning in the finest British tradition, form the cornerstone of later political philosophy. Perhaps most important is his notion of a 'social contract': the idea that by living in a society you are agreeing to a *quid pro quo*. You enjoy the security of a police force, a judicial system and so on, but in return you surrender certain liberties, such as the right to do whatever you want.

Hobbes annoyed almost everyone. Some called him an atheist because, even though he seems to have believed in God, he criticised aspects of Church dogma. Although a monarchist, he enraged other monarchists by refusing to say the right of kings to rule was 'divine' (i.e. ordained by God). At one point, he served as tutor to the young Charles II. His former pupil later granted him a pension, but blocked publication of his sequel to *Leviathan* on the grounds that it might be inflammatory.

David Hume, philosopher (1711–76)

USAGE: A relaxed agnostic might claim that his or her attitude regarding the existence of God was one of 'cheerful Humean scepticism'.

The French called him '*le bon David*': a reference to his mild and virtuous character. And David Hume does seem to have been a pretty nice guy.

One trouble with him is that it's hard to remember the names of his masterworks, *A Treatise of Human Nature* and *An Enquiry Concerning Human Understanding*, especially alongside similarly titled volumes by his near-contemporaries (for instance, John Locke's *An Essay Concerning Human Understanding*). Another is that his writings are so wide-ranging that they're hard to summarise. Add to this the fact that many of his insights were in fields of thought that to the layman seem rather obscure: for instance, the question of whether man is born with any innate ideas (Hume thought no) or whether it's possible to have free will in a determinist universe (Hume thought yes). All one really needs to know about him is that he's a biggie.

An empiricist (believing that reasoning should be based on experiment), he didn't say that God didn't exist, only that the arguments for His existence were rubbish. He once claimed the best argument he'd heard for believing in God was when an angry old woman refused to help him out of a bog until he'd admitted that He existed. A sceptical Scot, Hume gave out that when he died he planned to ask Charon (the ferryman across the river of the dead) for a few more years in which to watch men shrug off their superstitions. 'You loitering rogue,' Charon would (Hume anticipated) reply, 'that will not happen these many hundred years. Get into the boat this instant!' Possessed of a wry sense of humour, the philosopher once pointed out the ironical contradiction of the fact that some people complain how grim life is, and also that it's too short. It was an observation that Woody Allen would adapt in his opening monologue in the film *Annie Hall*: 'Life is full of misery, loneliness, and suffering – and it's all over much too soon.'

Loved by Woody

The film-maker Woody Allen is one of the arch intellectual name-droppers of our time. Practically everyone in this book has been name-checked in his films at one time or another. Here are a few prominent examples.

Walt Whitman, poet (1819–92)

USAGE: Disconcert anyone with a big beard by asking them if they're a fan of Walt Whitman at all.

In Woody Allen's excellent romantic comedy *Manhattan*, two pretentious characters sneeringly reel off a list of cultural figures whom they regard as overrated, including Carl Jung*, Norman Mailer* and the poet Walt Whitman. At this point, the horrified Allen leaps to their defence, saying, 'I think those people are all terrific, every one that you mentioned.'

Was Whitman terrific? He sort of was. This was a guy who wrote a novel in favour of the prohibition of alcohol (1842's *Franklin Evans*), then later admitted that he'd written it in just three days while he was blind-drunk. He sported an enormous manly beard, yet he was almost certainly gay. Among those who claimed to have kissed him were the young Oscar Wilde*. Whitman himself denied being that way inclined, but some of the passionate declarations of manly passion for other men in his best-known work, the poetry collection *Leaves of Grass*, suggest otherwise.

And yet that volume is regarded as a work central to America's idea of itself: the critic Harold Bloom said that, along with Mark Twain's *Huckleberry Finn*, it was a definitive expression of the American spirit. About half the book is taken up by the first poem, *Song of Myself*. A universal expression of an individualist philosophy, it begins: 'I celebrate myself, and sing myself, / And what I assume you shall assume, / For every atom belonging to me as good belongs to you ...' It aimed, unlike most poetry, to be read by the ordinary man, and it made Whitman a star. Two other footprints he left in popular culture. When Bram Stoker came to write *Dracula* (1897), he's said to have based his vampire's physical appearance on that of Whitman, whom he knew and admired. And remember the scene in the 1989 film *Dead Poets' Society*, when all the schoolboys stand up and exclaim, 'Oh Captain! My Captain!' They were quoting a Whitman poem.

Ingmar Bergman, film-maker (1918-2007)

USAGE: As an adjective, Bergmanesque tends to be used to describe films that have a bleak, serious, contemplative, Scandinavian mood.

In the list of the great auteur film directors (which is to say, intellectual ones, who write their films as well as directing them) Ingmar Bergman casts a long shadow. His themes are heavy: infidelity, death, religious faith, madness, etc. Yet with many of his 60 films, which include *Wild Strawberries* and *The Seventh Seal*, being hailed as masterpieces, his strike rate is rather better than that of his number one fan, the notoriously erratic Woody Allen.

The Swedish director endured a strict upbringing at the hands of his father, a Lutheran minister who used to lock him in a cupboard as a punishment for wetting the bed. The severity of this experience may help to explain the complete nervous breakdown Bergman suffered when, at the height of his fame, he was accused of tax evasion. While rehearsing a production of August Strindberg's* *The Dance of Death*, he was arrested by two plainclothes policemen. Did the great man fear he was about to be put back in the cupboard? In the event, he was cleared of wrongdoing, but – in scenes reminiscent of one of his own movies – he was plunged into depression, and declared he would never again make a film in Sweden. Instead he moved to Munich, where he sulked for eight years.

Bergman continued to make great movies until the end (e.g. 2003's *Saraband*), often using the same actors, such as Max von Sydow and Bibi Andersson. He had no trouble finding funding, he said, because he favoured projects that were cheap to make, and, secondly, he didn't make films in America, where the industry was obsessed with financial success. He spent his last years in mysterious seclusion at his home on the island of Faro in the midst of the Baltic Sea.

Gustave Flaubert, novelist (1821–80)

USAGE: The adjective 'Flaubertian' usually relates either to a kind of quiet scrupulous prose, or an absolute dedication to literary endeavour.

Gustave Flaubert is a serious candidate for the title of the novelist's novelist. That is to say, he took style incredibly seriously, labouring for years over each book, avoiding cliché and striving for harmony in his sentences. With *Madame Bovary* (1856), he practically invented the realist novel – the kind that tries to create a story as much like real life as possible – and every subsequent writer of the 'quiet style', avoiding flights of fancy in favour of a gentle accumulation of emotional force, owes a debt to the Frenchman.

The tale of a bored provincial wife cheating on her husband, the book was so realistic, its author's submersion in it so complete, that when he came to describe Bovary's suicide by taking poison, he literally threw up. This is the man whom Walter Pater described as 'the martyr of style'. 'Be regular and orderly in your life,' he famously declared, 'so that you may be violent and original in your work.' Bovary took him five years; *Salammbô* (an exotic tale set in the 3rd century BC) four; the autobiographical *A Sentimental Education* seven. They're all pretty good. The last is named by Woody Allen in *Manhattan* as one of the things that makes life worth living.

In his spare time, Flaubert smoked a lot and liked to read his works aloud to see how they sounded. If no friends were to hand, he would read them to the flowers. He travelled when he was young, but then settled and devoted himself to his writing. He never married. When he felt like a bit of slap and tickle he used to wander along to the local brothel: a classic writerly trait shared by one of the great figures of German literature ...

A Penchant for Prostitutes

'Love Isn't Free' runs the title to a
Dolly Parton song. In the case of these
four writers, she had a point.

Johann Wolfgang von Goethe, writer, scientist, statesman (1749–1832)

USAGE: When referring to a Faustian bargain – i.e. a deal in which someone swaps their soul for money, power or success – imply knowledge of one of the classic works of German literature by referring to 'the kind of bargain made by Goethe's Faust'.

When one person commits suicide, others are then more likely to do so. This 'Durkheimian* fact' is sometimes known as 'the Werther effect' in reference to the novel *The Sorrows of Young Werther*. When it was first published in 1774, it transformed its 26-year-old author, Johann Wolfgang von Goethe, into a celebrity. Another, less fortunate result of the book's success was that intense young men across Europe began following the example of its hero, who after being crossed in love, shoots himself in the head.

Scientist, poet, playwright, statesman, the aristocratic Goethe was a passionate fellow who lost his virginity to a prostitute, and at the age of 72 fell in love with a nineteen-year-old. (His friends gently dissuaded him from courting her.) He is regarded as being about as culturally important to the Germans as Shakespeare is to the English. As with Shakespeare's contemporary, Christopher Marlowe, perhaps his most famous work was a play about Dr Faustus, who sells his soul to the Devil in return for knowledge and power. Actually, in Goethe's case, that should be 'plays'. Being German, he couldn't say what he had to say in just one play, but felt forced to stretch the story to two: *Faust Part One* and *Faust Part Two*. *Part One* is thought to be better.

You can't exaggerate the significance of Goethe, but you can try. His poetry was put to music by all the great German-speaking composers, including Ludwig van Beethoven and Gustav Mahler. As well as a statesman serving at the court of the Duke Carl-August of Saxe-Weimar (who gave him the title 'von'), Goethe was a scientist whose theories about colour inspired the Austrian philosopher Ludwig Wittgenstein*. When Ralph Waldo Emerson* wrote his book *Representative Men*, praising the seven greatest men who had ever lived, he included Goethe alongside Plato* and Napoleon.

Charles Baudelaire, poet (1821–67)

USAGE: Declaiming French Romantic poetry is a sure sign that you have a passionate soul. You might follow the example of the character Uncle Monty in the film *Withnail and I*, and favour Baudelaire, exclaiming, 'Laisse-moi respirer longtemps, longtemps, l'odeur de tes cheveux!' (Let me breathe in for a long time, for a long time, the aroma of your hair!)

It was thanks to his frequent visits to prostitutes that the hell-raising French poet Charles Baudelaire caught gonorrhoea and syphilis while still at university. By his mid-twenties, he had squandered a substantial inheritance. He spent the rest of his life moving around from lodging to lodging to escape creditors. And then, at the age of just 42, he succumbed to a mixture of alcoholism and opium abuse.

His collection of poems *Les Fleurs du mal* (The Flowers of Evil) was his masterpiece. The poems lamented the new cleanliness of Paris (the city had just become industrialised in Baudelaire's day). Bring back the prostitutes and the beggars, said Baudelaire. Seek out wine and debauchery. And he insulted the reader, calling him a prig and a 'hypocrite' early on in the book. All these raucous sentiments he rendered in classical, rhyming verse. This didn't stop some of the poems – such as one called, simply, 'Lesbos' – from being banned by the French government.

Officially, Baudelaire was a Romantic – not the kind who sends flowers, but one of a group of artists who reacted against the machine age of the Industrial Revolution by writing about intense emotions. It's just that, whereas most Romantic poets of the day wrote about nature, Baudelaire wrote about sex and opium. For the last few years of his life, things calmed down for him dramatically: he went back home to live with his mother in a seaside town. After his death, his mother said she wished he had been a lawyer instead, observing, 'He would not have left a name in literature, it is true, but we should have been happier.'

Milton Friedman, economist (1912–2006)

USAGE: If the conversation turns to economics and how the government can get us out of the latest financial crisis, paraphrase Friedman: 'It's simple. We just need to drop money out of a helicopter.'

For an economist, Milton Friedman was surprisingly spicy. For starters, although he's not known to have frequented prostitutes himself, he was in favour of legalising the world's oldest profession. This was for the simple reason that he hated the government meddling with anything, even sex workers. For the same reason, he recommended that marijuana should be legalised. Forget conventional morality, was his position. You had to take the decision that would benefit the economy, which would lead to the greatest good for the greatest number of people. Following this line of argument to its extreme, he gave financial advice to Chile during the regime of General Pinochet, effectively abetting a murderer. Friedman explained that his aim was to help the Chilean people, not Pinochet.

Broadly speaking, you can say that economic theory in the first half of the 20th century was dominated by the

English economist J.M. Keynes*; in the second half, the American Friedman was the man. He is now best remembered for his theory of monetarism: the idea that the best way for a government to stimulate an economy was by printing more money. Before him, some had suspected this might be the case, but no one had proved it. Friedman produced reams of data supporting his claims. In his 1998 memoir, *Two Lucky People* (the title refers to himself and his wife Rose), he argued that the Great Depression had been triggered by the Federal Reserve's decision to restrict the availability of currency in the face of what might have been a common-or-garden-scale financial dip. Friedman advised the US president Ronald Reagan, inspired the British PM Margaret Thatcher, and outdid Keynes in one respect at least: he won a Nobel Prize in Economics.

Émile Zola, novelist (1840–1902)

USAGE: If someone tries insisting that your every action can be explained by your genetic code and upbringing, tell them to stop being such a Zola-esque Naturalist.

A man who practised what he preached – or, perhaps, a man who preached what he practised – the French novelist Émile Zola wrote sympathetically about prostitution in his debut novel *La Confession de Claude* (1865), which is about a guy who falls in love with a prostitute. So it's no surprise to learn that Zola's wife Gabrielle had worked as a prostitute when he'd got to know her.

In his day, Zola was criticised for producing *la littérature putride*, which is to say novels that dwelt on the sordid aspects of life. His riposte, perhaps, would have been that he was part of the literary movement known as Naturalism. Although to the uninitiated this might suggest that he fronted nature programmes, it actually meant he wrote novels rich with realistic details, which aimed to show that our lives are dictated by a combination of genetic inheritance and the social forces at work around us. Nevertheless, his books did have more than a whiff of the '*putride*'. In *Thérèse Raquin* (1867), a woman and her lover plot to kill her husband. *La Bête humaine* (whose terrific title means The Human Beast) is about a man wrestling with an irresistible desire to kill women.

As much as for his politically engaged and rigorously researched fiction, Zola is remembered for an article. Titled 'J'Accuse', it took up the front page of the newspaper *L'Aurore* in 1898, and was devoted to the defence of a Jewish soldier named Alfred Dreyfus who had been wrongfully convicted of espionage and imprisoned. The main reason his sentence wasn't overturned was anti-Semitic prejudice, but once Zola weighed in to the controversy, the tide turned. 'The truth is on the march and nothing shall stop it,' Zola declared. Dreyfus was eventually exonerated. Zola died in 1902 of carbon monoxide poisoning. This was, at first, thought an accident, but later a chimney sweep who disagreed with his political views claimed to have deliberately blocked the chimney.

Thomas Malthus, demographer (1766–1834)

USAGE: If you see reference to a 'Malthusian catastrophe', it means one that has been caused by a scarcity of resources.

Thomas Malthus, who should on no account be confused with the artist Balthus*, sounds like some crazed continental, to judge purely by his name (pronounced: MAL-thuhs). But he was, in fact, an Englishman, and rather a hard-headed one. He argued, for instance, that men should sleep with prostitutes – not because it's fun, but because they were then less likely to have children than if they slept with their wives. For Malthus' big idea was that the world's population will inevitably soar until the Earth can no longer support us. Then what? Famine. Disease. Warfare on a massive scale.

These three eventualities, inasmuch as they may serve to limit population growth, may be referred to as 'Malthusian catastrophes'. In his controversial 1798 essay *On the Principle of Population*, he himself called them 'positive checks', by contrast with 'preventive checks' such as birth control. His apocalyptic predictions and chilly recommendations (he suggested, for instance, that child allowances for labourers should be abolished, to discourage population growth) ran counter to the Enlightenment philosophy of the time, which accentuated man's ingenuity and the inevitability of positive progress. His conclusions were also hard to square with the idea of an all-powerful benign God (which, presumably, Malthus believed in. He was, after all, an Anglican priest).

Yet Malthus' contradictions serve to make him a rather endearing figure. If his parents had practised the birth control he advocated, he, as a seventh child, would presumably never have been born. A tall, handsome man, he had a cleft palate which made his speech indistinct. He taught at a university where the students nicknamed him 'Pop' (short for 'Population') Malthus. He had three children, none of whom produced offspring, with the result that the Malthus line died out). His wife was also his first cousin once removed …

Cousin Love

There's a stigma attached, these days, to the idea of marrying your first cousin (although the risks it poses to children are actually far smaller than is popularly supposed). It didn't used to be regarded as a big deal. Charles Darwin and Albert Einstein both married cousins. As did these two characters ...

Theodore Dreiser, novelist (1871–1945)

USAGE: When picking the less expensive of two travel options, you could claim to be adopting the Theodore Dreiser approach.

The American novelist Theodore Dreiser shocked the bourgeoisie by writing books involving amoral characters who didn't always get punished. To judge from his love life, he may have been an example of the type. He had a particular penchant for women twenty years his junior, one example being the teenage daughter of a colleague on a magazine he worked for, another an artist he lived with in New York after the end of his first marriage. A third was his second cousin Helen, who became his second wife. None of this prevented Dreiser leading an apparently charmed life. In 1912, he very nearly boarded the *Titanic*. But at the last moment, he decided to save money by switching to a cheaper berth on another boat, thereby eluding a watery grave.

Born in Indiana, the son of a German immigrant, Dreiser is best remembered for two novels, both made into big-budget Hollywood movies. The first, *Sister Carrie* (1900; filmed in 1952), told the story of a country girl who moves to the city and becomes the mistress of a businessman. When he loses his money, she leaves him and becomes a movie star. In the other, *An American Tragedy* (1925; filmed as *A Place in the Sun* in 1951), a young man from a humble background murders his pregnant girlfriend to free himself up for a relationship with a sexy heiress. In its depiction of an ambitious character who will do anything to get what he wants, the book seemed to express a dark truth at the heart of the American dream.

Nowadays, Dreiser isn't much read and it's fashionable to sneer at his clunky prose style. One literary critic complained that his books consisted of 'endless business deals with a seduction every hundred pages as light relief'. Another, F.R. Leavis*, declared scathingly that Dreiser wrote so badly it was as if English wasn't his first language.

André Gide, novelist (1869–1951)

USAGE: In any discussion of homosexuality, you should be familiar with Gide's argument that same-sex relationships have especially flourished in periods of high artistic and philosophical achievement.

André Gide had a reason for not marrying his wife Madeleine beyond the fact that she was his first cousin. It was that he knew by then he was more interested in young men. His travels in North Africa had clarified that one. Nevertheless

he tied the knot, and though the union was never consummated, the couple stayed together for twenty years. Then Gide
ran off with Marc Allegret, the fifteen-year-old son of the
man who had served as best man at his wedding. Madeleine
was so upset (with some justification, it must be said) that
she burned every letter he had ever written her. Gide and
Marc stayed together for a decade, though there was a *froi-
deur* after Gide sired a daughter as a result of a heterosexual
dalliance. Then Marc had the reverse of Gide's African experience. In 1927, he travelled to the Congo and fancied the
women so much that he realised he was heterosexual after
all. Nevertheless he and Gide remained friends.

And the books? Gide believed in working out what was
stopping you becoming the fullest version of yourself, then
battling it into submission. In *The Immoralist* (1902) an
austere intellectual discovers that the key to his happiness
is romping with small boys in North Africa. In *Strait is the
Gate* (1909) a woman in church hears a voice advising her
to reject her lover and devote herself to God. Needless to
say, this leads to misery all round. Gide himself held that his
greatest achievement was 1924's *Corydon*, four Platonic-style
dialogues discussing homosexuality. He uses them to argue
that homosexuality isn't unnatural: indeed, it has particularly
flourished in times of the highest achievements in the arts,
e.g. in Ancient Greece, Renaissance Italy and Elizabethan
England. In fact, exclusive heterosexuality is more artificial.

Gide received the Nobel Prize in Literature in 1947. A
few years after his death, the Vatican placed his *oeuvre* on its

Index of Forbidden Books: a prohibition that placed him in distinguished company with one of his fellow countrymen from four centuries earlier …

The Vatican Says No

*From time to time, the Catholic Church
feels moved to express its disapproval.*

François Rabelais, writer (1494–1553)

USAGE: The adjective 'Rabelaisian' is often used to describe a
likeable, larger-than-life character with an appetite for sensual
pleasures (especially food, booze and sex) and scant regard for
morality.

The novel (defined as a long story written in prose about
made-up characters) didn't always exist. It had to be invented.
And in its early days, it was often disreputable, involving
an unscrupulous character getting into scrapes. A classic
early example was the novel series known as *Gargantua and
Pantagruel*, which was considered so shocking in its day it
was banned by the Catholic Church. The author must have
anticipated scandal. He began publishing under the pseudonym Alcofribas Nasier, a peculiar anagram of his real name,
which was François Rabelais.

He was a man of many parts. Polymath. Doctor. Monk.
And the books were as shifting and various as the man who
wrote them. The first two centre on the activities of two giants
named Gargantua and Pantagruel who have enormous appetites for eating, drinking and general roister-doistering. The

others focus on a quest undertaken by several characters in search of something they refer to as the Divine Bottle. Rabelais was a genuinely funny guy. There's a story that his last will and testament consisted of one line: 'I have nothing, I owe a great deal, and the rest I leave to the poor.'

His style of writing is heavy with fantasy, jokes, puns and filthy *double entendres*. The motto of his main characters, which they repeat throughout the books, is 'Do what thou wilt', which is a maxim the author also observed in his writing. All rather surprising, you might say, from a man of the cloth. But there was something infectious about Rabelais' attitude to life, something incorrigible and, finally, honest. On his death-bed, the churchman made no assumptions. His last words were, '*Je m'en vais chercher un grand peut-être.*' 'I go to seek a great perhaps ...'

Federico Fellini, film director (1920–93)

USAGE: The word 'Fellini-esque' may be used to describe scenes of decadent partying. If there's a homoerotic element involved, you might say, 'It's like something out of Fellini's *Satyricon*.'

It was the flashes of nudity in Federico Fellini's classic movie *La Dolce Vita* (1960) that the Vatican objected to. The complaints were so shrill that the public flocked to the cinema to see what all the fuss was about. As a result, the film went on to break box office records in its native Italy, and the director, who until then had struggled to make ends meet, found himself a rich man.

Qualities that might qualify as Fellini-esque are exuberance, surreality, and a kind of despairing hedonism. His films are all terribly Italian, in other words. In the last years of the Second World War, when life was pretty grim, Fellini started out drawing caricatures of the American GIs with whom Rome was then swarming. His skill earned him a reputation and a few film-makers began popping into his shop, Funny Face. He got chatting to them and was soon trying his hand at writing screenplays. From there he made the transition to directing (key name drops: 1954's *La Strada* and 1957's *Nights of Cabiria*). Fellini's style, which found ultimate expression in *La Dolce Vita*, was welcomed as a trumpet blast of creativity: proof that the post-war hangover was finally over.

That film portrays a week in the life of a romantically inclined but spiritually aimless gossip magazine journalist played by the suave Marcello Mastroianni, who is chasing an American film star (the busty Anita Ekberg) around Rome. The best-known scene involved Ekberg splashing around in the Trevi Fountain. A couple of bits of trivia relating to the movie. The first is that the fountain scene was filmed in the middle of winter and the actress had to be warmed up with vodka shots before she could be persuaded to climb into the freezing water. The second is that we get our modern word paparazzi from *La Dolce Vita*. A minor character in the movie, a gossip-chasing press photographer, is named Paparazzo.

Charles Maurice de Talleyrand,
politician (1754–1838)

USAGE: The name Talleyrand has become a byword for amoral manoeuvring and skilful diplomatic shiftiness. To describe a dodgy but effective politician: 'He has a whiff of Talleyrand about him.'

The French statesman Charles Maurice de Talleyrand (pronounced: tal-ay-RON, though the n is almost silent) first embarked on a career in the Catholic Church and rose to become Bishop of Autun. However, when the French Revolution toppled the monarchy and proclaimed a godless state, he came out of the ecclesiastical closet and revealed he wasn't religious after all. The Pope excommunicated him. Talleyrand made the most of his new circumstances – as he would throughout his life – and married his mistress, the beautiful courtesan Catherine Grand. Devoting himself to diplomacy, he rose to be France's Foreign Minister.

For much of the career that followed, he served the interests of Napoleon – or at least, he made sure that that was what he seemed to be doing, while in reality he was lining his own pockets. Eventually when Napoleon discovered that Talleyrand had been secretly discussing the thorny question of who should ultimately succeed him as Emperor, he lost his temper and brilliantly told him that he was nothing more than 'a turd in a silk stocking'. Talleyrand (never one to take an unnecessary risk) waited until he'd left, then remarked, 'Pity such a great man was so badly brought up!'

After Napoleon's defeat, Talleyrand had a hand in the redivision of Europe that followed, and ceded too much land to Prussia, allowing for the rise of a powerful, militarily inclined Germany. Some even say it was he who sowed the seeds for the Second World War. In his private life, he was a witty conversationalist, an energetic womaniser, and a lifelong gourmet. It's said he spent an hour each day locked in discussion with his chef, Carème. He also suffered from a bizarre fear that he would kill himself by falling out of bed in the night. Accordingly he had a mattress designed with a dip in the middle, and wore fourteen nightcaps at a time, to protect his head in the event of a tumble.

Nicolaus Copernicus, astronomer (1473–1543)

USAGE: The phrase 'Copernican revolution' is used to describe a new theory that turns all previous thinking on its head.

The 'Copernican revolution' sounds like some little-known uprising. But here the word 'revolution' is used to refer not to bloody civil unrest, but rather to the circular motion of the planets. The Polish astronomer Nicolaus Copernicus was the first to work out a detailed theory of 'heliocentrism': the idea that the Sun, not the Earth, is at the centre of the universe. The 'revolution' he wrote about was the Earth 'revolving' around the Sun, as opposed to vice versa.

As well as a star-gazer, Copernicus was a doctor, economist, poet and administrator in the chilly northern European province of Warmia. He was understandably fearful that his heliocentrism would be seen as heretical by the Catholic Church, since it contradicted the Bible's 'geocentric' view of the Earth as the universe's centre. He delayed publishing *On the Revolution of the Heavenly Spheres* until 1543, when he was dying. The story goes that he revived from a stroke-induced coma, had a finished copy of the book placed in his hands, and died with a smile on his face.

After Copernicus' remains were unearthed beneath Frombork Cathedral in 2005, a plaque was installed identifying him as not only the founder of heliocentrism but also a church canon (a minor ecclesiastical official). It was an apology of sorts from a Church that had (as he had feared it would) denounced his works. Even the scientific community took decades to accept them: many felt that, in contradicting common sense, Copernicus was trying to be clever. For one thing, if he was right and the Earth really was travelling through space, why didn't an apple instantly disappear if you threw it in the air? Why did the apple simply fall to the ground? These questions had to wait another century before they would be answered by the English scientist Isaac Newton*. The latter also shared with Copernicus a fascination with the arcane study of alchemy – as too did Sweden's most famous playwright, who once asked a doctor to accompany him to a brothel and measure his penis ...

Alchemists

*Alchemy – the attempt to transform cheap
metals into gold – provides a handy metaphor
for all creative endeavour. For centuries many
believed it might literally be possible.*

August Strindberg, playwright (1849–1912)

USAGE: To drop the name of Strindberg into conversation,
a man could borrow a one-liner from Woody Allen: 'When
it comes to relationships with women, I'm the winner of the
August Strindberg award.'

In the film *Manhattan*, Woody Allen uses the line above to
allude to Strindberg's famously problematic relations with
women. But is Woody referring to the plot of the Swedish
playwright's *Miss Julie*, which after a lot of bickering ends
with the eponymous heroine's suicide, or did he have in
mind the horrifically brutal love affairs and break-ups that
Strindberg endured in his private life? It doesn't much matter,
as the point remains the same.

'Half-apes … mad … instinctively evil animals.' That was
how Strindberg described women in a characteristic rant. And
yet he is regarded as a feminist author. Let's just say that he had
his off days. Along with Henrik Ibsen* (who hated him) and
Anton Chekhov*, Strindberg is said to be one of the inventors

of the modern play: dramas, that is, in which people speak more or less as people really do speak, and which tackle significant contemporary themes such as the liberation of women.

In person he was extremely eccentric. For one thing, he was an obsessive alchemist. Then there was the time when, in a fit of insecurity brought on by a lover's taunt, he forced the local doctor to accompany him to a brothel. First he made the poor man measure his penis (a decent length, the doctor reassured); then he had sex with a prostitute and asked her to rate his performance. She told him it had been 'adequate'. It should also be noted that Strindberg had one of the silliest hairstyles in the history of literature, one that resembled a Mr Whippy ice cream. Despite these facts, he is revered in his native Sweden, as much for his novels as his plays, though he is mainly known for the latter in English-speaking countries.

Isaac Newton, scientist (1642–1726)

USAGE: The phrase 'Newtonian physics' refers to Newton's theories regarding the physical world, and how it acts according to a set number of simple universal laws.

Sir Isaac Newton died a virgin. At least, that's what Voltaire* said, after speaking to the doctor who had attended Newton on his death-bed. Despite being viewed as the father of modern science, Newton nurtured crazy secret passions such as alchemy and trying to work out the exact chronology of the Bible (he calculated that the world would end in 2060). In later life, working as Master of the Royal Mint, he used to disguise himself and hang out in taverns in the hope of catching counterfeiters. Sometimes he succeeded and the criminals were executed.

This, of course, is tittle-tattle beside Newton's titanic achievements in the field of science. As well as discovering gravity and inventing calculus (while Leibniz* was doing the same independently), he constructed the first practical (meaning small) reflective telescope, made huge contributions in the field of optics (explaining how white light is composed of all the colours of the spectrum), and in his book *Philosophiae Naturalis Principia Mathematica* (1687) laid down the basic laws of physics that govern the universe. These were accepted as gospel by later scientists until the corrective theories of Albert Einstein two centuries later.

'I do not know what I may appear to the world,' Newton once remarked, 'but to myself I seem to have been only like a boy playing on the sea-shore, and diverting myself in now and then finding a smoother pebble or a prettier shell than ordinary, whilst the great ocean of truth lay all undiscovered before me.' The world thought different. He is regarded by many as the greatest scientist who ever lived. This isn't to say he was perfect. In 1693 he suffered a nervous breakdown, during which he directed wild accusations against his friends. For example, he bizarrely claimed that the infinitely benign philosopher John Locke had 'endeavoured to embroil me with women'. As delusions go, this was pretty nuts. Though it would be outdone by a Scottish novelist who became convinced that T.S. Eliot was sending her coded messages in his verse …

I Can't Take it Anymore

*If you ever suffer a nervous breakdown (it's not
impossible), you can take comfort from the thought
that it has happened to many great cultural
figures of the past. Newton. Nietzsche. Bergman.
And here are a couple more examples ...*

Muriel Spark, writer (1918—2006)

USAGE: If you're ever accused of excessive levity, you could
raise Spark's point that people should have laughed at Hitler and
Mussolini, instead of taking them so seriously.

In 1954, while working on a book about T.S. Eliot*, the novelist Muriel Spark suffered a mental collapse. She became
convinced the poet was sending her messages encoded in his
verse. The delusions were at least partly caused by her use of
the slimming drug Dexedrine, instead of eating proper meals.
But they were also a product of an angst-ridden phase of her
life, which ended in her conversion to Roman Catholicism.
With this new spiritual support, Spark recovered well and in
1961 she published the novel for which she is best remembered, *The Prime of Miss Jean Brodie*.

It is the tale of an inspirational if controversial teacher
(haven't we all had one of those?) at a girls' school in Scotland,
who famously declares: 'Give me a girl at an impressionable

age, and she is mine for life.' The irony is that Miss Jean Brodie isn't really in her prime any more, though she keeps saying that she is, and that the story revolves around one girl who isn't 'hers', or not entirely, for she betrays her. (It was brilliantly filmed in 1969 with Maggie Smith in the lead role.) Spark's books – other examples are *Memento Mori* (1959) and *The Driver's Seat* (1971) – are notable for their wit and the caustic way in which the author skewers her characters' failings. Some critics said the style was lacking in empathy, to which Spark replied that satire was sometimes preferable: 'The masses should have laughed at Hitler and Mussolini, not been moved by them.' Others have argued that the books are too controlled, as if there were a touch of OCD in the author's make-up. In this vein, she insisted that any translators of her novels should be male.

This was particularly surprising given her history with men. Her husband Sidney turned out to be manic depressive. A lover, Derek, sold her letters when she became famous and wrote an inaccurate book about her. In her latter years, Spark lived in Tuscany with the sculptor Penelope Jardine.

More on 'I Can't Take it Anymore' overleaf

Carl Jung, psychologist (1875–1961)

USAGE: A Jungian approach to psychology is one that
emphasises the importance of the unconscious without seeking
to tame or explain it into submission.

On the shores of Lake Zurich stands a house known as the
Bollingen Tower. It was designed and largely built by the
founder of analytical psychology, Carl Gustav Jung (pronounced: YOONG), who used it as a retreat from the cares
of his professional life. Its style tells us something about its
maker. A simple place – there was no running water or electricity – it fitted with his ideas about the primitive nature
of the human unconscious, which he believed was to be
explored and celebrated, not deciphered and dominated, as
his one-time mentor Sigmund Freud* tended to argue.

Jung's ideas are often defined by contrast with those of
the older man. For instance, he believed that Freud over-
stated the significance of sexuality in the development of the
human psyche. This disagreement caused a rift between the
two, which was so traumatic that Jung suffered a nervous
breakdown. It was torment at the time, but he later claimed
this period of angst had given him special insight into the
workings of the unconscious.

Psychologists have tended to view religion as an emotional crutch. But for Jung, arguments about whether or
not God exists are missing the point. The point is that the
'archetype' of an omnipotent creator has an undeniable reality
in the human unconscious. In 1959, Jung was asked in an
interview if he believed in God. 'I don't believe,' he replied,

'I know.' 'Archetype' was one of several terms coined by Jung. He used it to refer to certain set figures and ideas – such as the trickster, the flood, and God – that occur in human psyches across different ages and cultures. Taken together, the archetypes form what Jung called 'the collective unconscious'. He also invented the terms 'introverted' and 'extroverted' …

Coining Phrases

*In addition to their other achievements, the
following all either invented – or inspired
the invention of – useful phrases.*

Denis Diderot, philosopher (1713–84)

USAGE: Whenever you use the phrase '*l'esprit d'escalier*', you
might add, 'an expression that, as you know, was invented by
Denis Diderot.'

You know that frustrating experience when you think up a
brilliant thing to say, but by then it's too late? There's a phrase
for this. It's known as '*l'esprit d'escalier*' (which translates as
'staircase wit') and it was invented by the French philosopher
Denis Diderot (pronounced: DEE-de-roe). The story goes
that, after being insulted at a dinner party, Diderot left the
room in a huff. He began to descend the stairs and by the
time he reached the bottom had thought of the perfect put-
down. But he realised that if he ran back upstairs and burst
into the room to deliver it, he would risk looking ridiculous.

Diderot was a leading figure in the Enlightenment – an
era in which the dangerous idea arose that people should
think for themselves instead of blindly trusting traditional
sources of authority such as the Catholic Church. To assist
them in this project, Diderot produced the work for which

he is now remembered, his *Encyclopaedia*. Crucially, he didn't write it all himself, but sought entries from many contributors, which he edited: the result was a more comprehensive book than previous encyclopaedias, which had been limited to the knowledge of a single author. This was revolutionary in itself, as were some of the entries in the work. For instance, the suggestion that the main concern of governments should be the welfare of citizens outraged the authorities of the time.

Surprisingly, for a man associated with such an optimistic project, Diderot himself was a pessimist. He believed human beings lacked free will and that our characters and behaviours were completely determined by our genetic inheritance (cf. the beliefs of Baruch Spinoza*). In essence, he was a progressive thinker who didn't believe in the possibility of progress. It goes without saying that he was vehemently anti-religious. His antipathy towards the Church was exacerbated when his sister, a nun, died young as a result of being overworked by her mother superior.

Edith Wharton, novelist (1862–1937)

USAGE: If someone seems about to deny themselves personal happiness for fear of what society might think, you might press a copy of *The Age of Innocence* into their hands.

The American novelist Edith Wharton was born Edith Jones, and as a young woman she was known affectionately as 'Pussy' Jones. Her father's family was so well-off that it's thought they inspired the phrase 'keeping up with the Joneses', since that was what their neighbours were always striving to do. It was hard to keep up with young Edith when she was a little girl, since her parents took her all over Europe. She was constantly on the move between the ages of four and ten. Her mother was by all accounts a cold fish. She forbade her daughter to read a novel until she was grown-up and married off, let alone to write one. When she was 23, Edith married a man named Edward Wharton, who was twelve years her senior. He turned out to suffer from chronic depression, yet despite being miserable in the marriage, she stayed with him for 28 years before finally filing for divorce. A brave move: divorce wasn't a walk in the park in those days.

So it's no surprise that thwarted love was the preoccupation of her fiction. Her best-known novel, *The Age of Innocence*, is about a man in New York society named Newland Archer who's about to marry a pretty wife when he falls in love with someone else. He 'does the decent thing' and goes ahead with the marriage, then pines for the rest of his life. The book's more fun than that makes it sound, elegantly written, acerbically critical of conventional society, and, in the end, heartbreaking. It won her a Pulitzer in 1921, making her the first woman to achieve that accolade. Wharton's 1905 novel *The House of Mirth* explores related themes, but is deeply depressing. Her 1911 novella *Ethan Frome* – another thwarted love narrative – is pretty downbeat too.

Stendhal, novelist (1783–1842)

USAGE: If you're ever caught escaping from an opera or a particularly long play before the end, you can claim to have been overwhelmed by 'Stendhal syndrome'.

The 19th-century French novelist Stendhal once predicted gloomily that his books wouldn't be appreciated until 1935. He was about right, as it turned out. For although he wasn't really lionised in his lifetime, since then he has come to be recognised as one of the early masters of the realist novel.

His masterpiece, *The Red and the Black* (1830), tells the story of an unscrupulous young man who rises from modest beginnings to achieve some degree of social success, before falling for someone and messing it all up. It is particularly admired for the depth and detail of its psychological insights. Indeed, these are held to be Stendhal's forte as a writer. The philosopher Friedrich Nietzsche* once referred to him as 'France's last great psychologist', and elsewhere declared that among novelists only Fyodor Dostoyevsky* was more impressive in that respect.

Apart from his novels, the author who wrote under the pseudonym of Stendhal (his real name was Marie-Henri Beyle) is now remembered for his analyses of two psychological syndromes. The first of these was love. In Stendhal's 1822 essay, *On Love*, he described the process by which, in his opinion, the emotion of love is 'crystallised'. There are four stages: first, admiration (when you notice and admire the qualities of the beloved); then, acknowledgement (when the beloved notices you have noticed, and you notice them noticing); then hope (when you entertain the hope that your passion will be returned); and then delight (when you take pleasure in magnifying the qualities of the beloved out of all proportion).

The other syndrome he identified (rather a more specific one, this) is now referred to as Stendhal syndrome. This denotes heart palpitations and a feeling of weakness or dizziness which can come over people in the presence of magnificent works of art. Stendhal first noticed it while he was walking around the churches of Florence. Others will have had a similar feeling in art galleries or at the opera, or possibly while reading this book.

J.K. Galbraith, economist (1908–2006)

USAGE: Discussing the 2008 financial crisis, you might mention that J.K. Galbraith believed such economic bubbles were an inevitable consequence of a capitalist economy.

The economist J.K. Galbraith is credited with having invented the phrase 'conventional wisdom', which is generally used with the negative implication that such wisdom is mistaken. And this was what Galbraith himself believed when it came to US economic policy. American economists had tended to favour a hands-off approach to market forces, but in his classic 1955 work *The Great Crash, 1929*, Galbraith argued that, far from being an isolated catastrophe, that crisis was actually one in a cycle of depressions that were an unavoidable downside of a free-market system.

According to Galbraith, reasons for this inevitability included the sheep-like psychology of the people, and general amnesia when it came to financial matters. (His theories seemed rather to be borne out just after his death by the crisis of 2007/08.) His critics accused him of being loftily patrician. Galbraith couldn't help the lofty bit. He was 6ft 8in. But it must have been galling to his academic colleagues that he had the ear of presidents, while they toiled away unheeded. He occupied several government roles, with notable success. For example, after the Second World War, he was tasked with controlling the inflation that was plaguing the US economy as a consequence of the cost of fighting Hitler. Heavily in debt, the government couldn't afford to raise interest rates. But with rates so low, the man in the street was tempted to borrow money and spend it. Which in turn drove up prices. Galbraith successfully combatted this vicious circle, mainly by persuading the government to freeze the price of bread and other essential goods.

It was a no-brainer, he claimed. He always liked to argue that economic matters were a lot simpler than most economists liked to pretend – which is one reason why his books, such as 1958's *The Affluent Society*, were so popular with the public. In the latter, he argued that a newly wealthy America had to devise new economic policies to avoid worse financial bubbles than ever before. Among the occupants of the White House who were impressed was JFK, who regularly consulted Galbraith on policy, and appointed him as his ambassador to India …

JFK

One of these fascinated John.
The other fascinated Jackie.

Philip Roth, novelist (b. 1933)

USAGE: If someone's offering a little too much information about their sex life, you might remark, 'Hey, take it easy. This isn't a Philip Roth novel.'

The year after John F. Kennedy's assassination, his widow Jackie dated the American novelist Philip Roth. By his account, she was startlingly confident. 'Would you like to come up?' she asked him, pausing a moment before adding: 'Of course you would.' Roth also mentioned, not entirely gallantly, that because she was so famous, kissing Jackie Kennedy was like 'kissing a face on a billboard'.

Being explicit about sexual matters was what brought the author to widespread attention with the publication of his 1969 novel *Portnoy's Complaint*. The main character spends that book 'complaining' to his psychoanalyst about the trouble his obsessive sex drive has been getting him into. On one occasion, for example, he was overwhelmed by the desire to masturbate using a piece of raw liver (which was then served by his mother for supper). As another author put it, 'I'd like to meet Roth, but not to shake hands with him.' (Or, we might add, to have dinner with him.)

His ex-wife, the actress Claire Bloom, has said he has a 'deep and irrepressible rage' towards women. But there's no denying the Jewish American novelist can be pretty funny. 'There is no punishment,' he once observed, 'too extreme for the crazy bastard who came up with the idea of fidelity.' His best books are also incredibly articulate, profoundly wise, and highly attuned to the times in which they're written. Whereas most novelists peak early, Roth has kept getting better. Other highlights of his literary career include *Sabbath's Theater* (1995) about the sexual exploits of 64-year-old Mickey Sabbath, and the ironically-titled *American Pastoral* (1997), which depicts a perfect American couple who raise a girl who turns out to be a bomber. Now in his eighties, he doubts whether many will read novels in the future. 'Maybe more people than now read Latin poetry,' he has suggested, 'but somewhere in that range.'

André Malraux, novelist and politician (1901–76)

USAGE: When visiting Paris, choose your moment, and then remark wistfully, 'Yes, isn't it beautiful. All thanks to the novelist André Malraux, of course.'

According to JFK, the French author André Malraux was the most fascinating man he'd ever met – and presumably he'd met a few. The American president was impressed, one might imagine, by the sheer breadth of Malraux's interests and experiences. At the age of 32, he was awarded the prestigious Prix Goncourt for *La Condition humaine*. This searing novel, which in English labours under the less musical-sounding title *Man's Fate*, describes the sufferings of the fledgling Chinese Communist Party, some of whose members were burnt alive in the furnace of a steam train (this was at a time when the few communists were being suppressed by the authorities).

Malraux was writing about the Far East when that was a novelty in itself. But he did more than write about things. He also fought against the Fascists in the Spanish Civil War, and after France was invaded by the Nazis, did sterling service for the Resistance. Or did he? The English historian Antony Beevor has argued that Malraux was a self-aggrandising 'mythomaniac' (a fine, cultured-sounding word for a compulsive liar). It's amusing, in the light of this claim, that after the war the French president Charles de Gaulle made Malraux his Minister of Information.

He went on to serve, from 1959 to 1969, as Minister of Cultural Affairs. It was Malraux who devoted public money to cleaning the blackened façades of Paris's city centre, restoring them to the bright condition in which you see them today. As well as other novels, he also wrote respected works about art and art history. The man achieved all this, it should be noted, in the shadow of horrific personal tragedy. His wife died in her thirties after a fall while boarding a train. And his two sons were both killed in their twenties, side by side, in a car crash ...

Car Wrecks

Ballard found an eroticism in car accidents.
The last years of Pollock's life were one waiting
to happen. Camus' seemed a fittingly absurd
end for the philosopher of absurdism.

J.G. Ballard, novelist (1930–2009)

USAGE: The adjective 'Ballardian' is used to describe bleak post-industrial landscapes, echoing warehouses, and outmoded technology. It usually implies a kind of value, perhaps even of beauty, in these apparently off-putting ideas.

J.G. Ballard's most famous novel is called *Crash*. It features a main character who, after a horrific car accident, discovers a group of people who are sexually turned on by car accidents. He tries to introduce this form of kinkiness into his moribund sex life with his wife. Sadly, it doesn't work out. By an odd twist of fate, the author was involved in a near-fatal car accident shortly after the book's publication, although history doesn't relate if he found it a turn-on.

Paranoia and near-deserted airports. Boredom and empty concrete swimming pools. And yes, perverse eroticism and near-fatal car accidents. These are the kinds of moods and props that most literature tends to avoid, preferring to focus on the conventionally beautiful things of life. Not Ballard.

The British author's novels, which critics politely refer to as 'dystopian', were so disturbed and disturbing that one publisher said of him: 'This author is beyond psychiatric help.' It's likely his dark preoccupations – he was particularly interested in how quickly supposedly modern technologies fall into disuse – were influenced by his grim experiences growing up in China during the Second World War: a period he wrote about in the (for him) conventional novel *Empire of the Sun*, which was later made into an acclaimed film by Steven Spielberg. He also suffered the trauma of his wife's sudden death from pneumonia when their three children were very young.

Ballard's bleakly humorous, cheerfully pessimistic science-fiction stories have influenced fellow novelists such as Will Self and Martin Amis, as well as inspiring the 1970s pop song 'Video Killed the Radio Star'.

Jackson Pollock, artist (1912–56)

USAGE: If you wanted to praise a piece of discordant, experimental music, you could say, 'I like it! There's a kind of beauty amid the chaos, like in a drip painting by Jackson Pollock.'

The Ernest Hemingway of art, the American painter Jackson Pollock lived hard, loved hard, and drank hard. Sometimes he did a painting. Latterly, he seemed split between self-adoration and doubt. His mistress Ruth Kligman recalled how once, at breakfast, Pollock declared that the only great modern artists were Pablo Picasso*, Henri Matisse and himself. At other times, he was tortured by the fear that he was 'a phony'.

The world was similarly split. Some claimed that anyone could pull off a 'drip painting' of the kind for which he became notorious. Pollock, who was filmed at work, laid the canvas down flat on the floor and moved over it with pots of paint, dripping, drooling and squirling lines and blotches of pigment around, using sticks instead of brushes, until he built up what looked like a huge cat's cradle of a picture. Somehow, it worked. There's a rightness to the overall visual impact of his paintings, a kind of harmony amid the chaos. Sadly, the artist wasn't able to find a similar peace in his private life. Reacting against an attitude in America that artists were effete, he proved his manliness by going on drinking binges and making outlandish, attention-grabbing statements.

When a critic observed that the weakness of his painting was that he didn't work from nature, Pollock replied: 'I am nature.' Now hailed as one of the pioneers of Abstract Expressionism, alongside the likes of Mark Rothko and Willem de Kooning, Pollock fetches millions at auction. As often, the extreme narrative of his life adds to the attractions of his works. The artist died in a car crash, blind drunk, at the age of 44.

More on 'Car Wrecks' overleaf

Albert Camus,
novelist and philosopher (1913—60)

USAGE: If anyone ever describes anything as 'absurd', you may ask: 'Do you mean that in the Camusian sense?'

In the admirably short novel *The Stranger* (1941) by Albert Camus (pronounced: CAM-oo), the main character kills an Arab for no reason (a moment immortalised in the Cure song, 'Killing an Arab'). The author had a knack for finding images that expressed what he saw as life's 'absurdity', which consists in the combination of facts that life has no meaning, but humans can't help forever desiring and looking for meaning. He explored this idea in detail in his long essay *The Myth of Sisyphus*, which presents as a metaphor for the human condition the figure of Sisyphus from Greek mythology, condemned eternally to push a boulder up a hill, only to watch it roll back down again. Life, according to Camus, is as pointless as that. So should we all commit suicide? Camus said no. At least Sisyphus had an occupation.

Unlike many philosophers, Camus wrote with grace and clarity. In 1957 he was awarded the Nobel Prize in Literature, becoming the second youngest recipient of that award, after Kipling. He died in a car crash at the age of 46. Thus Camus is remembered as, so to speak, the James Dean of philosophy, the intellectual rock star preserved always in his prime. For a Frenchman, he was unusually cool. He was handsome, highly articulate, and, despite being an intellectual who smoked cigarettes in Parisian cafés with dodgy characters such as Jean-Paul Sartre*, notably moral. He also claimed a certain kudos from having been goalkeeper for his university football team. It was a sporting feat equalled by another existentialist author, who played cricket (he was a bowler rather than a batsman) for Dublin University …

Athletes

*It's a rare feat for an egghead to be a
sportsman. But these two managed it.*

Samuel Beckett, playwright, novelist, poet (1906–89)

> **USAGE:** For maximum impressiveness, always refer to Beckett's
> most famous play by its original French title, *En attendant
> Godot.*

Samuel Beckett is the only winner of the Nobel Prize in
Literature to have an entry in *Wisden Cricketers' Almanack*.
He played a couple of games for Dublin University against
Northamptonshire as a left-arm medium-pace bowler,
although he failed to take a wicket. Fittingly, perhaps. For in
his plays, Beckett is the poet of failure, of bleak playfulness,
and of things that just don't happen.

In *Waiting for Godot*, which was first staged in 1953,
two characters named Vladimir and Estragon wait for a
character named Godot (the clue's in the title) who never
actually appears. Symbolic or what? Or rather, symbolic of
what? That's the question and the answer's up to us. Beckett,
who was born in Dublin but lived in Paris, was a master of
minimalism. Saying less. Short sentences. Like. This. He was
reacting against the extraordinary writing style of his friend
James Joyce, who he felt had taken linguistic richness as far

as it would go. Accordingly, Beckett wrote in French, which wasn't his first language, so he wouldn't waste time with a flowery style. (He did, however, translate most of his poems, novels and plays into English himself.)

To those who dislike them, Beckett's works are insufferably pretentious. To his fans, he dispenses with the mundanities of realism and has the courage to focus on the meaninglessness of existence and finality of death. His severity – which seems reflected in his pin-thin, hawk-like features – is lightened by his wry, spry sense of humour. (In his will he asked that his gravestone in Paris should be 'any colour, as long as it's grey'.) His plays are sometimes said to belong to the 'Theatre of the Absurd' – though less in reference to his wit than to the theories of another sportingly gifted author, one Albert Camus*.

Alan Turing, mathematician, computer scientist
(1912–54)

USAGE: If someone seems to be talking absolute gibberish, you could say: 'I'd need to be Alan Turing to decipher any meaning in what you just said.'

Working at Bletchley Park in Buckinghamshire during the Second World War, Alan Turing helped to crack the Nazi military codes, enabling the Allies to pre-empt the movements of the enemy's forces. As anyone knows who has seen Benedict Cumberbatch's performance in *The Imitation Game*, he also had a few problems relating to other people emotionally. His mathematical insights were too complex to be understood by non-specialists. Suffice to say that he was a maverick who pursued questions his colleagues thought were unanswerable, and that, for his later contributions at Manchester University towards developing the first computer, he is sometimes referred to as 'the father of computer science'. No one person can quite be said to have invented the computer, but Turing's name would arguably top the list.

The man's intellectual brilliance was matched by his personal eccentricities. A gifted long-distance runner, he would sometimes jog the 40 miles from Bletchley Park to London for high-level meetings. He received little official recognition during his lifetime. This was partly due to the confidential nature of his war work, which meant he couldn't even be rewarded for it after the event. Partly, though, it was because he was gay. Homosexuality was still then illegal in England and Turing was eventually prosecuted for 'gross indecency'. He agreed to submit to chemical castration, meaning he was injected with oestrogen, which rendered him impotent.

Two years later, he killed himself with cyanide at the age of 41. This was the man who, according to Winston Churchill, had contributed more than any politician or general to the ultimate defeat of fascism in Europe.

Fascists

It's not thought so hot, these days, to be a fascist.
But there was a time when it was all the rage.

Filippo Marinetti, writer (1876–1944)

USAGE: Any work of art that extols the virtues of speed,
machinery and all things modern, at the cost of humane
considerations, may be said to be influenced by the spirit of
Marinetti.

The art theorist Filippo Marinetti was once praised by the
murderous Italian leader Benito Mussolini as 'a fervent fascist'. And to be honest, that was what he was. He was also a
dandy who styled his moustache to resemble the bow-tie he
liked to wear around his neck. By his own account, Marinetti
had an epiphany after driving his car into a ditch to avoid a
couple of cyclists. He resolved to forge a new Italian culture
called 'Futurism': vigorous, masculine, and, well, fascist. His
Futurist Manifesto was published in the French newspaper
Le Figaro in 1909. 'We will glorify war – the world's only
hygiene,' Marinetti raved, 'militarism, patriotism, the destructive gesture of freedom-bringers, beautiful ideas worth dying
for, and scorn for woman.' Clearly a charming individual.

Despite the fact it was all clearly unhinged, Marinetti's
manifesto found a lot of supporters in those days before

anyone really understood the horrors of modern warfare. Like André Breton*, he is better remembered for his manifesto than for anything else he did. He was no artist (though some of the Futurist paintings he inspired, by the likes of Umberto Boccioni or Tullio Crali, are quite cool). He did write plays, though these were often ridiculed as a load of rubbish. Marinetti declared that this had been his intention all along. If Futurists got heckled, he claimed, this just proved they were doing their job properly. Oh, and you should know that his play *Elettricità sessuale* (Sexual Electricity), apart from having an excellent title, is credited with inventing the idea of a humanoid robot.

Marinetti joined the Fascist party as soon as he got the chance and helped to write its manifesto. He was later disappointed that Il Duce didn't adopt Futurism as the official artistic style of the new Italy – even more so when the Nazis included Futurist works in their touring exhibition of 'degenerate art'.

Günter Grass, novelist (1927–2015)

USAGE: If a work of art strives to come to terms with a nation's dark past, you might observe that it is engaging in a type of '*Vergangenheitsbewältigung*, in the manner of Günter Grass'.

Vergangenheitsbewältigung. It doesn't trip off the tongue, but it's a key word for post-war German literature, since it means 'coming to terms with the past'. It is used to refer to one of the major preoccupations of novelists such as Günter Grass, whose message is that the atrocities of the Second World War must not be concealed. Nor must it be concealed how certain people have tried to conceal them. In his most famous novel, *The Tin Drum*, one character dies after swallowing his Nazi Party pin, in an attempt to disguise his affiliation from the invading Soviet army.

The Tin Drum is a work of magical realism, meaning a lot of crazy stuff happens in it. The hero stops growing on the occasion of his third birthday, for example. His most treasured possession is the tin drum of the title, which he receives as a present on that same day. The book was the first in a series (along with *Cat and Mouse* and *Dog Years*) known as the Danzig trilogy, which established Grass not only as one of his country's great post-war novelists, but also as its moral arbiter. He was awarded the Nobel Prize in Literature in 1999.

After that, Grass's reputation took something of a hit. In 2006, he caused outrage when, while publicising his memoirs, he confessed in an interview that he had been a member of the Waffen SS during the war. Why had he not taken the trouble to reveal this before? He had been ashamed, he admitted. Some accused him of hypocrisy; others argued that he shouldn't have been held to account for a decision he took aged seventeen.

More on 'Fascists' overleaf

Ezra Pound, poet and critic (1885–1972)

USAGE: Commenting on an author with extreme, but not insane, political views, you could say: 'Don't get me wrong. We're not venturing into Ezra Pound territory here. But yes, they're a little controversial.'

The poem 'In a Station of the Metro' by Ezra Pound – a two-line stanza juxtaposing a vision of faces in a crowd with the image of petals on a tree-branch – tells us a lot about its author. First of all, he was one of the founding fathers of Imagism, a movement in poetry that strove for clear images described without old-school, overly poetic flourishes (none of your Tennysonian waffle). It also favoured 'modern' subject matter: a glimpse of people in a Metro station, for instance.

That's the Paris Metro, note, not the New York subway. An American, Pound was a quintessential ex-pat, swanning around first in London and later Paris and Italy. While doing so, he helped give birth to modern poetry, not only by the example of his own work, but especially by the aid he gave to those even more gifted than himself. He was the first to publish James Joyce's novel *Ulysses*, for instance, and edited T.S. Eliot's *The Waste Land*: two of the most significant literary works of the 20th century.

The difficulty with Pound was that he was a 100 per cent, dyed-in-the-wool, raving, blazing anti-Semite. He referred to the Italian Fascist leader Benito Mussolini as 'the boss', signed letters 'Heil Hitler', and made pro-Fascist broadcasts during the Second World War. In his defence ... actually, there isn't really anything that can be said in his defence. He spent several years in a lunatic asylum after the war. But it seems he wasn't really mad. He just hated Jews. This may make one dislike him as a man (he also treated women badly), but it doesn't affect the quality of his best writing, as for instance the sprawling, imperfect, unique *Cantos*. Unsurprisingly for a man of his sympathies, his activities were monitored with special interest by the FBI – as too have been those of a certain controversial philosopher, notorious for accusing the US government of enormous crimes …

Investigated by the FBI

*It's almost a mark of distinction, arguably,
when the FBI opens a file on you. Here
are a few who have achieved it.*

Noam Chomsky, philosopher (b. 1928)

USAGE: Anyone who believes the world is run by a conspiracy
of evil capitalists who control the media (and by extension our
minds) may be said to have 'read a little too much Chomsky'.

It's hardly surprising that the FBI decided to keep a file on
Noam Chomsky, since the philosopher has been one of the
American government's severest public critics. He first made
a name for himself in the less obviously controversial field
of linguistics. Specifically he argued that all human beings
are born with the innate ability to acquire language, and
with structures in place in the brain that mean this language
will conform to a 'universal grammar', or – an instance of
Chomsky's dry sense of humour – 'ug' for short. In any conversation about linguistic theory, just keep saying 'Ug'.

Professor Chomsky would probably have remained little known outside of academia, if the Vietnam War hadn't
driven him, in his forties, to start attacking US foreign policy. In this arena, he is best known for his analysis of the way
the media tends to support the authorities. In his 1988 book

Manufacturing Consent, he outlined 'distorting filters' that prevent journalists from writing the truth. For instance, if they annoy the government, they'll be excluded from state sources of information: coverage will suffer, they'll lose readers and their paper will go bust. One of the attractions of holding Chomskyan beliefs is it allows you to sneer at anyone who thinks that most of what gets presented as the news is more or less true. This doesn't, of course, mean he's wrong.

More broadly, Chomsky has attacked the hypocrisy of US foreign policy: for preaching the virtues of democracy while offering secret support, whenever it's convenient, to right-wing dictatorships and to armed militias working against anti-US regimes. This last tactic, according to Chomsky, is by any normal definition a form of terrorism.

Carlos Fuentes, novelist (1928–2012)

USAGE: Anyone rejecting the left-wing idealism of their youth, and espousing more right-wing views, may be said to resemble a character in a Carlos Fuentes novel.

For Carlos Fuentes (pronounced: foo-EN-tez), Mexico's most famous novelist, being investigated by the FBI was a vital part of his identity. A lifelong communist, he enraged Fidel Castro by visiting New York, which the Cuban leader regarded as the centre of capitalist corruption. Fuentes was mortified to have annoyed the great Castro, but knowing the FBI were keeping a file on him was a great source of solace to him during the difficult days that followed: proof that the Americans, at least, didn't doubt his allegiance to the communist cause.

It was a commitment Fuentes also proclaimed in his novels. In his debut, *Where the Air is Clear* (1958), a social reformer sells out, abandoning Marxism for capitalism. But capitalism doesn't make him happy. The book was written in Spanish, which was itself a statement. As Fuentes himself put it, 'Although the English language didn't need another writer, the Spanish language did.' His later novels, which explored similar themes (key name-drop: 1962's *The Death of Artemio Cruz*), cemented his status as one of the foremost authors of the Latin American literary boom (along with Jorge Luis Borges*, Gabriel García Márquez, Pablo Neruda* and Mario Vargas Llosa*).

Like some of his characters, Fuentes was a champagne socialist, enjoying a luxurious lifestyle and hobnobbing with the rich and famous. He was friends with the actress Shirley MacLaine, and had affairs with the actresses Jean Seberg and Jeanne Moreau. He claimed that the idea for his 2006 novel *The Eagle's Throne* had been given to him by his buddy, the former US president Bill Clinton. Forgiving his double standards, Fuentes' fellow Mexicans adored him. So many mourners attended his funeral, they brought the traffic in Mexico City to a standstill.

Dorothy Parker, humourist (1893–1967)

> **USAGE:** If someone tries the old line (particularly popular with men) that there aren't many genuinely funny female comedians, you might mention Dorothy Parker among your counter-examples.

Suspecting her of being a communist, the FBI compiled a 1,000-page file on Dorothy Parker. As a result, she lost her job writing screenplays for Hollywood movies. It wasn't her only career setback. She was also sacked by MGM boss Sam Goldwyn for refusing to give a script a happy ending. 'I know this will come as a shock to you, Mr Goldwyn,' she told him, 'but in all history, which has held billions and billions of human beings, not a single one ever had a happy ending.'

As well as film scripts, Parker wrote verse, short stories, and theatre reviews for *Vanity Fair*. Back in her journalism days, she used to go for lunch every day at New York's Algonquin Hotel with colleagues such as Robert Benchley and Robert Sherwood. These gatherings became so famous for the witty one-liners that flashed back and forth that the group became known as the Algonquin Round Table (in reference to Arthurian legend, as if they were verbal knights-in-shining-armour). It is for her witticisms on these and other occasions that Parker is now best remembered.

'Men seldom make passes at girls who wear glasses.' 'This is not a novel to be tossed lightly aside. It should be thrown with great force.' 'Tell him I was too f***ing busy. Or vice versa.' These examples give a taste of the great Parker wit: acerbic, misanthropic, but pretty damn good. She had a miserable personal life by all accounts. Both the men she married turned out to be bisexual, and she ended up a hopeless alcoholic. She left everything she had to Martin Luther King. Yet it's hard not to think there must have been good times in the Algonquin, given how linguistically dexterous the participants were. And she had enjoyed enormous success in her day, bagging the prestigious O. Henry Award for her short stories, and twice receiving Oscar nominations for her screenwriting.

The Oscars

Pablo Picasso* has been played on screen by Anthony Hopkins; Che Guevara* by Benicio del Toro; Hunter S. Thompson* by Johnny Depp. The following two were also portrayed in Oscar-winning movies.

Pablo Neruda, poet (1904–73)

USAGE: In order to stake your claim to be one of the last of the great romantics, you might declare your passionate admiration for the love poetry of Pablo Neruda.

In the fictional, Oscar-winning film *Il Postino* (1994), a simple postman on the island of Capri enlists the aid of the Chilean poet Pablo Neruda to woo a local beauty. His kind of writing – open, erotic, passionate – made Neruda a rare example of a serious poet who was accessible to, and adored by, the general public. It was a style he perfected in his teens with the publication of *Twenty Love Poems and One Song of Despair* (1924), which would remain his best-known work.

The hot-blooded precociousness came to seem like a form of arrested development as the decades passed. A diplomatic career took him to Spain in the 1930s, where he became friends with Federico García Lorca*. The latter's murder at the hands of the Fascists politicised Neruda. He remained a committed communist for the rest of his life, long after the horrors of Stalinism became widely known. His refusal to condemn Soviet oppression made him a controversial figure. Jorge Luis Borges*, for instance, characterised him as 'a very fine poet' but 'a very mean man'.

He was awarded the Nobel Prize in Literature in 1971. Two years later, during his final illness, his home in Chile was searched by the forces of the right-wing dictator Augusto Pinochet. 'Look around,' Neruda is reported to have told them. 'There's only one thing of danger for you here – poetry.' And if the judgement of Gabriel García Márquez, that Neruda was the greatest poet of the 20th century in any language, may seem dubious, it's an indication at least of the admiration and affection in which he was held, not only by his fellow writers, but also by the public at large.

Stephen Hawking, physicist (b. 1942)

USAGE: To express the idea that something is a small beginning of a much larger project, you could say: 'This, if you like, is the Hawking singularity from which everything else will follow.'

Although wheelchair-bound, intellectually the acclaimed astrophysicist Stephen Hawking has roamed the outer reaches of the universe. As a PhD student at Cambridge, he wrote his thesis on black holes (the extreme regions left after a star collapses). His further researches led to theories that can't be meaningfully summarised for the non-specialist in a paragraph. (They would cause the 'star' of your brain to collapse, creating a cerebral black hole.) Suffice to say that he concluded, firstly, that the universe must have started as a 'singularity': the point within a black hole where space and time have no meaning. Another of his theories, that a black hole radiates heat (so-called 'Hawking radiation'), was later proved right – and most significantly, successfully combined what had previously been thought to be the irreconcilable theories of quantum mechanics and Einstein's* general relativity.

The British scientist's achievements are all the more extraordinary, given that he was diagnosed with motor neurone disease in 1963. At the time, he was given two years to live. As anyone knows who has seen Eddie Redmayne's Oscar-winning performance in *The Theory of Everything*, he was first plunged into depression, but saved by a combination of love and work.

In addition to his other abilities, Hawking has proved to be a consummate salesman. His book *A Brief History of Time* has shifted an incredible 10 million copies. And this is despite the fact that books about physics are not usually runaway bestsellers. Nor are books on economics, as a rule – but again, one author has confounded expectations in this respect, even earning praise from multi-billionaire Bill Gates …

Surprise Bestsellers

The phrase 'surprise bestseller' is a tautology: the publishing industry is so hard to predict, every bestseller comes as a surprise. Having said that, the following hits were particularly unexpected.

Thomas Piketty, economist (b. 1971)

USAGE: You can invoke Piketty's name in relation to the idea that if we don't do something about it, the wealth gap will just keep widening.

What can account for it? In 2014, a 700-page book by an obscure French economist became the must-read of the moment. Politicians left, right and centre claimed to have fought their way through it. Some may even have done so. But *Capital in the Twenty-First Century* by Thomas Piketty (pronounced: to-MA PEE-ket-ee) proved popular with the general public too.

The book's central argument is that the gap between rich and poor is getting wider, and unless we do something about it, that's going to continue. Why? Because in a free-market economy the fastest way to make money is not by working hard, but rather by investing the money you already have. In other words, the rich inevitably get richer, while the poor are increasingly doomed. The only way to put a stop to this malign trend, according to Piketty, is to impose heavy taxes on the rich.

Of course, one reason for Piketty's success is that in the wake of the global financial crisis of 2007/08 people were angry with bankers and capitalism generally. Any book that gave an intellectual underpinning for this emotion was always going to be a winner. Naturally, there were also those who dismissed its left-wing macroeconomic analysis. (N.B. Always try to refer to 'macroeconomics'; it basically means the same thing as 'economics' but it sounds more complicated.) These critics, who usually came from the other end of the political spectrum, pointed out that the data for the past 250 years, which was Piketty's focus, didn't actually support his theory. In fact, since the beginning of the 19th century, the wealth gap has not widened but narrowed. Indeed, in the years between 1910 and 1970, when Europe was devastated by two world wars, the gap narrowed drastically. Piketty – a suave-looking young man born after the end of that period – dismisses it as an interval that went against the flow of history. His critics counter that it may be the decades of capitalist prosperity that followed which prove to be the exception rather than the rule.

Who will turn out to be right? In any conversation about macroeconomics, a handy get-out is to say that the whole business, like the publishing industry, is impossible to predict.

Alexis de Tocqueville, philosopher (1805–59)

USAGE: When expressing a controversial view, you might recommend that, before anyone condemns you, they should bear in mind de Tocqueville's warnings about the 'tyranny of the majority'.

Democracy in America may sound an unlikely title for a bestseller, yet that's what Alexis de Tocqueville's extensive and rigorous tome became after its publication in 1834. Three years earlier, the Frenchman had secured a commission to produce a report on the way the prison system was being run in the US. He crossed the Atlantic with a mate of his named Gustave, and spent nine months travelling around, keeping his eyes open, and making notes. But the end product had a scope far wider than the penal system. It was nothing less than a portrait of a nation.

And it's worth remembering that what was going on in America was a pretty exciting experiment in the eyes of jaded Europeans. The land of opportunity! De Tocqueville served up a work that fed that appetite, with its fair share of praise and enthusiasm. Hence its success in his lifetime. The fact that it still gets cited today rests more on the reservations and criticisms expressed by the author. He was personally a believer in liberty more than in equality, since the 'depraved taste' for the latter 'impels the weak to want to bring the strong down to their level'. In America, he said, there is no automatic respect for anyone, neither for aristocrats (fair enough) nor for educated, talented men (this was going a bit far). The result was a culture that was inclined in favour of mediocrity.

De Tocqueville – who would later serve as France's Foreign Minister – also argued that the problem with democracy on the American model was that it could foster intolerance if you didn't side with the consensus view: a problem he dubbed 'the tyranny of the majority'.

Bertrand Russell, philosopher (1872–1970)

USAGE: A philosopher who bases his arguments on mathematical forms of logic may be said to be an analytic philosopher in the tradition of Bertrand Russell.

A London taxi driver once gave a ride to a man he recognised as England's premier philosopher, Bertrand Russell. So he asked him: 'What's it all about?' To the driver's dismay, Russell had no answer. But the story tells us something about a man who refused to sugar-coat the truth. For Russell, the question 'What's it all about?' was meaningless and he wasn't going to pretend otherwise.

As mathematicians go, Russell was pretty racy. Having established his reputation with the joint authorship of *Principia Mathematica* (with A.N. Whitehead, whose wife he later pursued), he went on to outrage public opinion with his controversial stances on many of the key issues of the day. An atheist who believed in free love, Russell was a pacifist in a time of war, for example. This had the beneficial side-effect of making him a celebrity – he was arguably the first media academic – who could command large sums for his newspaper articles. In 1945, his accessible *History of Western Philosophy* became a surprise bestseller and ensured his financial security. For unlike most philosophers, he wrote with clarity and charm. He was awarded the Nobel Prize in Literature in 1950.

He is respected by academics as a founder of analytic philosophy, who made major contributions to logic and the philosophy of language. Yet by most he's more likely to be remembered for his wispy white hair, his public atheism (he was the Richard Dawkins of his day), and his roving libido, which was forever flinging him into affairs with married women. As far as one can judge, Russell had a better time of it with women than did the following poet, who was so openminded that he allowed his wife to run off with Salvador Dalí ...

The Resistance

*After the war, practically everyone in France
claimed to have been secretly fighting in the
Resistance. A few people really did.*

Paul Éluard, poet (1895–1952)

USAGE: If anyone tells you enthusiastically that they're in an
open relationship, you might warn them of the fate of Paul
Éluard, who lost his wife to Salvador Dalí.

During the Second World War, the French poet Paul Éluard
risked his life by putting together a volume of anti-Nazi verse
by like-minded poets. His own passionate, lyrical, moving
ode '*Liberté*' was thought to be so inspiring that the RAF
dropped thousands of copies of it over occupied France, in
the hope of raising the morale of locals. It was stirring stuff,
which cemented Éluard's status as a kind of poet laureate of
the French Resistance.

Compared with the rest of his work, the poem was also
relatively straightforward. Éluard was one of the founders of
the Surrealist movement, which believed in breaking down
the doors of perception and releasing the deep subconscious
energies that are normally experienced only in dreams. What
this often meant in practice was writing a lot of nonsense,
though occasionally it could produce a line that made some

kind of sense. Try, for instance, his love poem 'The Curve of Your Eyes'.

Like the true Bohemian he was, Éluard shared more than ideas with his fellow artists. He and his Russian wife Gala (whom he had met in a Swiss sanatorium) famously entered into a *ménage à trois* with the artist Max Ernst*. Sadly, this created tension in the marriage. They divorced and Gala married Salvador Dalí instead. In later life, the poet became a devoted communist. So committed was he to the cause that even after a friend of his (a Czech author named Zavis Kalandra) had been executed by Stalin, Éluard continued to praise the Soviet dictator.

Simone Weil, philosopher and activist (1909–43)

USAGE: In a discussion of how long it took most of Europe's left-wing intellectuals to recognise the vices of communism, you could mention that Simone Weil had foreseen them in the 1920s.

It was only natural that Simone Weil should have joined the Resistance during the Second World War, since all her life she believed in practising what she preached – and to a pretty extreme degree. Aged six, she refused to eat sugar as an act of solidarity with French soldiers suffering in the trenches. As she grew up, she became increasingly opposed to extremist ideologies – not only fascism but also communism. She was one of the first to see that a danger with the latter was the opportunity it gave revolutionaries for becoming as cruel as the masters they had sought to overthrow. She argued her case so well that even Leon Trotsky* was impressed. Despite their differences, the ever-generous Weil arranged for him to stay at her parents' apartment when, exiled by Stalin, he came to Paris.

Although she wrote no big book, her influence, through her brilliant essays, has been substantial. She's also unusual among 20th-century intellectuals for being passionately religious. This led her to develop crazed views on theological matters. She explained the 'problem of evil' – the mystery of why a benign, all-powerful God would allow evil in the world – by a tortuous argument involving the claim that He was an 'utter fullness', which meant for humans to exist, they had to exist outside him, in a space that included evil (since only goodness, and no evil, resided with Him).

'The only way into truth is through one's own annihilation', Weil once remarked. She lived according to this belief – and ultimately, died by it. Having escaped to London, she starved herself in empathy with her fellow countrymen who were suffering in Nazi-occupied France, and, as a direct consequence, expired of a heart attack at the age of 34. Self-sacrificing, always passionate and engaged, full of love but clumsy, brilliant but impractical – that was Weil. In fact, there's a story that, working for the Resistance, she dropped a suitcase in the street, causing a sheaf of secret papers to spill out over the pavement. At least, though, she didn't leave the suitcase on the Tube. It's easily done, as could be attested by a certain Indian man of letters …

Suitcase Mishaps

These days most of us back things up regularly on our computers, but there was a time when there was such a thing as 'the only copy'. Ernest Hemingway* famously divorced his first wife partly because she'd mislaid a suitcase containing all his early writing. These two also suffered suitcase-related misfortunes.

Rabindranath Tagore, poet and novelist (1861–1941)

USAGE: A good example of a man who once enjoyed an almost Shakespearean level of acclaim, whose star has subsequently waned.

Rabindranath – it's a name worth mastering, since Rabindranath Tagore is, or was, a big deal. The first non-European to win the Nobel Prize in Literature, he introduced many in the West to Indian literature (particularly his own), while also educating Indians in his native Bengal about new developments in European culture.

A handsome man from an aristocratic Brahmin background, Tagore only really hit the big time in his fifties. In 1912, he sailed to England with his own English translation of a book of his poems entitled *Gitanjali*. Having come so far, he lost the suitcase containing the manuscript on the London Underground. Fortunately, it was returned to him.

He persuaded W.B. Yeats to read it and the latter hailed it as a work of genius. When it was published the following year, it created such a sensation that Tagore was awarded the Nobel practically on the spot. The book went on to be translated into French and Russian by André Gide* and Boris Pasternak respectively. Before he was killed in action, the poet Wilfred Owen inscribed a quotation from Tagore in his notebook: 'When I leave, let these be my parting words: what my eyes have seen, what my life received, are unsurpassable.' Poems by Tagore form the lyrics of three national anthems: those of India, Bangladesh and Sri Lanka.

Almost inevitably, there has been a backlash against the towering status achieved by Tagore in his lifetime. Even Yeats backtracked, complaining that some of the great man's later work was a bit sentimental (Tagore described the Taj Mahal as 'a teardrop on the face of eternity'). He's now regarded in India rather as Alfred Tennyson is in Britain: good stuff, but a bit old-school.

Robert Capa, photographer (1913–54)

USAGE: While taking an extreme close-up with your camera phone, you might murmur, 'As Robert Capa used to say: "If your photographs aren't good enough, you're not close enough."'

Capa is the Hungarian word for shark. It was the nickname of a sharp-witted Jewish kid named André Friedmann at school in 1920s Hungary. Moving to Paris to escape the threat of fascism, he launched himself as a photojournalist, claiming to be an American named Robert Capa. The ploy worked and he went on to become the best-known war photographer of his time.

A dashing, dark-haired fellow with a face like a falcon, Capa chased wars and women with equal energy. There are those who say his most famous photograph – *The Falling Soldier* (1936), which purports to show a Spanish soldier at the moment he's struck in the head by a bullet – is actually a fake. (The guy may not have been dying; he may merely have missed his footing.) Others point out that, charming as Capa was, one can't wholly admire a man who was happy to bed his friends' wives (as he regularly did). It should be noted, though, that the photographer had lost the love of his life – fellow-photographer Gerda Taro, who was crushed by a tank in 1937 – and after that, he was never the same. A risk addict, he used to say: 'If your photographs aren't good enough, you're not close enough.' In 1954, he pursued this philosophy to its logical conclusion on assignment in Vietnam. Treading on a landmine, he had one of his legs blown off. It took him a while to die.

A large number of Capa's photographs of the Spanish Civil War can be seen in the International Center of Photography in Manhattan. Many of them were discovered in the 1990s in a suitcase that had been lost for half a century. The photographer had mislaid it while fleeing from the Nazis in 1939.

Harassed by Nazis

Say what you like about the Nazis … No, really,
say what you like: they deserve it. In addition
to their more sickening crimes, they oppressed
writers and suppressed freedom of speech.

Rudolf Steiner, philosopher, spiritualist, educationist
(1861–1925)

USAGE: Ask a friend who's into organic food whether they
subscribe to Rudolf Steiner's broader spiritualist beliefs.

The man must have done something right. The Nazis hated
him, trying to disrupt one of his lectures in Munich by turning the lights out and throwing stink bombs at the stage.
What was it about Rudolf Steiner that bothered them so
much? He had some strange theories about race, which
didn't fit with their own strange theories. Then again, most
of Steiner's theories were barking mad. The Austrian's big idea
was to take a kind of scientific approach to spiritualism: that's
to say, ghosts, karma and reincarnation. Steiner believed he'd
seen the ghost of his aunt when he was nine. He also believed
he had met Jesus. He called his philosophy, if you're interested
to know more, anthroposophy. It was a benign kind of lunacy,
emphasising the importance of love and things like that.

Putting aside his interest in complementary medicines, and advice to farmers to plant their crops according to the alignment of the Moon and planets, Steiner had a few ideas that weren't completely crazy. (One thing to be said for him, he certainly had no shortage of ideas – so some were bound to hit the mark.) When it came to organising the state, he advocated a separation between political, economic and cultural institutions. He was an early supporter of organic farming practices. But of all the areas of thought into which his feverish mind strayed, it is in education that he made the deepest mark. In the thousand or so Steiner schools that are still in operation today, pupils are given a more freewheeling kind of educational experience than is traditional, with equal emphasis on arts and sciences. Controversially, Steiner didn't believe children should be taught to read until they had grown adult teeth, which often results in Steiner pupils being a bit behind on the literacy front.

Sigmund Freud, psychologist (1856–1939)

USAGE: The commonest notion of 'Freudianism' is that everything is, ultimately, all about sex. In almost any conversation, you may ask, 'What would Freud say?' Then waggle your eyebrows.

Where to begin? The Oedipus complex. Sigmund Freud believed that the Greek myth of Oedipus, who inadvertently killed his father and married his mother, represented a deep truth about human nature. We all fancy our mothers and resent our fathers, but pretend we don't, which leads to other psychological problems. To which one might reply: speak for yourself, Sigmund!

The fact many of his theories can't be disproved is problematic (see Karl Popper*). But he practically invented psychotherapy, and his influence is clear from the sheer number of concepts he developed, which are still in use today. Infantile sexuality: children have basic sexual urges. The talking cure: speak about your problems and you'll feel better. The pleasure principle: urge for sensual gratification. The death drive: a self-destructive urge. Penis envy: women secretly wish they had penises. Id, super-ego and ego: basic desires, social morality, and the will that governs between them. Repression: denial of unpalatable experiences. Transference: self-deception regarding the true source of resentment or desire. Freudian slip: accidentally saying something that reveals a hidden truth.

Bear in mind that Freud was carrying out his research in late 19th-century Vienna, where almost everyone was barking mad. Also, he was doing a massive amount of cocaine (he thought it was therapeutic). After the Nazis showed up at his Vienna home one day, demanding a large sum of money and taking his daughter Anna away for questioning for 24 hours, he escaped to London, where he spent the rest of his life. He died of jaw cancer caused by smoking large and (as he might have put it) phallic cigars. His remains were interred at the Jewish cemetery in Golders Green.

André Breton, writer (1896–1966)

USAGE: There's nothing more boring than someone banging on about a dream they had. Call a halt to any such conversation by insisting they follow Breton's advice and write a poem about it.

André Breton made Frida Kahlo* famous. He 'discovered' the artist while on a visit to Mexico, and invited her to show her work in Paris. He didn't particularly like the woman herself, so when she arrived at the airport, instead of going to pick her up, he sent his wife Jacqueline. The unforeseen consequence, it's said, was that the two women embarked on a passionate affair.

Kahlo had more than one cause to be grateful to Breton – as does anyone with an interest in Surrealism, the iconoclastic cultural movement the Frenchman launched in 1924 with his *Surrealist Manifesto*. This document (the achievement for which he is best remembered) declared the vital importance for the creative artist of freeing him or herself from the tyranny of logic. Most people when they think of Surrealism think first of self-consciously bizarre paintings by the likes of Salvador Dalí, but it should be noted that as well as painters, it was a movement for writers such as Breton himself. He recommended automatic writing: i.e. jotting down ideas as they come into your head without trying to shape the words into anything particularly coherent. A flavour of his poetry can be got from one in which he describes his wife as having 'the waist of an otter in the teeth of a tiger'. Come again? Surrealism seems to have worked better for visual artists.

Breton's anarchic tendencies and communist sympathies led to his having to flee Europe after the Nazi occupation of France. He spent much of the rest of his life globe-trotting, collecting friends and Surrealist disciples, artworks and curios. A wall of Breton's apartment, complete with some of his favourite paintings, is preserved at the Centre Georges Pompidou in Paris.

Paul Valéry, poet (1871–1945)

USAGE: On a windy day, you might quote Valéry: 'Le vent se lève! … Il faut tenter de vivre!' (The wind rises! … We must try to live!)

The French poet Paul Valéry never won the Nobel Prize (despite being repeatedly nominated for it) but, revered as a literary giant, he held several distinguished posts in the cultural firmament (e.g. membership of the Académie Française). These positions, though, were all stripped from him during the Second World War as punishment for his refusal to collaborate with the Nazi-supporting Vichy regime.

His career demonstrates the advisability of waiting until you're ready before launching yourself on the literary scene. Aged 21, Valéry, then a budding young poet, was devastated by the death of his friend and mentor, the poet Stéphane Mallarmé*. The loss triggered an existential crisis that finally prompted him to stop writing. He was staring out of a window at a storm in 1898 when he realised the pointlessness of everything and decided to lay down his pen. It wasn't until nineteen years later that the death of another mentor – the former head of an advertising agency, for whom he had worked as a secretary – persuaded him to end what has become known as 'the great silence'.

It took him four years to write it, but when his 512-line poem *La Jeune parque* (The Young Fate) appeared in 1920 it was hailed as a masterpiece. 'Qui pleure là, sinon le vent simple', it begins. 'Who is that weeping, if not the wind …' Written from the point of view of a young woman staring out to sea, wondering whether life is worth living, it was taken as a comment on the horrors of the First World War and is viewed as one of the greatest French poems of the 20th century.

Paul Klee, artist (1879–1940)

USAGE: If you want to name an example of a genius, Klee's a good one, because he's not as well known as Albert Einstein, say, or Leonardo da Vinci.

A Swiss school teacher once took his pupils out for a picnic. When he suggested they all do a sketch of a nearby aqueduct, one of them drew shoes at the bottom of the structure's pillars. As an eminent critic has put it, 'All aqueducts have walked since that day.' The idea is that even at the age of eleven, Paul Klee (pronounced: CLAY) was touched by genius.

Yet at first he wasn't sure of his vocation. Like the film-maker Michelangelo Antonioni*, as a child he excelled at the violin. He later abandoned music, believing it to be a dying tradition, and instead devoted himself to art.

What do we mean when we describe someone as a genius? It tends to refer to the sheer diversity of their achievements. A glance through Klee's *oeuvre* reveals an astonishing range of styles, as if he had rethought his whole approach from one picture to the next, in most cases with total success. The other relevant aspect of Klee in this regard was his child-like playfulness (a quality also found in Picasso or Einstein, for example), sometimes incorporating stick men and humour in his works.

A shy man, the artist used to shuffle backwards into the classroom where he taught at the Bauhaus School in Weimar in the 1920s, and address his students without looking at them. His lectures, later published, were revolutionary, one of the most important tracts on art theory of the 20th century. Inevitably his avant garde ideas brought him into conflict with the Nazis. Although he wasn't Jewish, he was modern. That was enough to get him classed as 'degenerate'. He was dismissed from a teaching post in Düsseldorf, his works were removed from public galleries, and anyone who had bought one was persecuted. In later life, Klee suffered from scleroderma, a progressive hardening of the skin that made movement difficult and eventually killed him.

More on 'Harassed by Nazis' overleaf

Marc Chagall, artist (1887–1985)

USAGE: You may praise any infant's doodle by murmuring that, to you, it's a little reminiscent of mid-period Chagall.

There's a lot more to Marc Chagall (pronounced: sha-GAL) than his child-like sensibility and use of attractive colours: two traits that find expression in his favoured motif of a cello-playing goat. As well as his paintings, he made stained glass windows for cathedrals, painted the ceiling of the Palais Garnier opera house in Paris, and produced an acclaimed series of illustrations for an edition of the Old Testament.

Loss is a constant theme in the artist's work, which is nostalgic for the traditional Jewish ways of life among which he'd grown up in the Russian town of Vitebsk, where his father worked in a herring factory. Many of the motifs in his paintings, which include the frequent appearance of herrings, originate in his memories of this home. Chagall's experience of loss didn't end when he abandoned Russia for Paris. In due course, he also felt forced to leave Europe and made his home in New York, after the Nazis, targeting him as a Jewish artist, set fire to books about his work in the book burnings of 1933. Some of his later works speak not only to his own sufferings but also to those of the Jewish people. Although he usually only hinted at the theme, in 1938's *White Crucifixion* he spelt it out, showing Jesus on the Cross, surrounded by Nazi hate crimes.

But it would be a mistake to think of Chagall as a painter of grim or gruelling scenes. A more characteristic work, perhaps, is *La Mariée* (The Bride), which depicts a woman in a bridal veil accompanied by that ubiquitous goat playing the cello. The image is surreal, swooningly romantic, and at the same time, rather wistful. (The figure of the bride may be inspired by Chagall's first wife Bella, who had died a few years earlier.) It achieved a new stratosphere of fame after playing a key role in Richard Curtis's romantic comedy *Notting Hill*. Julia Roberts, playing a mega-wealthy movie star, expresses her affection for Hugh Grant by giving him the painting. Quiz question: Elton John sings the song 'But Not For Me' over the opening scene of Curtis's *Four Weddings and a Funeral*, but who wrote the music and lyrics?

Four Weddings

The Richard Curtis romantic comedy Four Weddings
and a Funeral *begins with repeated uses of
the word 'f***'. Later, a character recites the
entirety of a W.H. Auden poem. A classic
combination of high and low culture, which
was something of a calling card for Curtis.*

George Gershwin, composer (1898–1937)

USAGE: If someone is attempting not to express their own talent
but to copy someone else, you might remark, 'Why be a second-
rate Ravel, when you can be a first-rate Gershwin?'

What do the films *Manhattan* and *Four Weddings and a
Funeral* have in common, besides being two of the most suc-
cessful romantic comedies ever made? The answer is they
both kick off with music by the American composer George
Gershwin. In the former case, it's his explosive *Rhapsody in
Blue*, a daring symphony that established his place in the
canon alongside popular composers such as Strauss and
Tchaikovsky. In the latter, it's the Broadway song 'But Not
For Me', with lyrics by Gershwin's older brother Ira. 'They're
writing songs of love, but not for me …'

Writing songs of love was how the young Gershwin, whose
father made women's shoes, first earned a crust in New York's

Tin Pan Alley in the 1920s. His breakthrough hit was the song 'Swanee', performed by Al Jolson ('I'd walk a million miles for one of your smiles …'). It was the first of a long list, which also included 'Fascinating Rhythm' and 'Oh, Lady Be Good!' But these light, throwaway classics belie Gershwin's ambition, which also extended to *Porgy and Bess* (1935). Featuring a nearly all-black cast, the opera, which includes the wonderful 'Summertime' and 'It Ain't Necessarily So', is considered a classic.

What the man might have accomplished had he lived longer (he died aged 38 of a brain tumour) is an intriguing but unanswerable question. In any case, his achievements are huge. Gershwin once asked to study under the French composer Maurice Ravel. Ravel replied: 'Why be a second-rate Ravel when you can be a first-rate Gershwin?' When he asked Igor Stravinsky* for pointers, he received the reply that, given what Gershwin earned, he was the one who should be giving lessons.

Franz Kafka, writer (1883–1924)

USAGE: If you want to insult someone (while also showing off your cultural awareness), you might describe spending time with them as 'a Kafka-esque experience'.

In the romantic comedy *Annie Hall*, a girl in bed with Woody Allen tells him: 'You know, sex with you is really a Kafka-esque experience.' Allen looks taken aback – and understandably so, for the works of Franz Kafka are associated with emotional alienation (*The Castle*), punishment for a crime you didn't commit (*The Trial*), and being transformed into a bug (*Metamorphosis*). Which also explains why it's amusing, in the Richard Curtis-scripted *Bridget Jones's Diary*, when the heroine has to promote a new novel surreally entitled *Kafka's Motorbike*.

Kafka's observational powers, combined with his themes, which encapsulate the atrocities of his era, have made him one of the most highly regarded fiction writers of the 20th century. The achievement came at great personal cost. An embodiment of the writer as a victim of his own sensitivities, the Jewish Czech author was assailed by feelings of paranoia. From an early age, he suffered from tuberculosis. Eventually his throat was so painful he couldn't eat, and he died of starvation at 41. This excruciating death was prefigured in his haunting short story *The Hunger Artist*, which tells the tale of a man who literally starves himself for the entertainment of an increasingly indifferent audience.

In person, Kafka could be a little intense. Yet his friends attest that he was also capable of being hilarious company. If Woody Allen can make Jewish paranoia entertaining, mightn't there also be something amusing about the opening line of Kafka's short story (and probably most famous work) *Metamorphosis*: 'One morning, when Gregor Samsa woke from troubled dreams, he found himself transformed in his bed into a horrible vermin'? Haven't we all had that feeling, at one time or another? The man's impact on his fellow writers was huge, influencing everyone from Vladimir Nabokov* to a certain Italian postmodernist, who once in an interview referred to Kafka as 'my author' …

Love Letters

There aren't many upsides to having an affair with a writer. One is that, if you're lucky, they might write you a nice letter.

Italo Calvino, novelist (1923–85)

USAGE: In a discussion of Christopher Nolan's films, you might comment that they have 'a labyrinthine unreality, like some story by Borges or Calvino'.

'We are drugged,' Italo Calvino wrote to his mistress, the actress Elsa de Giorgi. 'I can't live outside the magic circle of our love.' The passion and intimacy was typical of the love letters he wrote her over the course of their long affair. That last phrase, in which he calls their love 'a magic circle', might also be applied to the strange alternative reality in which Calvino's fiction operates. It is a strange, unique world, in which nothing is quite as it seems.

The opening sentence of his 1979 novel *If on a winter's night a traveller* gives a flavour of his style: 'You are about to begin reading Italo Calvino's new novel, *If on a winter's night a traveller*. Relax. Let the world around you fade.' The words are comforting, because they include ideas and phrases familiar from traditional storytelling (the traveller, the winter's night), but at the same time disorienting, because the author constantly reminds you you're reading a fiction. This is what's known as postmodernist self-reflexiveness, and it can be intoxicating or extremely irritating, depending on taste.

Calvino does without the emotional impact of traditional novels, which relies on the suspension of disbelief. In its place, he offers brilliance, inventiveness, a wry sense of humour, and fluency. Brought up in northern Italy, he started out as a realist, but launched into experimentalism in the 1950s (around the time he became disillusioned with communism). *The Cloven Viscount* tells the tale of a viscount cut in two by a cannonball; *The Baron in the Trees* that of a baron who lives in a tree. Again there's the combination of the familiar (the aristocratic protagonist) with the surreally disorienting.

Too much of his work, perhaps, can seem like castles in the air – almost literally in the case of his 1972 novel *Invisible Cities*, which describes in short colourful sketches a number of invented cities, as reported (Calvino imagines) by the explorer Marco Polo to the Mongolian emperor Kubla Khan. These are wonderful and wearisome, intricate and endless. You have the sense that he could have gone on for thousands of pages in this way, if he had wanted: that taken as a whole, the book is a remarkable achievement of style and intellect, but an achievement of those qualities only.

James Joyce, writer (1882–1941)

USAGE: The adjective 'Joycean' refers to a writing style or personality that revels in linguistic richness and the realm of senses and appetites.

A publisher once paid a visit to James Joyce and his wife Nora in Paris. At a certain point, he murmured to Nora, 'You are married to a great man.' To which she replied, 'You don't have to live with the bloody fool!' They were devoted to each other really, staying married until the author's death, and exchanging passionate (and extremely pornographic) letters whenever they were apart. And although she sometimes insulted him, Nora was fiercely proud of her husband's status as one of the great writers of the 20th century.

His best-known novel is called *Ulysses*, which makes it sound like it's about a Greek mythological hero, when in truth it concerns a single day in the life of a cuckolded Dublin advertising agent named Leopold Bloom. (The structure is loosely based on that of Homer's *Odyssey*, whose hero's Latin name is Ulysses.) This is deliberate. The book glorifies the mundane – there are adventures, its title implies, concealed in the most ordinary of days – and pays tribute to the common man. The interior thoughts of the 'hero' are expressed in language of such rich mellifluousness, at times it's like listening to music, even when Joyce is describing Bloom's sexual shenanigans with his wife Molly: 'he kissed the plump mellow yellow smellow melons of rump', and so on. What does 'smellow' mean? It's hard to say, but you get the idea. Joyce took liberties with language, delighting in alliteration, word-play and obscure references. With his next novel, *Finnegans Wake*, he went too far. Most people agree it's total gibberish, and few have managed to read it the whole way through.

Although born and brought up in Dublin, Joyce lived most of his adult life in Italy and France. He often travelled to Switzerland for treatment for various eye problems from which he suffered. In the same country he took his daughter Lucia to have her schizophrenia treated by Carl Jung*. But after reading *Ulysses*, the great psychologist was more interested in diagnosing Joyce himself, who he concluded was schizophrenic.

Anaïs Nin, writer (1903–77)

USAGE: Don't bungle the pronunciation. Her first name is 'ann-a-EES'. Discussing pornography, you could point out it's not just men who are the authors: 'You only have to look at Nin's *Diaries*.'

After her death, a stash of steamy love letters was discovered among Anaïs Nin's belongings, from, of all people, Gore Vidal* (famous for his graphically homosexual novels). In her diary, as well as praising Gore's 'poise', she wrote of his 'manliness' (not a word commonly associated with the fey Vidal). In his memoirs he denied their relationship was ever physical, though Nin said it was. In matters of sex, she wasn't backward about coming forward.

Born in Paris, brought up in New York, Nin lived and wrote with a freedom that inspired and shocked in equal measure. For starters, she kept two husbands on the go at the same time. One was a banker on the East coast of America, the other an actor on the West coast. Her double life was so complicated, she had to keep a 'Lie Box' in order to sustain it, which contained such essentials as two sets of cheque books (her simultaneous marriages had naturally resulted in two surnames).

Nin wrote novels and poetry, but is best remembered for her voluminous *Diaries*. As well as being full of graphic sexual encounters – she was the first serious female author of high erotica – they're a rare source of information about many male 20th-century writers and artists, as seen from a woman's perspective. Her insights were helped by the fact that in several cases, she had also slept with them. Nin's circle of friends and lovers included John Steinbeck, Lawrence Durrell – and, most famously, a particularly uninhibited American writer, the only man to give Nin a run for her money when it came to writing explicitly, and some might say pretentiously, about sex …

Henry Miller, novelist (1891–1980)

USAGE: As with Nin, Miller's name is a shorthand for the place where pornography and high art meet. If you were fond of puns, you might say that *Fifty Shades of Grey* is merely 'Miller lite'.

At the height of their affair, the balding Henry Miller, who somewhat resembled a myopic bloodhound, wrote to Anaïs Nin*: 'I came away with pieces of you sticking to me; I am walking about, swimming, in an ocean of blood, your

Andalusian blood ...' He was an intense man. As prolific in his sex life as in his writing, he was still at it (in both senses) in his eighties, penning 1,500 letters in the last four years of his life to a young *Playboy* playmate, the pneumatically well-endowed, if rather implausibly named, Brenda Venus.

The apex of Miller's authorial achievements was his 1934 novel *Tropic of Cancer*. (He wanted to use the word 'cancer', he said, to suggest 'the disease of civilisation'.) This work describes Miller's time as a struggling writer in Paris, and the incredible amount of sex he had after the break-up of his first marriage in New York. Making liberal use of the C-word (and we don't mean cancer), the book was so pornographic it was banned in the US for 30 years. (One government official decried it as 'a slimy gathering of all that is rotten in the debris of human depravity'.) It's an unusual read, nauseating or invigorating, depending on your taste. Here's a sample: 'We wriggle into the [lavatory] cabinet and there I stand her up, slap up against the wall, and I try to get it into her but it won't work and so we sit down on the seat and try it that way but it won't work either.' In 1964, the Supreme Court finally ruled that Miller's masterpiece was 'non-obscene', and all right after all.

The man's real achievement, arguably, wasn't that he wrote graphically about sex, but that he pioneered the autobiographical novel so popular today, the kind where readers are tempted to guess if the incident described actually occurred in real life. With Miller, one senses it very often had. He had a lot of life experience to work with – not least because he had been married five times: a milestone in matrimony that would be surpassed by Norman Mailer* and equalled by the author of *Henderson the Rain King* ...

Much Married

The prize goes to Norman Mailer, who was married
six times. But these two weren't far behind.*

Saul Bellow, novelist (1915–2005)

USAGE: The adjective 'Bellovian' is used to refer to a style of
sonorous, freewheeling, intellectually voracious prose, similar to
that found in the novels of Saul Bellow.

The Bible states that King Solomon had 700 wives. His
namesake, Solomon Bellows, who would find literary fame
under the pen-name Saul Bellow, managed only five. But he
is reputed to have had a considerable sex drive. Not that this
was accompanied by much in the way of bedroom technique,
by all accounts. One mistress noted that the author 'didn't
know a clitoris from a kneecap'.

But don't pity him too much. The only man to have won
the National Book Award three times, he has a claim to being
the greatest American novelist of the 20th century. The opening
words of *The Adventures of Augie March* (1953) give a flavour
of his prose: 'I am an American, Chicago born – Chicago, that
somber city – and go about things as I have taught myself, free-
style, and will make the record in my own way …' The book is
about a man who drifts around, flitting from one dead-end job
to the next – he works in a dog training parlour at one point

– and from woman to woman. The book was notable for its striking blend of cool accessibility and intellectual engagement with the major issues of its time.

The way he wrote was very American in its musical eloquence, its intellectuality, and, perhaps, its garrulousness. In the eyes of the English author Martin Amis (a famous Bellow fan), his sentences simply 'seem to weigh more than anyone else's'. Yet for some, that may represent a problem. As with Roth*, say, or DeLillo*, it's hard to encounter Bellow's erudition (other key novel name-drops: 1964's *Herzog* and 1975's *Humboldt's Gift*) without an uneasy sense of how much you, by contrast, don't know. On receiving the 1976 Nobel Prize in Literature, Bellow appealed to authors to 'awaken [people] from intellectual torpor'. His detractors have called him a literary conservative, his larger-than-life characters harking back to 19th-century novels by the likes of Charles Dickens. There are, of course, worse authors to be compared to.

Max Ernst, artist and poet (1891–1976)

USAGE: 'Are you a fan of Ernstian frottage?' would be an interesting opening gambit to grab the attention of an attractive art-lover.

Max Ernst knew everybody and everybody knew him. He was friends with Alberto Giacometti, collaborated with André Breton* and the Surrealists, and when, in California in 1946, he married the British artist Dorothea Tanning, it was in a joint ceremony along with the photographer Man Ray* and his bride.

To his fans, Ernst is an artistic giant, his restless intellect leading him to experiment in different forms and styles, with always interesting results. Others say the German was a show-off, less interested in serious art than in the vital importance of being Ernst. Certainly some of his works seem calculated to shock. *The Robing of the Bride* (1940) is a riot: a naked woman is swamped in a huge orange furry or feathery cloak that obscures her face but still reveals her bare breasts. An arrow is pointed suggestively at her genitals by a weird half-man, half-bird creature. The latter was a symbol, the artist confessed, for himself (he called the birdman 'Loplop' and he recurs in several of his works), and indeed there is something bird-like in Ernst's odd demeanour, his bright eyes and somewhat beaky nose – and also in his inquisitive, distracted temperament. He couldn't decide on an artistic style, just as he couldn't decide on a wife. He was married four times in all.

Ernst experimented with techniques of what he called frottage (similar to brass rubbing) and grattage (scraping paint around with a palette knife). Meanwhile he darted from woman to woman, having an affair with one prominent British Surrealist, Leonora Carrington, and later marrying another – but only after divorcing a certain prominent art collector. The woman in question was Peggy Guggenheim, who once, on being asked how many husbands she had had, replied, 'My own, or other people's?' And in fact, sex seems to have been a major preoccupation of the American heiress's life (to read more, turn to page 1) …

Index of main entries